KOHIMA

ARTHUR SWINSON was a British army officer, playwright, historian and BBC producer. He served in the 2nd British Division at Kohima. The author of some twenty works of non-fiction, Arthur Swinson died in 1970.

ARTHUR SWINSON

KOHIMA

First published in the UK in 1966 by Cassell & Company Ltd

This edition published in the UK in 2015
by Head of Zeus Ltd.

9 7 5 3 1 2 4 6 8

A catalogue record for this book is available
from the British Library.

ISBN (HB) 9781784081782
ISBN (E) 9781784081775

Printed and bound in Germany
by GGP Media GmbH, Pössneck

Head of Zeus Ltd
Clerkenwell House
45-47 Clerkenwell Green
London EC1R 0HT

WWW.HEADOFZEUS.COM

To All Those Who Fought
At Kohima
And Especially My Friends
Who Still Lie There

Contents

List of Images

Brigadier 'Daddy' Warren, commander of the 161st Indian Brigade (*Inter-Services Public Relations Directorate, India*)
Lieutenant-General Kotoko Sato, commander of the Japanese 31st Division (*Kyodo News Service*)
Lieutenant-General Renya Mutaguchi, commander of the Japanese 15th Army (*Kyodo News Service*)
Kohima in 1965

List of Maps

Preface

According to Admiral Lord Mountbatten 'the battle of Kohima will probably go down as one of the greatest battles in history'; according to Field-Marshal Wavell 'when the history of this war comes to be written, the fight here will be put down as one of the turning points of the war... when the Japanese were routed and their downfall really began'. They were both speaking soon after the battle, when its horror and fury were still vividly in mind; since then, though it cannot be said that Kohima has been forgotten, there is no doubt that it has not acquired the fame of comparable battles, such as Alamein or Cassino. The reasons for this are many, but probably the most important is that the battle was fought over terrain so extraordinary that its tactical pattern is difficult to grasp. Even the Chiefs of Staff were mystified by the battle while it was going on and asked why the fighting was characterized 'by so many company and platoon actions'. What had eluded them was the paradox of Assam as a theatre of war; that while the country is so large that it rapidly absorbs vast numbers of troops, it denies the deployment of large formations, operating *en masse*. One should not imagine though that because an action in this battle was small it was necessarily unimportant. Assam is a country where a platoon well dug in can hold up a division, and a company can hold up an Army Corps; a country, therefore where the success or failure of a battalion attack may have momentous results.

Another reason why Kohima may still be so relatively unknown is that no full account of it has yet appeared. Two narratives of the siege have been published, concentrating on the action of the Royal West Kents; but the siege occupied only fourteen days out of the sixty-four, and after it was over there came the long and bitter action to clear Kohima Ridge and open the road to Imphal. I hope, therefore, that so far as the general reader is concerned, this book will go some way towards filling a gap in the history of the war in Burma.

During my discussion with Field-Marshal Slim, he warned me: 'Whatever you do, don't forget that Kohima and Imphal were twin battles, both fought under 14th Army control'. I hope this point has been sufficiently emphasized in my narrative, as even after twenty years I'd hate to disobey an order from my old commander. From an Army, from a strategic viewpoint, of course, the two battles were inextricably linked; but to the officers and men at Kohima, their battle was distinct and separate. For the most part, their only information about Imphal was that they had to open the road and get there—and the sooner the better. Fortunately, for those interested, a complete account of the battle of Imphal is already available, in the work of Sir Geoffrey Evans and Antony Brett-James.

In my researches for this book I have been greatly assisted by many people who were in the battle, and to them I would like to express my thanks. Field-Marshal the Viscount Slim, K.G., G.C.B., G.C.M.G., G.B.E., G.C.V.O., D.S.O., M.C., formerly commander of the 14th Army, patiently submitted himself to my interrogation and put me right on a number of points. I am most grateful to him. My thanks are also due to General Sir Montagu Stopford, G.C.B., K.B.E., D.S.O., M.C., D.L., commander of the 33rd Indian Corps during the battle, for making available a large amount of documentary material, and for answering questions in correspondence; and to my old divisional commander, Major-General John Grover, C.B., M.C., for letting me have material and for sparing the time to answer endless questions. Sir Charles Pawsey, C.S.I., C.I.E., M.C., has helped me considerably over a number of matters concerning Assam and the siege of Kohima; and I would also like to thank General Sir Ouvry Roberts, G.C.B., K.B.E., D.S.O., who has advised me on a number of matters. Lieutenant-General S. Matsutani has carried out research for me in Tokyo and I would like to express my gratitude to him.

Many officers have helped me by making available their diaries and personal narratives, or other unpublished material, and to these I am very indebted: especially to Brigadier Victor Hawkins, D.S.O., M.C., for his account of 5th Brigade operations; to Brigadier Hugh Richards, C.B.E., D.S.O., for his account of the siege; Brigadier D. G. T. Horsford, C.B.E., D.S.O.; Lieut.-Colonel L. P. Waterhouse, M.C.; Major John Nettlefield, M.C.; Major Arthur Marment, M.C., T.D.; Major Sir Christopher Nixon, M.C.; Major Colin Hunter, M.C.; Major W. G. Graham, M.C.; Major David Graham, M.C.; Major H. Elliott, M.C.; and Captain David Young, M.C.

I am also grateful to those officers who have found time to discuss the battle with me and suggest lines of research: Lieut.-General Sir Richard Collingwood, K.B.E., C.B., D.S.O.; Major-General E. H. W. Grimshaw, C.B., C.B.E., D.S.O.; Colonel H. R. R. Conder, O.B.E.; Colonel W. A. Bickford, D.S.O.; Colonel E. R. W. Tooby, O.B.E., M.C., T.D.; Lieut.-Colonel John Brierley, M.C.; Lieut.-Colonel G. E. Braithwaite; Lieut.-Colonel Hugh Conroy, D.S.O., M.C.; Lieut.-Colonel G. A. E. Keene, M.B.E.; Major R. A. J. Fowler, M.C.; and Major E. Lloyd Jones, M.C.

My thanks are also due to those who kindly gave me information or advice in correspondence: Major-General F. J. Loftus Tottenham, C.B.E., D.S.O.; Major-General J. D. Shapland, C.B., D.S.O., M.C.; Brigadier W. G. Smith; Lieut.-Colonel D. J. S. Murray; Major R. Kensington; and Captain S. S. F. Hornor.

Officers at the various regimental headquarters have helped me in many ways; apart from supplying material, they have tracked down officers at my request, and on many occasions suggested subjects for research. I would therefore like to express my thanks to: Colonel D. A. D. Eykyn, D.S.O. (Royal Scots); Major W. G. Cripps (Royal Norfolk); Major T. P. Shaw (Lancashire Fusiliers); Lieut.-Colonel C. P. Vaughan, D.S.O. (Worcestershire Regiment); Lieut.-Colonel D. G. W. Wakely, M.C. (Dorsetshire Regiment); Lieut.-Colonel J. C. Vyvyan (Royal Welch Fusiliers); Lieut.-Colonel C. L. Spears (Duke of Edinburgh's Royal Regiment); and Major G. Browne (Durham Light Infantry).

In Tokyo, members of the Society of the 58th Regiment have most kindly supplied me with information and a copy of *The Burma Front,* a symposium of individual narratives: Mr Susumi Nishida; Mr Shyo Nishida; Mr Jiro Tamura; Mr Kiyoji Kumijura; and Mr Shuishi Nakamura. I am most grateful to them, also to Mr Mutsuya Ngao who has carried out research and interviews for me in Tokyo.

When I was beginning my researches, Brigadier E. Lucas Phillips, O.B.E., M.C, was already at work on his book concerning the siege of Kohima: but he generously suggested a number of contacts, for which I am most grateful. Lieut.-Colonel A. J. Barker, an authority on the Japanese aspects of the campaign, has found the time to discuss various problems with me, and has made available most useful material from his researches. I would like to express my thanks to him. I am also grateful to Mr Antony Brett-James for all the advice and help he has given me; to Lieut.-Col. O. G. W. White and Gale & Polden for allowing me to quote from his book *Straight on for Tokyo;* to Major-General M. Utsunomiya, the Japanese Defence Attaché in London; and to Colonel P. S. W. Dean, formerly Military Attaché in Tokyo.

Finally, my thanks are due to the Imperial War Museum for permission to reproduce some of the photographs in this book; to Sir Charles Pawsey for kindly supplying a photograph of his bungalow; to Mr T. S. Krishnamurti, Private Secretary to the Governor of Assam and Nagaland, for sending me the photograph of Kohima as it is today; and to the B.B.C. for permitting me to use the eyewitness report by their correspondent, the late Richard Sharp.

Before concluding this Preface, I should like to add a few words concerning accuracy, as I suspect that readers who were at Kohima themselves may not find my account of some actions in strict accord with their own memories. All reasonable efforts have been made to ensure accuracy, though no doubt it has not been achieved completely, and concerning several episodes of the battle may never be achieved. Regimental histories and Divisional histories are often inaccurate and disagree completely as to dates, times and dispositions of units; war diaries are notoriously inaccurate also. Individual memories, though often accurate as to mood and detailed observation, play curious tricks with time, and place incidents in the wrong order. More than once during my researches I have discovered instances where both parties were convinced that they were on the left (or right) of each other. Considering the close and often hectic nature of the fighting at Kohima, this is not surprising; nor is it surprising that men attending the same meetings or conferences have very different recollections as to what was said and what was decided. This may happen in ordinary civilian life and in a much calmer atmosphere. Faced with such wide disagreement as to time and place or cause and effect, I have tended to place more reliance on diaries or other documents completed during the battle, before victory was achieved and the forces of hindsight began to operate. In some cases where doubt still remains, or there are two or more distinct schools of opinion, I have indicated this in the text. Naturally, all opinions expressed in this work, except where otherwise stated, are the responsibility of myself and not of the many people who have assisted me.

Khabvuma 2 m.
Bokajan 33 m.
Cheswem
<32 m. from Dimapur
Zubza
Sachema
Dzuza R.
Jotsoma
Mozema
TWO T
Khonoma
Dzuna R.
7522
PULEBADZE
Pulomi 7 m.
Maram 27 m.

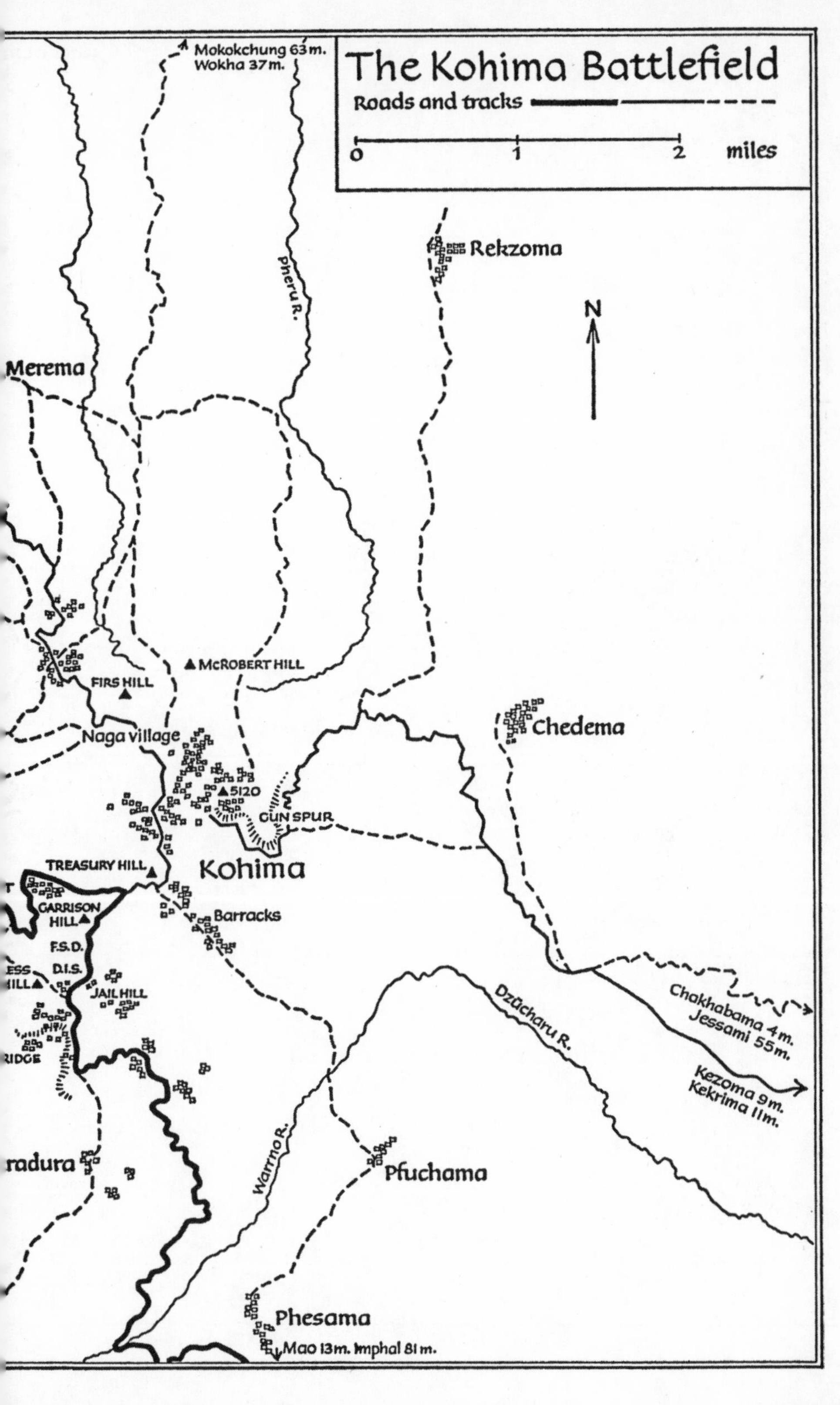
The Kohima Battlefield
Roads and tracks
0
1
2
miles
N
Mokokchung 63 m.
Wokha 37 m.
Pheru R.
Rekzoma
Merema
McROBERT HILL
FIRS HILL
Naga village
5120
GUN SPUR
Chedema
TREASURY HILL
Kohima
GARRISON HILL
Barracks
F.S.D.
D.I.S.
JAIL HILL
Dzücharu R.
Chakhabama 4 m.
Jessami 55 m.
Kezoma 9 m.
Kekrima 11 m.
Warrno R.
radura
Pfuchama
Phesama
Mao 13 m. Imphal 81 m.

Chapter One

Four Generals; One Rendezvous

On Wednesday, 15th March 1944, the Mechanical Engineers of the 33rd Indian Corps (in military parlance the R.E.M.E. and I.E.M.E.) arranged what they called a 'Waterproofing Festival and Workshop Exhibition' at a place called Audh, some eight miles from Poona in central India. It was an elaborate and highly-organized affair, laid out like a country show in England, and the visitors included officers from G.H.Q. India, from S.E.A.C. (Lord Louis Mountbatten's headquarters), and 11th Army Group, the formation above General Slim's 14th Army in Burma. In the morning they were invited to inspect exhibits of various R.E.M.E. trades, and instructional films; and in the afternoon, demonstrations such as 'Testing A and B Vehicles through Splash', 'B Vehicles—Recovery', and 'Drowned Vehicles—Recovery by Breakdown Crew'. 'I have never been to a better show in my life...' wrote the Corps Commander, Lieut.-General Montagu Stopford. 'The organization was perfect, and everything was laid on in a pleasant, informal atmosphere.'

Stopford at this time was fifty-two years old, a large, solidly-built man, whom journalists liked to picture in farming terms. 'When he walks round his units,' one of them wrote, 'he might be inspecting his barns, or noting the progress of his crops. He is calm, unflappable. He has the unhurried walk of a man who has lived close to the land.' Though superficially correct, the portrait was, of course, ludicrously inadequate. The most important thing about Stopford was his ability, his achievement, and his potentiality as a soldier. Though his walk was unhurried, his mind moved very fast; and his ostensibly calm exterior often concealed the explosion already working its way to the surface. He had the courage and the power of command, two of the most important qualities of a soldier. He could write and speak powerfully and lucidly. He was very ambitious; some would call him ruthless; but that he was a very professional commander, there could be no doubt whatsoever. Commissioned to the Rifle Brigade in 1911 he had fought through the First World War. By 1935 he was a Lieut.-Colonel; and in 1939 he took the 17th Infantry Brigade to France. After Dunkirk, he commanded the 56th Division for a period before returning to the Staff College, Camberley, as Commandant. In 1943 he was promoted to the rank of Lieut.-General and took over the 12th Corps, but the same year was posted to the newly forming 33rd Indian Corps in India.

The role of this Corps—and the *raison d'être* of the Waterproofing Exhibition—was to act as an assault force in combined operations, and during 1943 it had taken part in large-scale exercises on the western coast of India. These had come to a sudden halt when in December 1943 it was discovered that the assault craft were needed for the Anzio landing, so the Corps devoted its energies to jungle training. At this moment there was only one infantry division in the Corps, the 2nd British, commanded by Major-General John Grover, and it was strung out over tens of thousands of square miles from Poona to Bangalore, to remote areas in the jungles below Belgaum. The 2nd British was one of the two regular divisions of the British Army and carried with it a long and proud tradition. It had fought under Wellington in the Peninsula, in the Crimea, in South Africa, and throughout the long horror of the Western Front. Its regiments included some of the finest in the whole of the Army: the Royal Scots, the Royal Norfolk, the Lancashire Fusiliers, the Worcestershires, the Dorsetshires, the Cameron Highlanders, the Durham Light Infantry, the Royal Berkshires, and the Royal Welch Fusiliers. It was highly trained, highly equipped, and highly mobile. When on the move its transport took up 165 miles of road. The Division was detested by G.H.Q. India and by almost every officer in the Indian Army, many of whom would have liked to see it broken up. Obversely many people in 2 Div. (as it was generally called) had no great opinion of the Indian Army and were not shy of saying so. Unfortunately, not having made contact with any fighting formations, their opinion of Indian troops was based on the somewhat low-grade men they saw wandering round the base areas. Both sides, in fact, were prejudiced and ill-informed; and the situation was a most unhappy one.

The 2nd Division had left England in April 1942 in the largest military convoy ever to be organized. Its orders were to sail west out into the Atlantic to avoid the Focke-Wulf bases, turn south and east for the Cape, then to continue up the eastern shores of Africa to Suez. The plan was for the Division to join the 8th Army for its next campaign in the desert; but some time in May, after the widespread riots and unrest organized by the Indian Congress Party, new orders reached the convoy commander, and, somewhat to their amazement, the 16,000 troops found themselves disembarking at Bombay. That they were neither expected nor welcomed by the military authorities soon became evident, as the administrative chaos slowly unwound itself; it was a month or more before the troops could be found acceptable rations. But apart from G.H.Q. the Indian politicians also viewed the arrival of the Division with disfavour. Had anyone considered the cost? They asked; then pointed out forcibly that the burden of maintaining the Division and paying its officers and men would be three times the cost of an Indian division. There had never been a whole British division in India before, they argued, except for the 5th which had made a brief stay, and there was no need for one now. In 1943, after representations had been made in London, a plan was concocted to send the division overland to Teheran, and staff officers began energetically working out schemes for setting up supply and petrol points right across the Persian desert. But the plan fell through. And with the arrival of Mountbatten, ideas were formulated to use 2nd Division for Combined Operations... so it soldiered on, its unpopularity increasing.

John Grover, the Divisional Commander, was at this time forty-seven years old, a passionate professional soldier with a great eye for detail. Of medium height and slender of physique, he was highly charged with nervous energy and drove himself and his staff mercilessly hard. He was correct, punctilious, and perfectionist; always demanded the highest standards and obtained them. A few weeks previously in jungle training a new staff officer had been asked to produce some loading tables, and rather than trudge round collecting first-hand data had used what was readily available. Grover took the document, glanced at it a second, then angrily thrust it back again, saying: 'Take it away and do it properly.' Faced with incompetence, sloth, or any failure of duty, even the slightest, Grover would explode with rage; and there can be no doubt that many officers were afraid of him. But on the other hand, he was selfless and extraordinarily generous; and would spare no efforts whatsoever to do a thing, once convinced it was his duty. But the most remarkable thing about him was his moral command over the division. By some miracle he seemed to acquire the personal allegiance of every officer and man, and his personality not only pervaded every single unit but seemed to permeate the very guns and equipment. Wherever the General walked the air quivered with nervous excitement and apprehension. Would he spot the one fire bucket in the area which wasn't full of water?

Would he find a cook with dirty fingernails? Or, the worst horror of all, would some misbegotten soldier come round the corner of a hut without his hat on? The whole place was on tenterhooks until the inspection was over and he'd been safely steered into the Mess. A subaltern in the Royal Scots (now a well-known actor and playwright) earned a tremendous reputation throughout the Division for his imitation of the General, and not infrequently would be invited to regimental messes so that people could hear it. On one occasion, so the story went, after a brush with his commanding officer, the subaltern crept outside his tent, put on the General's voice, and made some caustic remarks about the battalion lines. The C.O., who was having a quiet afternoon nap, leapt from his *charpoy,* seized his hat and belt and stumbled out into the blazing sun. Only a thorough inspection of the whole area convinced him that there was no General around.

But if some officers were scared of Grover, the troops never were, and regarded him with great affection. They would talk to him quite freely about pay, leave, amenities, the qualities of the char, and what they would like to do to the man who invented 'soya links', the wartime substitute for sausages. Grover would listen to them patiently, and if there was anything he could do, he would do it. In time the troops came to believe that their welfare was his vital concern; and there was nothing they wouldn't do for him. The relationship was quite remarkable.

Like Stopford, Grover had served in the First World War, having been commissioned to the King's Shropshire Light Infantry in December 1914, and earned the M.C., being wounded three times. By 1938 he was commanding the 1st Battalion of his regiment, but later became G.S.O.I (that is the senior staff officer) to the 5th Division, and in that role saw it over the beaches at Dunkirk. He spent a year as a Brigadier, then in 1941 was appointed to command of the 2nd Division.

Grover did not attend the Waterproofing Festival. He was

in Delhi on this particular date for discussions at G.H.Q. India concerning a recent threat to take 100 men from every unit in the 2nd Division as reinforcements of the 14th Army. This threat had already been the subject of heated correspondence, but realizing that only a personal interview with the G.O.C. 11th Army Group, General Sir George Giffard, would produce any results, Grover had pleaded to see him. On the 15th he saw a number of staff officers, but the following day was ushered into Giffard's office. Here he received the news that three Japanese divisions were crossing the Chindwin, to threaten 4th Corps; and so immediately asked if 2nd Division couldn't be of some help in this situation. But Giffard shook his head, replying: 'There's no chance of employing 2nd Division in the 14th Army area—we couldn't maintain it there.' Grover therefore mentioned that his formation had just finished its jungle training, and was about to disperse on leave. 'Is that in order?' he asked. Poker-faced, Giffard said: 'Yes, that's quite in order.' So Grover left G.H.Q. and took the train back to 33rd Corps headquarters, where he arrived on the morning of the 19th.

*

While Stopford and Grover were thus engaged, Lieut. -General Kotuku Sato, the commander of the Japanese 31st Division, was at his headquarters at Homalin, a town on the River Chindwin. It had been a very busy day. From first light he had been supervising the administrative arrangements for ferrying his Division across the river, from 9 p.m. onwards. Things seemed to be going very smoothly, and the men together with their guns and equipment were moving swiftly towards the embarkation points. The plan was that the division (with the 15th Division on its left flank) should move in three columns. The right-hand or northern column consisted of a battalion of the 138th Infantry Regiment, with a battery of the 31st

Mountain Artillery Regiment, engineers, signals, and medical attachments; the centre column consisted of an advance guard of the 138th Infantry Regiment (that is three battalions, the equivalent to a British Brigade) with a battalion of the 31st Mountain Artillery Regiment; while the main body consisted of the divisional headquarters, the 124th Infantry Regiment, a battalion of the 31st Mountain Artillery Regiment, with engineers, signals, a field hospital and a transport unit. The left-hand or southern column moved under the divisional second-in-command, Major-General Miyazaki, and this included the 58th Infantry Regiment and the remainder of the 31st Mountain Artillery Regiment.

General Sato at this time was fifty-one years old and he had served in the Japanese Army since December 1913, when he was commissioned 2nd Lieutenant. From 1918–21 he was at the Staff College and the following year returned to regimental duty as a company commander in the 321st Regiment. Later he had a period on the staff of the 7th Division before being posted to the Kumamoto Military School as an instructor. By 1928 he was a Major on the General Staff, but three years later he was promoted to command a battalion in the 18th Infantry Regiment. By 1937 he was a Colonel, and in December 1939 he was a district commander in Manchuria. In December 1942 he took over the 31st Division with the rank of Lieut.-General and the following year moved into Burma. Initially, at least, he wasn't very pleased about the posting and remarked to a journalist accredited to his Division: 'I've been sent here because Tojo detests me.' As can readily be seen he was a very highly trained soldier, though his experience of action was somewhat limited. As to character, he has been described as 'of great courage, of easy manner, of open-hearted nature and inclined to be unconventional'. He has also been called stubborn, one-track-minded, and painfully orthodox. Whatever the truth of this, one fact is quite clear: he knew how to make his division get a move on, and commanded one of the most remarkable advances in military history.

'When we strike, we must be absolutely ready... reaching our objectives with the speed of wildfire....' The author of this directive was Sato's superior, Lieut.-General Renya Mutaguchi, commander of the 15th Army. One cannot help wondering if he knew what he was asking, as the country facing Sato's men was some of the wildest and toughest in the world. Vehicles, even jeeps, were out of the question, and loads were to be carried on mules, oxen, and elephants. The engineering companies could carry no heavy equipment and would have to improvise, making rafts and bridges, and improving the tracks as they went along. Apart from small arms, the regiments were to carry their infantry and anti-tank guns with up to 300 rounds of ammunition for each. There were also seventeen mountain guns to be carried by the ten elephants. The division had been allocated 3,000 horses and 5,000 oxen, the principal task of which was to carry ammunition and rations for the troops. Even so every man was laden with as much rifle ammunition as it was thought he could carry, and food for three weeks. 'Personal effects,' Sato had ordered, understandably, 'must be kept to the minimum.'

As he watched his men pouring over the Chindwin, Sato must have been proud and confident; at last he was commanding a division in battle; at last a military triumph was within his grasp. Already reports indicated that the British and Indian troops were in headlong retreat before the 33rd and 15th Divisions to the south; and he had a shrewd suspicion that his own division would be well on the way to its objective before the enemy realized what was happening. The objective was only seventy-five miles away as the crow flew, two hundred perhaps on the ground, but he'd be there in fifteen days. And once he'd captured it, he could turn south and slaughter the British as they retreated. The name of his objective was Kohima.

*

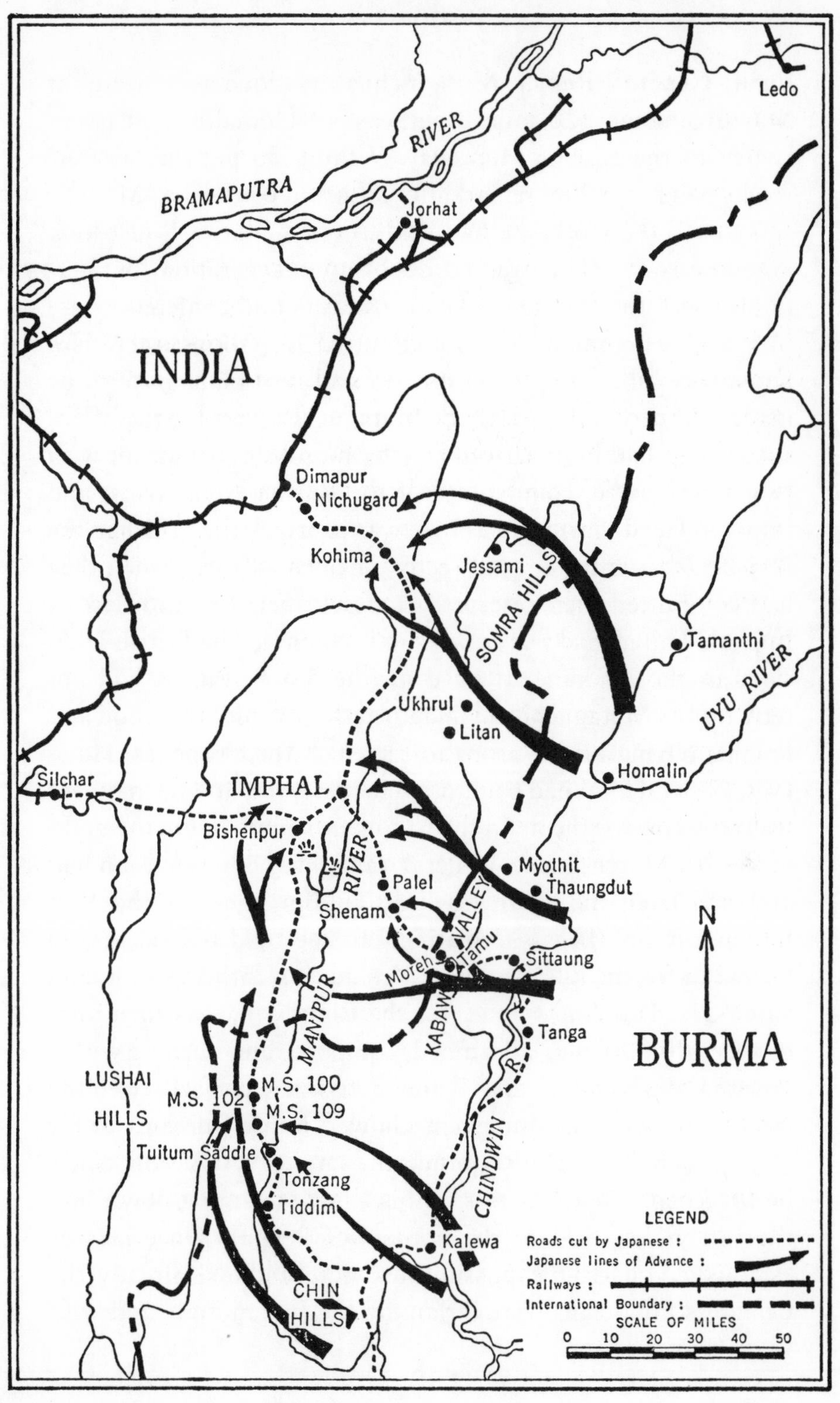

Ledo
RIVER
BRAMAPUTRA
Jorhat
INDIA
Dimapur
Nichugard
Kohima
Jessami
SOMRA HILLS
Tamanthi
UYU RIVER
Ukhrul
Litan
Homalin
Silchar
IMPHAL
Bishenpur
RIVER
Palel
Myothit
Thaungdut
Shenam
VALLEY
Moreh
Tamu
Sittaung
N
MANIPUR
KABAW
Tanga
BURMA
LUSHAI
HILLS
M.S. 100
M.S. 102
M.S. 109
Tuitum Saddle
Tonzang
Tiddim
CHINDWIN
R
Kalewa
CHIN
HILLS
LEGEND
Roads cut by Japanese :
Japanese lines of Advance :
Railways :
International Boundary :
SCALE OF MILES
0 10 20 30 40 50

Lieut.-General Renya Mutaguchi's headquarters were at Maymyo, some 220 miles Southeast of Homalin, and twenty-five to the east of Mandalay. Visitors during the last few weeks had found him remarkably calm and confident. 'My officers do all the work,' he had said to one of them. 'I just look after the roses.' This was no doubt an exaggeration, but certainly, once the frantic weeks of planning and conferences are over and a commander has committed his troops, there is a temporary lull, till reports come in and new plans have to be made and new orders drafted. Mutaguchi's plan for the offensive, which had been arrived at after months of argument with General Kawabe, commander of the Burma Area Army, and Imperial Headquarters in Tokyo, was to attack the British in the Arakan (that is the coastal sector of Burma), then, when they had committed their reserves, to attack their forward base at Imphal. Things had not gone exactly to plan. The British Divisions in the Arakan, attacked on the 5th February, had not retreated as Mutaguchi had imagined they would, but stood and fought, relying on air-drops to replenish their supplies. However, General Slim had committed his reserves, and the moment was now ripe for the main thrust towards Imphal. On the night of the 7th March, Lieut.-General Yanagida's 33rd Division had attacked from the south towards Tiddim, then, as the 17th Indian Division began retreating, cut the road behind it, and moved in for the kill. And now Yamauchi's 15th Division, and Sato's 31st Division were across the Chindwin, making a total of over 100,000 men, all trained, equipped, and burning with a fanatical desire for victory. Though he knew perfectly well the limit of his orders, Mutaguchi allowed himself dreams of far greater conquest. If the mountain barrier of Assam could be breached, what was to stop his army streaming down into the valleys beyond—to the borders of Bengal? Once he was established there, the possibilities were endless; already the Congress politicians were inflaming the Indian mob, and with a Japanese army sitting on their borders, the whole population would rise, tearing the British Raj to pieces. In one such moment of daydreaming, as he admitted later, Mutaguchi saw himself riding through Delhi on a white charger.

At this time he was fifty-six years of age and had served in the Japanese Army since 1910. Promotion had come regularly, staff and regimental appointments alternating. As a Major he had been Instructor of Military Science at the Staff College, then in 1936 had commanded the 1st Infantry Regiment during the war with China. From there he went on to the appointment as Chief of Staff 4th Army, with the rank of Major-General, and then left active service to take over as Director of the preparatory course at the Military Academy. In 1940 he was promoted to Lieut.-General and in April 1941 given command of the 18th Regiment which he led in Malaya and Burma. It was here that he made his military reputation, with a spectacular dash for Singapore. According to Colonel Masanobu Tsuji, Chief of Operations and Planning on the 25th Army staff, Mutaguchi was a man of great courage, always up with the forward elements. During the crossing of the Johore Strait he was wounded in the shoulder, but carried on, refusing any suggestions that he should go to the rear. He was a big man by Japanese standards, with what they describe as 'a ruddy complexion'. He had a strong personality and great powers of command; but he wasn't afraid of emotion and knew the value of a theatrical gesture. In the days when he was a divisional commander, he would go up to the forward units before an attack to see their colonels. When a staff officer once protested that his presence at this time would cause difficulties, he replied: 'I must shake hands with them before they die.' Mutaguchi had an explosive temper; and though he treasured his friends, he never forgot a grudge nor forgave his enemies. There can be no doubt that his staff officers were afraid of him, and sometimes they withheld unpleasant facts, merely telling him what they thought he would like to know. Because of this, he was sometimes unaware of the real situation. Lieut.-Colonel A.J. Barker, who knows him personally, has said: 'He had followed the star of General Araki as a member of the Kodo-ha—an Imperial Forces group—which held the cause of the Emperor to be higher than the law of the land, and advocated the direct rule of the Son of Heaven.... He was also a member of the Cherry Society—formed in the early 1920s by a group of Army officers who were intensely pro-service, and "anti" the politicians. Sato was a fellow member of the society.' Barker adds that Mutaguchi tended to see things in black and white, and overcame opposition by steam-roller tactics. Also, he believed passionately in the comradeship of soldiers and accepted that death in battle was the highest honour that could befall a Japanese. Despite his defects and his dreams he was a formidable soldier; and whether his plan was a sound one only time could tell.

*

Kohima lies on a saddle connecting two mountain ridges, some 5,000 feet up among the Naga Hills, in central Assam. The name is a corruption of 'Kew-hi mia', meaning 'the men of Kewhi'; a plant found growing on the hillside. It is a beautiful place with great panoramic views; to the south the green mountains roll upwards some 10,000 feet towards Mao Songsang, while to the north-west the ground drops away precipitously into a deep valley, pointing towards Dimapur. To the west the wooded slopes of the Aradura Spur run up towards Mount Pulebadze and Mount Japvo, dark, spectacular peaks which dominate the country for many miles. To the east the land rises, hill after hill, towards Chedema and Jessami, then disappears into a wild untrodden region left bare on the map and marked simply 'dense mixed jungle'.

The Naga Hills form the northern sector of the great mountain barrier between Burma and India, which runs down from the Himalayas to the sea. To the south lie the Lushai Hills and below them the Chin Hills. From end to end the barrier is some six hundred miles long and up to two hundred across; it is a very inhospitable region indeed. The ridges, and therefore the valleys and rivers between them, run from north to south, making any lateral movement extremely hazardous and difficult, even in fine weather. But Assam is wet and includes Chara-punge, the wettest place on earth where eight hundred inches of rain have been recorded in a single year. In the monsoon, which lasts from mid-May till early September, the jungle paths sink deep in the mud, and the smallest streams swell quickly into great rivers and cascade towards the south. There is no comfort for man or beast in 'those hellish jungle-mountains' as General Slim called them; and the insects are an endless torment. There are sandflies, ticks, mosquitoes, and leeches. The latter crawls up your legs during the night and suck your blood till they become swollen to bursting point. The mosquitoes must be the largest and most persistent in the world; some strains, such as those around Mao, bringing up great septic sores, and anyone whose face has been attacked might well be in the terminal stages of smallpox. Where insects abound, there is always disease; and in Assam one is prey to dengue, scrub typhus, malaria, cholera, scabies, yaws, sprue, and every known form of dysentery. There is also the Naga sore, caused by pulling off leeches, and leaving their heads beneath the flesh. After four to five days a small blister appears which grows steadily till it is five or six inches across, and destroys not only skin but flesh, and even muscles. The stink from this putrefaction is foul in the extreme, and, unless adequate medical care is available, the victim may die. The correct course (as the troops soon learned) is to let the leech have his fill of blood and drop off, or burn it with a cigarette end. In this case no harm is done.

Climbing the saddle, the Kohima road curves in a half-circle, then for a quarter of a mile runs due east. At the very top, it forms a hair-pin bend, runs on for another half a mile then bends towards the south. Roughly, one might say it traces the outline of the head of a jay, with its pointed beak. In March 1944 the apex of the beak was occupied by the charming bungalow of the Deputy-Commissioner, Charles Pawsey, with its lawn and tennis court, flanked by flowers, rhododendron bushes, and thick copses. Running south from this on a series of hillocks were the club, and a number of army installations, the Field Supply Depot, and the Daily Issue Store. Kohima at this time was a staging post between the railhead at Dimapur, forty-six road-miles to the north-west, and Imphal sixty-five miles to the south, and during the last few years the Army (in its usual fashion) had been steadily expanding its hold. A mile or so to the north on the Merema ridge, and beyond the Naga village, there was the 57th Reinforcement Camp, and on a spur to the west was sited the 53rd Indian General Hospital. There were also such installations as a bakehouse, a transport workshop, and numerous offices. To the Southeast of the D.C.'s bungalow, on a relatively flat stretch of ground, lay the Assam Barracks, the depot for the 3rd Assam Rifles. They were a body of militarized police, who had first come to establish a post at Kohima as long ago as 1877.

Kohima, and indeed the whole of Assam, has known war since the beginning of recorded history and, most probably, centuries before then. The Koch and Cachan races fought each other without respite for generation after generation, till the beginning of the thirteenth century, when the Ahoms invaded the country, Shan peoples of the great Tai races of Burma. They ruled firmly, if barbarously, for seven hundred years until the British took over in 1825, at the end of the first Burma War. At that time the country was almost entirely without communications, but in 1830 a Mr Bruce prospected the Brahmaputra and Surma Valleys, which form a crescent on the western flank of

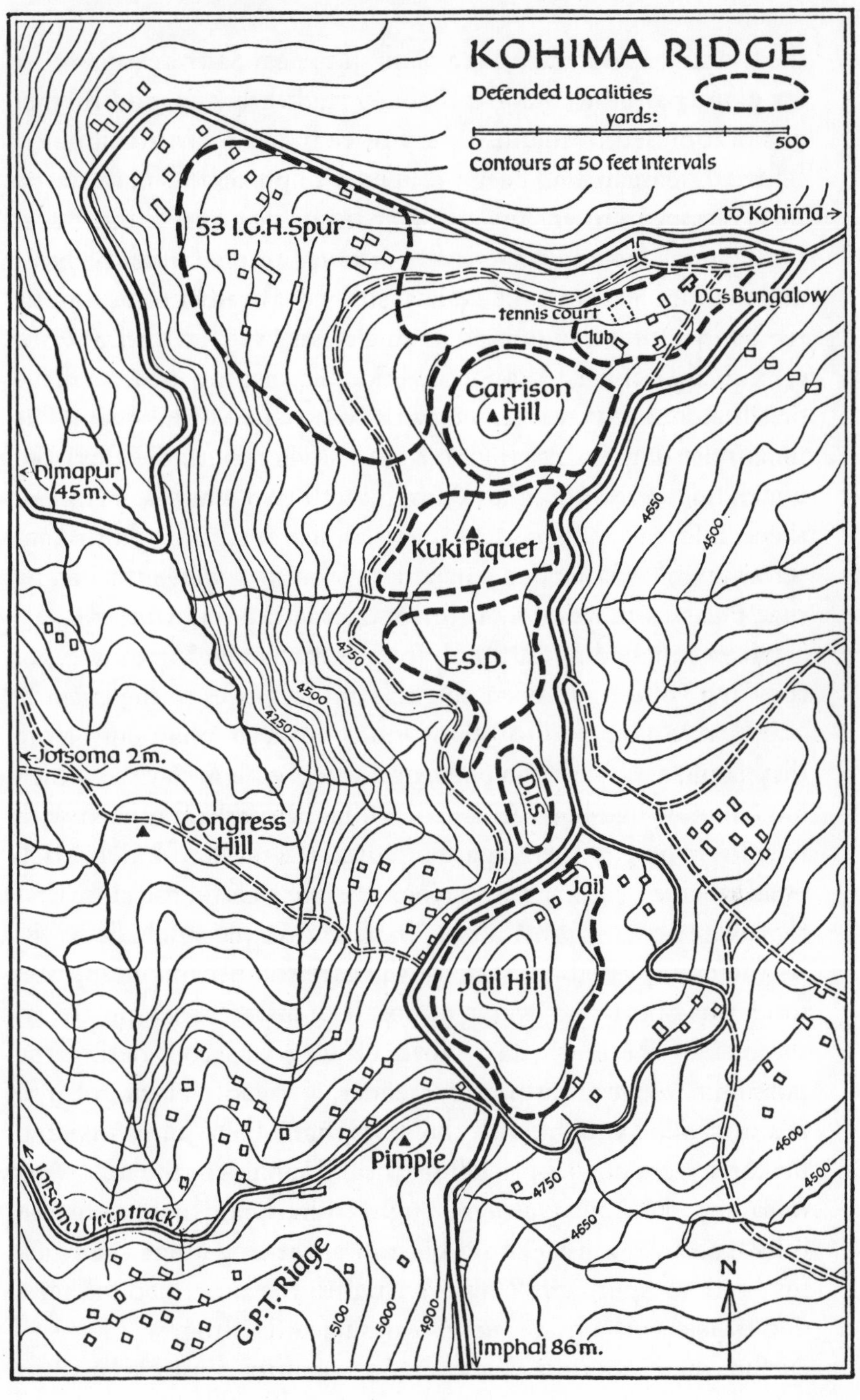
KOHIMA RIDGE
Defended Localities
yards:
0
500
Contours at 50 feet intervals
to Kohima
53 I.G.H. Spur
D.C's Bungalow
tennis court
Club
Garrison Hill
Dimapur 45 m.
Kuki Piquet
F.S.D.
4750
4500
4250
4650
4500
Jotsoma 2 m.
D.I.S.
Congress Hill
Jail
Jail Hill
Pimple
4750
4650
4600
4500
Jotsoma (jeep track)
G.P.T. Ridge
5100
5000
4900
N
Imphal 86 m.

the country, and started a tea plantation near Sadiya. Soon other tea planters followed and a thriving trade grew up; and further exploration led to the discovery of coal and oil in the jungles. By 1850 steamers had been brought in to ply on the main rivers, then European townships grew up and clubs were built. But if civilization flowed up the rivers, it failed to penetrate the hills; and their inhabitants, the Nagas, still went head hunting among rival tribes, and slaughtered intruders. In 1879, a Political Officer called Damant led an expedition against the armed village of Khonoma, but was killed with twenty-five of his men. The remainder of the party fled to Kohima where with the garrison, which numbered about a hundred, with two white women and their children, and some 240 non-combatants, they shut themselves up in two wooded stockades. Soon they were attacked by the Nagas from Khonoma, Jotsoma, and other hostile villages, a force estimated at 6,000 all told. Fortunately, Mr Cawley, of the Civil Police, had been able to send messages to the friendly Nagas at Wokha and to Major Johnstone at Imphal; but before they could send help the enemy attacked with arrows to which burning tow had been attached, while the garrison replied with rifle fire. Some of the Nagas employed the old Red Indian trick of advancing behind a rolling log, one party getting so close that they were able to throw a human head over the stockade walls. As the days passed the state of the garrison became desperate; food was short and water almost exhausted. Fortunately, at the end of the tenth day, when Cawley was considering the possibility of negotiating a surrender, a friendly Naga got into the stockade by night with the news that Major Johnstone and his force were now approaching from Imphal. On the following morning, the 27th October, bugles were heard in the distant hills, and by noon he could be seen advancing along the track by Aradura Spur. The Nagas retired to their fortified villages, and the siege, the first siege of Kohima, was lifted.

But there was no peace in Assam; and by 1924 no less

than fifty-two punitive expeditions or campaigns had been launched. In one of them, the Lushai Expedition of 1871, the chief staff officer was Colonel F. Roberts, later to become the famous 'Bobs', Commander-in-Chief India. He was the first soldier of any eminence to take the field in Assam, and his writings leave no doubt as to what he thought of it. Ambushes were frequent and casualties high, and even the elephants fell down, exhausted. 'Every bit of road had to be cut and cleared, entailing endless labour, while in addition, much bridging work had to be carried out.' Even a British officer carried a load of 80 lbs. on his back; and the coolies started going down with cholera, even before the expedition had left its base. Later and more highly equipped expeditions proved just as uncomfortable.

According to their own legends, the Angami Nagas, who have a large village on the northern slopes of Kohima, emerged from the bowels of the earth in some land to the south. Anthropologists aren't so certain, some relating them to the head-hunters of Malaya, others to the Polynesians, and a few to the hill races of China. Undoubtedly they worked their way up Assam from the south, but when the migration took place and how long it lasted, it is impossible to say. Travellers and others living among them for long periods have often noticed their fancy for marine shells, and there is little doubt that they have strong cultural affinities to the natives of Borneo and the Philippines. Some people would say they have physical affinities too. The Naga languages have been studied by numerous philologists and with varying results; but it appears that the classification arrived at by Sir George Grierson in 1911 has obtained fairly general acceptance. He considers that the Angami Naga is of the Tibeto-Chinese family.

But whatever their origin, the Nagas are now firmly settled in their fortified villages on the Assamese hilltops. Generally the men are about five feet nine inches tall, though some go up to six feet. Their bodies are brown and lithe and agile. Their powers of endurance are remarkable, and men have been known to complete forced marches of thirty to forty miles a day, for several days on end. They can stand the sun and the rain, and carry considerable burdens, usually passing a sling round the forehead to take the strain. Their calves, chests and shoulders are magnificently developed; and through constant climbing in bare feet their toes become widely separated, the big toe branching away from the others. Their features are pleasant, sometimes handsome; though their hair is black from puberty onwards, their eyes are always brown. Their voices are musical and they have a wonderful laugh. As to dress, they wear a short kilt, and are bare above and below this, except for a wide band of beads round the neck. They also wear bangles on arms and legs, and a wide variety of other decoration according to individual prowess in love and war. A fourth row of cowries on the kilt, for example, indicates 'an intrigue with a married woman living with her husband' or 'a double-barrelled intrigue with two girls of the same name'. Some of the older men wear sleeveless red coatees; and those in authority carry rolled umbrellas, which appear ludicrously incongruous.

The Naga village is invariably built on the summit of a hill, on a high saddle, or on a spur running down from a high range. It is always sited with a view to defence. Writing in the last century, Captain Butler described it thus:

> 'Stiff stockades, deep ditches bristling with panjies, and massive stone walls, often loop-holed for musketry, are their usual defences. In war-time the hillsides and approaches are escarped and thickly studded over with panjies, sharp-pointed skewers or stakes, some of them as thin as a pencil, which give a nasty wound and often cause complete lameness for some hours.... The approaches to the villages are often up through tortuous, covered ways, or lanes, with high banks on either side, with an overhanging, tangled mass of prickly creepers and brushwood, sometimes through a thick ravine

> and along the bed of an old torrent, in either case admitting of only the passage of one man at a time. These paths lead up to gates or rather doorways, closed by strong, thick and heavy wooded doors, carved out of one piece of solid wood.'

By 1944 the panjies and stockades had largely disappeared, but the ditches and walls remained, as did the narrow, hollowed approaches. The villages were still difficult to attack.

Another feature of the land inhabited by the Angami Nagas is the terracing. Great hillsides are stepped and irrigated, and planted with rice. By this method of agriculture, the Nagas kill two birds with one stone: the clearing of the jungle not only makes the land available, it provides a field of fire. To the south of Kohima, large areas were stepped and cleared in this manner.

What was happening at Kohima on the 15th March 1944 it is now impossible to say; though almost certainly it was nothing spectacular. The men of the Assam Rifles no doubt drilled on the *maidan*; the troops at the reinforcement camp lay idling on their *charpoys*; the Deputy-Commissioner, Charles Pawsey, went up to see his Nagas; the doctors, sisters, and nurses in the 53rd I.G.H. went on quietly with their work; and at lunch time and in the evening the officers congregated in the club to sip gimlets and chatter. Perhaps a few of them went down to the D.C.'s bungalow for a quiet game of tennis. Few if any of the officers knew that a Japanese offensive had begun on the Imphal front; none imagined that it could really affect Kohima. The place was too remote, too inaccessible. So the sun went down slowly behind Mount Pulebadze, the lights came on right across the great crescent of mountains, then one by one went out again. Tonight, at least, Kohima slept at peace.

*

During the 16th and 17th March General Stopford occupied himself with administrative matters; and the 2nd Division rounded off its jungle training. On Sunday the 19th John Grover met Stopford after breakfast and they talked of training and leave. It was high time, Stopford said, that Grover took some leave himself. Whatever was decided, Grover left for his headquarters, and Stopford studied a paper on 'the handling of the M.T. Division in the jungle'. Then, as he was preparing for dinner a signal arrived to say that the 2nd Division was to concentrate at its brigade stations. At midnight a further signal came to advise Stopford that the division would probably be required with 14th Army. This was followed by administrative orders, warning that road parties were to start moving to the Burma front on the 24th, and rail parties on the 26th. No mention had been made of the 33rd Indian Corps or its commander, so Stopford's initial reaction was that his troops were being taken from him, and he and his headquarters would now be serving no useful purpose. At 9.0 a.m. Grover arrived, having driven hard through the night from Belgaum. He had already given orders for his division to start concentrating, but was somewhat astonished at this new development. 'It was only on Saturday,' he said, 'that General Giffard told me there was no likelihood of the Division being employed in Burma this year.' Then at 6.0 p.m. yet another signal arrived, from Southern Army, informing Stopford of the Japanese offensive against Imphal. It also gave him orders to report to H.Q. 14th Army at Corrulla in two days' time with a skeleton staff, and to bring up the remainder of his headquarters as quickly as possible. No doubt he experienced some excitement at this sudden turn of events; instead of losing his Corps as he'd feared, he was going to command it in battle. But, as always, he remained a realist, and noted: 'We are going to buy a very sticky show unless we are careful....'

By now the advance guard of Sato's 31st Division was less than fifty miles from Kohima; Stopford, Grover, and the 2nd Division were 1,500 miles by plane, and well over 2,000 by road or rail. But such were the extraordinary chances of war, the twists of fate, and the decisions of the generals, that it was here they were to meet in a bloody and prolonged battle of attrition; a battle which was to prove one of the great turning points of the War.

Chapter Two

A Colonel from Delhi

To understand the causes for the Allied predicament in March 1944, and the background to the Japanese offensive in Burma, it is necessary to trace briefly the events of the previous two years. In May 1942 the Japanese had contemptuously swept the weak British forces out of Burma, but did not pursue them across the border into Manipur, the small state which acts as a buffer between Burma and India. Their reasons for calling off the chase may have been many; the lengthening of their line of communications, the difficulty of campaigning in the monsoon, or their official reason, which was to avoid arousing ill-feeling among the Indian masses. But whatever the reason for it, the lull was fortunate for the British, as only one division now remained to protect the Northeast frontier of India, the 23rd Indian.

The capital of Manipur is Imphal, which lies sixty-five miles to the south of Kohima. It is situated on a plateau some 2,600 feet up in the mountains, known as the Imphal Plain. This plateau (which extends forty miles by twenty) is formed by an opening in the Manipur River gorges and originally formed the bottom of a lake. The soil is fertile, the vegetation lush, and all manner of flowers, fruits, and vegetables abound. The duck-shooting has been renowned for many years, and Logtak Lake has been the scene of shooting parties since the British penetrated into the country in the last century. The Manipuris are clean and prosperous, take a keen delight in songs, music, and dancing, and instituted a State Ballet Company many centuries before the French or the Russians.

It was to Imphal that many refugees came when the Japanese invaded Burma, over 150,000 of them. There were Indian coolies, dock labourers from Rangoon, household servants, Anglo-Indians, Anglo-Burmese, along with British families who had been engaged in oil or timber, and random representatives of many other nations. They were attacked by exhaustion, hunger, disease, and stumbled into the refugee camp more dead than alive. Many did die, and it is said that the columns of vultures wheeling above the camp could be seen for miles.

After the refugees came the troops, ragged, almost like scarecrows, but still in the ranks and still carrying their rifles. They had been defeated, humiliated, and were somewhat bewildered. The fact that they had not been disgraced seemed merely academic at the moment; what mattered was sleep, food, and a lot more sleep.

To General Slim and his commanders this was no time for sleep; it was now perfectly obvious that if the Allied Armies were ever to launch an offensive against the Japanese and clear them out of Burma, Imphal must be the springboard. Slim conferred with Lieut.-General Scoones who was responsible for the northern front, and plans were set in motion to build it into a vast base. Slim has said: 'The Japanese Army seemed as little prepared as we were to advance in the monsoon, and we might reasonably look for a breathing space....' In fact, one Japanese staff officer, Lieut.-Colonel Hayashi, was already arguing with his superiors that it was imperative that Imphal should be captured at once, *before* the British could carry out their plans. His arguments found favour with the High Command in Tokyo, but the divisional commanders in Burma wanted to pause and consolidate—and Slim got his breathing space.

So, on the central front during 1943, operations were confined to patrolling and air activity. But politically, and among the military commanders, there was tremendous activity and by August the entire command structure had been changed. Till that date, Slim was commanding the old Eastern Army, and, apart from dealing with the Japanese, had vast internal security responsibilities in Behar, Orissa, and most of Bengal. The job was palpably impossible. Furthermore, he had to take his orders from G.H.Q. India, and, as became increasingly obvious with every week that went by, the idea that this ramshackle organization could prosecute a successful campaign was quite ludicrous; and some other headquarters must be formed. Not only the Chiefs of Staff at home were worried, but the Americans who had a special concern for China. By the beginning of 1943 it had seemed likely that Chiang Kai-shek's armies were near defeat, and if they did quit the field not only would large forces of Japanese be freed for other fronts but the American Air bases would be lost. This possibility led to consideration of the reopening of the Burma Road; but the latter could obviously not be effected until northern Burma had been retaken from the Japanese, and the mention of northern Burma led to the command situation, which was bristling with problems. General Stilwell, old 'Vinegar Joe', the American who had commanded the Chinese forces in the retreat from Burma, was convinced that the British had no fight left in them, and openly said so. However, a new road was proposed running from Ledo in Assam and following the Hukawng and Mogaung valleys to Myitkyina, before crossing to Bhamo to join the old Burma Road where it crossed the Chinese frontier; and Stilwell was given the job of driving it through. The railway from Ledo, it is worth mentioning here, ran down the Brahmaputra Valley to Jorhat and Dimapur (railhead for Kohima and Imphal) before curving away east for Gauhati and Bengal.

In August 1943 the South-East Asia Command was created at the First Quebec Conference by the British and American

Governments. The intention was that all campaigning should be taken out of the hands of G.H.Q. India, and a new unified command set up with Admiral Mountbatten as Supreme Commander. Under him there were to be three Commanders-in-Chief for the three services: Admiral Sir James Somerville, General Sir George Giffard, and Air Chief Marshal Sir Richard Peirse. Slim's forces were to be put under Sir George Giffard's 11th Army Group; and Slim would thereby be relieved of all his internal security responsibilities, and could concentrate on training his men and defeating the Japanese.

But the setting up of new commands and the appointment of new commanders does not necessarily bring order out of chaos; and in this instance it appeared for some time that the chaos would become even worse. None of the three C.s-in-C. understood the concept of a Supremo, and it did not take Mountbatten very long to decide that he would have to get rid of them as soon as possible. Sir George Giffard with his dry, factual, down-beat manner depressed him especially; when he was merely stating difficulties, Mountbatten assumed that he was creating them. The personalities refused to mix. Sir James Somerville was senior to Mountbatten in naval ranking, and had commanded a fleet in action (which Mountbatten had never done) and therefore considered the notion of serving under him as somewhat comic. But, apart from matters of personality and rank, there were other enormous problems to be solved. Mountbatten found, for example, that his naval units were controlled by the Admiralty in London, and his American Air Force squadrons took their orders from Washington. His headquarters, at present sited in Delhi, were right outside his own area of command; and most of the thirty departments were at war with each other. His directives came from the Combined Chiefs of Staff in Washington, but Churchill had a habit of weighing in with his own interpretation of these, or even issuing supplementary directives which conflicted with the originals. And, furthermore, action or even the initial planning for it had to be preceded by a good deal of tiresome horse-trading with Chiang Kai-shek, President Roosevelt, and Wavell, who had now taken over as Viceroy of India. More tangled still were Mountbatten's relations with Stilwell; this commander was not only his deputy, he was Roosevelt's accredited agent and had his own responsibilities for keeping China in the war, and therefore for the flow of supplies over the Hump. Such unlikely arrangements have worked, of course, but only with a constant supply of goodwill; and none came from Stilwell. He was acidly anti-British; did not believe they ever wanted to fight the Japanese. And he caused trouble at every turn. The basic cause of difference between the British and the Americans was China; the British had no faith in it whatsoever and wanted to hit the Japanese in Burma to restore their own damaged prestige, while the Americans thought Burma a side-issue and believed firmly that if only the supplies could be pushed through, Chiang Kai-shek's armies would keep fighting. The views were quite unreconcilable.

However, Mountbatten went ahead with great courage and energy to overcome the mountainous difficulties confronting him. He moved his headquarters from Delhi to the less political atmosphere of Kandy in Ceylon. (This enraged Sir George Giffard as he was tethered to G.H.Q. India, and there was not even a telephone line between Delhi and Kandy.) He directed and spurred on a great administrative build-up on the Burma front; and he endlessly explored every possible means of getting at the Japanese by land and by water. But, as his Command came at the end of the queue for arms and equipment, these projects were gradually whittled down, and in December 1943, as already mentioned, the landing craft were recalled for the Anzio battle. Somewhat dispirited, Mountbatten reported to the combined Chiefs of Staff that 'the possibility of our engaging large numbers of enemy troops at numerous points now depends largely on the initiative of the Japanese themselves'.

But if the overall strategic picture was depressing, the situation in the 14th Army had improved. The personality of Slim and the tonic of Mountbatten's whirlwind visits had improved morale considerably. And the administrative build-up at Imphal, at Dimapur, and in the Arakan had gone on steadily. In the latter sector, there were the 5th and 7th Indian Divisions, both battle-hardened formations constituting the 15th Corps under Lieut.-General Christison; and at Imphal there were the 17th, 20th and 23rd Indian Divisions in Scoones' 4th Corps. It was not a very large Army; but it was much bigger than the force which had been thrown out of Burma in 1942.

The Japanese forces had been reinforced, too, with the arrival of the 31st Division in August. The following month Mutaguchi, who had taken over command of the 15th Army in March 1943, ordered his divisions to prepare for the offensive. In 1942, as a divisional commander, he had strongly opposed an attack on Imphal, but now he was just as strongly for it, and urged his views on General Kawabe, the Burma Area Army commander. It is said that Mutaguchi had been impressed by the achievements of Wingate's first operation, and argued that, given dry weather and detailed planning, an army could advance over the jungle-mountains and still retain the strength to fight a battle. General Kawabe was not so certain, and pointed out the difficulty of maintaining an army at the end of such a long and tenuous line of communication; but, in his usual manner, Mutaguchi bulldozed his ideas through, until gradually they were accepted by Southern Army and Imperial Headquarters. As it happened, Mutaguchi's plan came at the right time for the Tojo government. With the succession of defeats in the Pacific at Guadalcanal, at Midway Island, and in New Guinea, the strategic situation was changing. Also, as the American blockade was tightening its grip, the shipping losses were mounting, and the morale of the civilian population needed a fillip. A victory in Burma would undoubtedly provide this; and would pay other dividends too. The Chinese divisions hovering on the northern Burmese borders, like vultures waiting for the kill, would be hurriedly withdrawn; the British, with the loss of Imphal, would be paralysed, so far as any future offensives were concerned; and India might well rise in rebellion. Subhas Chandra Bose, commander of the renegade 'Indian National Army', was confidently predicting that revolt was simmering just beneath the surface, and with one more British reverse nothing could stop it bursting into fury from Bombay to Calcutta, from Madras to Delhi. Mutaguchi believed him; and the High Command believed Mutaguchi.

So in October and November the staffs got down to detailed planning. The object of the operation was: 'To upset the British base around Imphal in order to suppress the British counter-offensive. To strengthen the defence of Burma and to exercise political control over India.' The 'Scheme of the Operation' was '... to rush into Imphal as quickly as possible and give the Allies no chance to make a counter-offensive.' As the conferences went on week after week plans were modified, and at one stage it was decided that if the 15th Army was successful at Imphal it would then occupy Kohima with powerful forces and 'expect to secure that area in order to establish permanent occupation'. Later on, however, when the tactical importance of Kohima was more fully appreciated, it was decided that a whole division should march there. Having seized the town, it would prevent the British sending down reinforcements to Imphal, slaughter the troops retreating *from* Imphal, and, if called on, send a regiment to join in the main action. On the 7th December, the second anniversary of the attack on Pearl Harbour, the Japanese Prime Minister's broadcast from Tokyo: 'Now, on the threshold of a new year, Japan will seek to consolidate her gains; she will go on doing so until ultimate victory is attained.'

By January 1944 Mountbatten and Slim were quite aware that the Japanese offensive was coming. In December the 31st

Division had been identified at Homalin, and some weeks later the 15th Division was identified also. To quote Slim:

> 'Enemy activity and strength all along 4 Corps front were noticeably increasing. Documents, diaries, marked maps, and even operation orders taken from Japanese killed in these patrol clashes were being brought in almost daily. All these clues, painstakingly fitted into the mosaic of our intelligence at Corps and Army Headquarters, began to give us a general picture of the enemy's intentions.'

Air reconnaissance brought back information of camouflaged rafts being concealed in the lower reaches of the Uyu River, opposite Homalin, and herds of cattle near Thaungdut on the Chindwin. And agents from 'V' Force, the Intelligence Screen, also brought in stories 'of the massing of transport, mechanical and animal, even of elephants'. By the end of January, Slim had a fairly comprehensive picture of the whole Japanese order of battle. As to Mutaguchi's intentions, Slim in conference with Scoones decided that these would be as follows:

> '... first, to capture Imphal, and second, to break through to the Brahmaputra Valley so as to cut off the Northern front and disrupt the air supply to China.... A Japanese regiment would, we foresaw, make for Kohima to cut the main Imphal–Dimapur road and threaten the Dimapur base. We calculated the offensive would begin about the 15th March.'

To meet the threat to Imphal, Slim decided to let the 17th and 20th Indian Divisions fall back on the Imphal Plain, and fight the battle there. 'I was tired,' he said, 'of fighting the Japanese when they had a good line of communications behind them and I had an execrable one. This time I would reverse the procedure.' Nevertheless, Slim was conscious that the forces available to cover Assam were most inadequate and discussed with General Giffard the movement of the 5th Indian Division from the Arakan, and, later on, the 7th Division, when a formation could be brought from India to replace it. The staff at 11th Army Group, however, considered that these movements would overstrain the railway system; and, after considerable argument, Giffard suggested a compromise. This was that he would send Slim the 50th Indian Parachute Brigade, consisting of two battalions, and would put in hand 'arrangements for moving the 2nd British Division if it became urgently necessary to do so'.

Believing that only a Japanese regiment would advance on Kohima, and even this must move slowly and painfully over the difficult country, Slim did not greatly concern himself with the situation there. He was soon to be disillusioned.

*

Executive orders from Tokyo for the Burma offensive reached Kawabe on the 7th January, and after a fortnight's delay he issued his orders to Mutaguchi. (This was about the day that Churchill was writing in a memo to General Ismay: 'This report [by the Joint Intelligence Staff on Japanese Intentions in Burma] confirms the view I have held for some time that the danger of invasion of India by Japan has passed.') A month later Chandra Bose was exhorting the I.N.A. troops with a 'Special Order of the Day'. 'Comrades, Officers and Men of India's Army of Liberation. Let there be one solemn resolve in your hearts— "Either Liberty or Death". And let there be but one slogan on your lips—"Onward to Delhi"... Victory will certainly be yours.' Three days later, on the 18th February, Mutaguchi issued his own Order:

'The Army has now reached the stage of invincibility and the day when the Rising Sun shall proclaim our definite victory in India is not far off.

This operation will engage the attention of the whole world and is eagerly awaited by 100,000,000 of our countrymen. By its very decisive nature, its success will have a profound effect upon the course of the war and may even lead to its conclusion....

I will remind you that a speedy and successful advance is the keynote of this operation... despite all the obstacles of the river, mountain and labyrinthine jungle. Aided by the Gods and inspired by the Emperor and full of the will to win, we must realize the objectives of this operation.... Both officers and men must fight to the death for their country and accept the burden of duties which are the lot of the soldier of Japan.

The will of the Emperor and our countrymen must be fulfilled.'

By this time the Arakan diversion launched by the 55th Division on the 4th February had shot its bolt, but learning that the 5th Indian Division was now committed, Mutaguchi was not unsatisfied. The second stage of his plan could go ahead as scheduled.

*

While Mutaguchi was issuing his Order of the Day, a unit called the 1st Assam Regiment was packing up at its quarters at Digboi in northeast Assam to move to Kohima. This regiment had only been raised in June 1941, with some initial help from the Assam Rifles, and had mobilized six months later. Commanded by British officers, the sepoys included Nagas, Lushais, Khasis, and Assamese, and the language problems were almost insoluble.

However, under the leadership of an energetic commander, Lieut.-Colonel 'Bruno' Brown, these and a good many other problems were overcome, and in April 1942 the battalion moved up to join the 23rd Indian Division, and patrolled towards the Chindwin. A year later it was back in Digboi, more experienced, but pitifully short of clothing and equipment. The orders for a ceremonial parade on the 23rd May are nothing short of Gilbertian and make one wonder why on earth the unit didn't disintegrate:

> 'C Coy will borrow side caps from D Coy.
> D Coy will borrow steel helmets from C Coy.
> A Coy will borrow side caps from B Coy.
> Headquarters Company will lend D Coy any further steel helmets of which they may be deficient.'

However, as Napoleon put it, 'the moral is to the physical as three to one' and six months later the unit was ready for battle. On the 22nd February it arrived at Kohima and took up its quarters in the 57th Reinforcement Camp. Initially, it came under command of Brigadier Hope-Thompson of the 50th Indian Parachute Brigade, which was to be positioned near Ukhrul, thirty-five miles Northeast of Imphal; and its orders were to form firm bases at Jessami and Kharasom, and Phakekedzumi (commonly known as 'Phek') and guard all exits from the Somra Tracts east of Kohima by extensive use of patrols. The battalion would have a company of the 1st Burma Regiment under command to man the position at Phek; and it was to maintain close liaison with the forward screens of V Force and the Assam Rifles.

On the evening of the 23rd February, Charles Pawsey gave the officers of the battalion a farewell cocktail party in his bungalow. This was the last social occasion to be held there; and the last time that all the officers would be together and enjoying themselves. One of them, Peter Steyn, was later to recall the beauty of the garden as he looked out into the evening sunlight, and the laughter and good fellowship inside.

Next morning the battalion marched for Jessami; and on the 27th, after slithering downhill to the Laniye River, climbed up to Jessami Ridge. By the following day, the whole unit was concentrated there, with the exception of 'A' Company under Captain Young which had moved nine miles to the south (eighteen miles along the track) to establish its post at Kharasom. Colonel Brown decided to site his firm base around the junction of two jeep tracks, a quarter of a mile to the south of the village. The spot wasn't ideal for defence, as it had no permanent water point, and was overlooked by the high ground to the south. But it did have an excellent command of the approaches from the east, north, and west; and there was ready access to the bridle paths leading into the Somra hills, and to Mol-he near the Burma border. Temporary bivouac headquarters were set up to the south of the base; and in the latter the battalion (or such men as weren't on patrol) got quickly to work making bunkers and foxholes, then linking them up in a defensive system. Meanwhile, food, ammunition, petrol and engineering stores arrived daily by jeep convoy. The perimeter was surrounded then criss-crossed by barbed wire and by the first week of March the whole position presented a very formidable obstacle indeed. From now on the battalion was to patrol—and wait.

On the 5th March, having flown to Hailakandi to watch the departure of the 77th L.R.P. Brigade for operation 'Thursday' (Wingate's second and most ambitious campaign), Slim flew to Imphal. Here he discussed with Scoones the plans to meet Mutaguchi's coming offensive, and agreed to the withdrawal of the 17th and 20th Indian Divisions, provided that Scoones gave the orders personally when he was certain that a major offensive had begun. Later Slim asked Giffard to earmark additional troops, in case the situation on the Plain became difficult, and

Giffard promised the 25th and 26th Indian Divisions, and the 14th and 23rd L.R.P. Brigades. Slim then arranged to relieve the 5th Indian Division, now engaged in the Arakan, by the 25th Division, as soon as it could arrive. Before he went to bed that night, after a long and anxious day, Slim could be cheered by one thing at least: after withstanding the onslaught of Sakurai's 55th Division, the 7th Division had now resumed its advance.

On the 6th March Mutaguchi began to show his hand. Near Tonzang, on the Manipur River, troops of the 214th Regiment began a series of attacks on the British covering detachments. Gradually these increased until it was evident that the whole regiment was coming across. On the 7th March Scoones set his administrative plan in motion; supply points along the lines of withdrawal to Imphal were stocked up, non-combatant units were ordered back to Dimapur, and self-contained boxes around the town of Imphal were set up. On the same day Slim sent orders to the 5th Division that it was to go to Imphal just as soon as it had been relieved by the 25th, and he moved the 50th Parachute Brigade to Imphal. Also that day Tokyo radio announced: 'The March on Delhi has begun… we shall be in Imphal by the 27th.' And, by a malicious stroke of fate, Mountbatten was injured near Ledo. Jeeping down a track on the northern front, he had been caught in the eye by a bamboo branch and was taken to an American hospital. Here he remained for four days, during this critical phase of the operations, bandaged and unable to see.

Meanwhile the Japanese offensive gained momentum, and on the 8th the 215th Regiment crossed the Manipur River several miles to the south of Tiddim, then moved north to cut the road behind the 17th Indian Division at milestone 100. On the 9th a Jap column was reported at Kaptel, fifteen miles to the west of Tiddim. On the 10th the pressure grew, and the next day 'Punch' Cowan, commander of the 17th Division, having orders to defend Tiddim at all costs, ordered the digging of defensive boxes. On the 12th the advance of the 33rd Japanese

Division became known and Scoones was now quite certain that a major offensive had begun, so next day he ordered Cowan to withdraw, and sent forward his only reserves, to help him fight the encircling Japanese columns, clear the road blocks, and gain the safety of the Imphal Plain. But the fact that he had committed his reserves changed his tactical position; it was now imperative that the 5th Indian Division should be flown up at once. Scoones had an intellectual, analytical brain. Slim rates it as the best brain among senior commanders on this front. Also, by nature, he was equipped for the waiting game; though some people considered he did not inspire and encourage sufficiently, that, like Giffard, he over-dwelt on problems and difficulties. However, Slim was confident that he had the right man in the right place and never wavered from this view.

Three days earlier, on the 10th, with the bandages still covering his eyes, Mountbatten had asked Lieut.-General Sir Henry Pownall, his Chief of Staff, to ascertain what reserves could be moved up to help 4th Corps. The following day he was told that 14 L.R.P. Brigade, a brigade group of the 5th Indian Division, and 23 L.R.P. Brigade were moving up, and that Giffard intended to concentrate the 5th Division in the area immediately it had been relieved from the Arakan. Mountbatten apparently imagined that the relief (and therefore the move of the 5th Division) would take place immediately, as when he learned on the 14th that the Division was still in the Arakan, the situation grew somewhat explosive. The Supremo blamed Giffard for not moving the Division earlier, and for not keeping him informed of the situation while he was in hospital. What Mountbatten did not realize was that on the 6th the Division had gone into action and could not be disengaged any earlier; and also that it was only when Scoones committed his reserves that the situation became desperate. However, this unpleasant interlude had two results, one personal and one military. Mountbatten never trusted Giffard again; and he intervened personally to rush the

161st Brigade from the Arakan to Dimapur. This action was to have a vital effect on the situation at Kohima.

The circumstances of Mountbatten's intervention were as follows: *En route* for Delhi, he touched down at Comilla airstrip for a short conference with Slim. The latter explained the situation and asked for aircraft to expedite the move of the 5th Division to Imphal. Mountbatten promised to put matters in hand at once, and proposed to borrow the necessary aircraft from the air ferry. On the 20th March, six days later, he received word from Washington that the United States Chiefs of Staff had agreed that he could divert thirty Dakotas.

Meanwhile, on the 18th March, there was a further development; Giffard and Slim decided that the 2nd British Division should be moved up to Chittagong and be placed in 14th Army Reserve, the idea being that it should relieve the 7th Indian Division which would then follow the 5th from the Arakan to the Imphal front. Giffard sent this signal off at once, but, as we have already seen, it wasn't decoded and delivered to Stopford till 7.0 p.m. on the 19th. And it was the 21st before Grover was able to reach Corps headquarters to report.

Something else happened on the 18th. Lieutenant Lloyd Jones of the Assam Regiment who had taken out a patrol to Mol-he, near the Burma frontier, was surprised to see a column of Nagas approaching in some agitation. He says: '... they were full of a story that 300 Japs had crossed the Chindwin and were advancing this way across the Somra Tracts.'

Lloyd Jones' first reaction was that it was probably only a Jap patrol, and that the best course was to continue with his own. However, during the night he was woken up by a sentry who pointed to columns of torches moving up the hill towards the stockade—evidence that the panic was widespread, and the villagers were leaving their homes. On the morning of the 19th, the Deputy-Commissioner, Charles Pawsey, arrived with a large party of women and civilian officials; his information was that V Force headquarters at Kuki had been captured. Convinced that the Japanese were in force and carrying out a swift encircling movement, Lloyd Jones rushed back the information to his unit at Jessami, to prevent their being surprised. He also sent a message to V Force headquarters at Imphal, via an Indian Signals unit, though what happened to it once it arrived is not certain.

However, it was on the 19th also that the 5th Division began its move from the Arakan; and that Sato's second-in-command, Miyazaki, who was commanding the southern column of the 31st Division, bumped the 50th Parachute Brigade, which had come down from Kohima on the 10th March, at Sangshak, eight miles from Ukhrul and thirty-six from Imphal. Miyazaki's orders were to move through Ukhrul to Mao, on the Kohima-Imphal road, then turn north for Kohima. But learning about Hope-Thompson's brigade he decided to deal with it, as he did not wish to leave such a powerful force in his rear, threatening his line of communications to the Chindwin. This, as he was to discover later, was a great mistake. Slim, of course, did not know the identity of Miyazaki's column, or whether it had been ordered to turn south to Imphal or north to Kohima; he had to fight the battle as it came.

Next day, the 20th March, Slim and Giffard flew to Imphal for a meeting with Scoones. Slim did not yet realize the extent of the trouble that was brewing for him at Kohima, but he did realize that he'd made one big mistake. Knowing 'the big picture' he should have ordered the withdrawal of the 17th and 20th Indian Divisions himself, before they got embroiled. As it was, Scoones had left things too late and the battle was starting very untidily; 17th Division was having a very hard fight to get back at all, and whether it would do so without a severe mauling was still in doubt. However, one thing had become apparent, and that was that a new Corps commander was needed to operate south from Dimapur and reopen the communications to Imphal should these become cut. As it will be appreciated, both the Dimapur–Kohima–Imphal road, and the railway behind it, ran laterally across the front and were therefore vulnerable. ('Whoever designed Burma,' said Slim, 'designed it for the Japanese.') So, for the first time, it would appear, the suggestion was made that Stopford and his headquarters, now troopless in India, should be brought up to join in the battle. It was also arranged that the 1st Burma Regiment, then *en route* for Fort Hertz, should be diverted to Dimapur to act as local protection, and that the first brigade of the 5th Division to arrive, the 161st Brigade, should be based there as a mobile striking force. 'These measures,' says the Official History, 'it was believed would enable IV Corps to hold up the Japanese while a counter-stroke was prepared.' Whether this is a fair reading of the situation, it is impossible to say, but, knowing the characters of the three men involved, one very much doubts it. However, if that was what they hoped, they were to be disappointed. And before very long.

*

On the 22nd March Colonel Hugh Richards flew to Imphal and reported to Scoones at 4th Corps headquarters. He had been commanding the 3rd West African Brigade, which had been training for Wingate's Chindit expedition, but when Wingate learned that he was fifty years of age, he promptly sent for him and announced that the maximum age for any officer on the show was forty. (Wingate, of course, was forty himself.) Richards was therefore out of a job, so Giffard found him a place on his headquarters at Delhi, until something suitable turned up. So, it happened that on the 20th, when it was rapidly becoming obvious that someone must take charge of Kohima, Giffard wired Richards and told him to come at once. At the 4th Corps headquarters, he was given an operation order which stated quite categorically: 'You will be in operational control of all the troops in Kohima and of 1 Assam Regt. You will be directly under command of 4 Corps. Your role will be to hold Kohima, and to deny the area JESSAMI-KHARASOM-KOHIMA to the enemy by the use of 1 Assam Regt.' From this last paragraph it would appear that 4th Corps had either not received many of the intelligence reports flooding through its signal offices, or did not believe them. In fact, the information paragraph showed that the advance of three columns was now known, each estimated to have a maximum strength of one battalion. It added somewhat sinisterly: 'There may be one more regiment in reserve.' So the probability was that with one battalion Richards would have to defend a triangle of country thirty-five miles in length and ten miles at the base against a force of three battalions; and at the worst, six. To comfort him, perhaps, a staff officer gave an assurance that 'it was most unlikely that the enemy would have any artillery, as the tracks were too bad'.

Pocketing the order, Richards walked out of 4th Corps headquarters and next morning travelled the sixty-five miles to Kohima, where he arrived that afternoon. The first of the principal actors in the Kohima drama was now in position. An hour later, a second arrived in the person of General Stopford who reported to 14th Army headquarters at Comilla. While he was having tea with General Slim, General Auchinleck, C.-in-C. India, was addressing the Council-in-State in New Delhi: 'I am satisfied,' he said, 'that the quality of the men and the strength at the Allies' disposal should enable the latest Japanese "counter-attack" to be dealt with. There is no need to be unduly concerned about the fact that the enemy columns are advancing....'

But a lot of people were concerned; Stilwell and his Americans, for example, who were expecting the railway to be cut and, with it, their only line of communications; also the seething denizens of the base at Dimapur. There is no uglier spectacle on earth than a base in a flap; and here the temperature was mounting as quickly as the barbed wire fences round the Area offices. Only Mutaguchi at Maymyo, and Sato, sweating along the jungle paths with his advance headquarters towards Jessami, had any cause for contentment.

At Kohima, Colonel Richards went on inspecting the defences till it was too dark to see.

Chapter Three

A Conference at Midnight

Two main problems confronted Richards: to decide how much of the Kohima area he could put into a state of defence before the Japanese arrived, and to discover how many men he would have to fight under him when they did. As his reconnaissance soon revealed, the whole place was in a complete mess. Various people had been toying with the job of preparing defences, before being replaced by others, who in turn had been replaced by someone else. Such trenches as had been dug were too wide and lacked head cover. Some of them were badly sited too. On making inquiries Richards discovered that they hadn't been dug by troops at all, but by Naga labour, working under inadequate supervision. Worse still, there seemed to be a complete lack of defence stores—especially barbed wire; in his whole reconnaissance he didn't see a foot of it.

The defence was organized into four boxes. The main one was sited in the central area, from the Treasury (north of the D.C.'s bungalow) to Jail Hill. It included the series of wooded hillocks enclosed by the road: Kuki Piquet, D.I.S. Hill, and F.S.D. Hill, and, in its northwestern sector, the I.G.H. Spur. In short, the 'duck's head' shaped region, enclosed by the road. Stationed in the box was a medley of administrative units, including a petrol depot, an ordnance store, a field bakery section, a transport company, and a cattle conducting section. As to fighting troops, there were some rear details of the Assam Regiment, some platoons of the Assam Rifles, and the bulk of a State Forces battalion. This force was totally inadequate. A second box was sited at the Reinforcement Camp, a couple of miles along the Bokajan road, to the north of the main position. A third box was sited at milestone 44, two miles along the Dimapur road; and a fourth on G.P.T. Ridge, below the Aradura Spur. Out at their boxes at Jessami and Kharasom, thirty-five miles to the east (sixty along the track), were the rifle companies and headquarters of the Assam Regiment, who were under Richards' command. Guided by Major Giles, of the R.I.A.S.C., Richards toured the whole area for two days; he had to see and study the ground now, for, as he realized, he wouldn't get another chance.

On the afternoon of his arrival, Richards had been taken to the D.C.'s bungalow, where he met Major-General Ranking (commander of 202 Area), and Brigadier Haines (commander of 253 Sub-Area), and Lieut.-Colonel Borrowman, who was adviser to the State troops. They gave him all the information they could, but concerning one of the main problems facing him, they were vague in the extreme: and that was the number and composition of the troops available to defend the place. The plain fact, as he soon realized, was that they did not know; and it was very doubtful whether 4th Corps or anyone else knew either. All Richards could do was keep working and planning from day to day, and see what turned up.

On the 24th March, the 2nd Battalion West Yorkshire Regiment turned up, to his great relief and delight. This was a famous unit which bad already fought the Italians and the Germans, apart from the Japanese; and by a happy coincidence, Richards had at one time been second-in-command of it for three years. His old adjutant was now the commanding officer. The obvious task for the battalion was to dig themselves into the central box and constitute themselves the main buttress of its defence. As far as Richards had been able to ascertain from his subsidiary commanders, the number of men in the area, at the moment, thought to be capable of bearing arms, was about eleven hundred; but the difference between a collection of troops from various detachments and a crack British infantry unit is immense. The arrival of the West Yorks virtually quadrupled his strength; it made the defence of the main box at least feasible.

But there was one big snag; and that was that the local administration of Kohima still came under 253 Sub-Area. As Richards was soon to discover, troops were coming and going all the time, without any reference to him, so the total of weapon-bearing men rose and fell with every hour that passed, and would continue to do so. He had absolutely no powers to detain anyone for the garrison; and it was possible, at least, that by the time the Japanese arrived his 'eleven hundred' would be reduced to nine, or even six. Seldom in history can a commander have prepared to defend a vital position in circumstances of such chaos.

Two other events happened on the 24th, though Richards heard of neither of them. The Chiefs of Staff told Mountbatten that the Americans' view of his role was 'to develop, maintain and protect the air link with China'. And General Wingate was killed in an air crash.

On the 25th, Richards ordered the West Yorkshires to send out a detachment to liaise with the Assam Regiment. Though he could sense that the tide of war was sweeping closer, his information concerning the enemy was vague and fragmentary—all intelligence reports were still being routed via the Sub-Area ! The officer commanding the West Yorkshire detachment arrived at Jessami to find the Assam Regiment evacuating its bivouacs to occupy the bunker position. Patrols were still going out, however, and recently had reported increased Japanese activity in the Laruri area, which had caused the withdrawal of all V Force personnel to Phek. This information was carried back to Kohima before nightfall.

In fact, the exact point reached by the Japanese that day was Layshi, some sixty miles from Kohima, and eighty along the track. Jessami lay directly in their path, still twenty-five miles off. The column commanded by Colonel Torikai was still going well, even after ten days of tremendous exertion. Very little opposition had been encountered so far, and the information reaching the advance guard commander, and relayed to Sato who was moving with his tactical headquarters, indicated that even less lay ahead. Mutaguchi was evidently right: the British had not expected such a lightning thrust and were unprepared for it. A few more days and Kohima would be in sight.

Behind the forward troops things were not going so smoothly, and it is difficult to understand how the momentum of the advance was maintained. According to the Divisional War Correspondent, Yukihiko Imai:

> 'It was cold on the journey and the rivers were full. Large numbers of horses and oxen fell down into the ravines. The horses kept going to the limit of their strength, but the oxen were much more trouble. When tired they would sit on the path and would not move a step even though the soldiers beat them. As a last resort the troops had to set fire to their tails.
>
> As soon as we reached a village we caught the women and children and locked them up. We then asked the men folk to guide us to the next village, promising to release their families as soon as they had done so. This was the only way we could get guides or labour to help with the transport. By the time we had got half way we had lost most of the horses and oxen, either through their falling down the hillside, or being shot by enemy gunfire.'

While Sato was passing through Layshi, Mutaguchi was at Torburg near Tiddim, where he had gone to see Lieut.-General Yanagida, commander of the 33rd Division. Mutaguchi was in great spirits, for not only was the news from Sato good, but the British were falling back on Imphal, just as he knew they would, and already much of the Kabaw valley was in his hands. Yanagida, however, was pessimistic. He'd lost a considerable number of men in his fight with the 17th Indian Division, and it was still moving back in good order. No one had panicked; no one had thrown their arms or equipment away and this Yanagida did not like. He'd never had much faith in the operation, and now things were going wrong, just as he'd predicted. He told Mutaguchi: 'You'd better give up your idea of the March on Delhi.' This outburst did not deter Mutaguchi; he merely noted that Yanagida was unfit to command a division in action, and resolved to replace him with a younger, more vigorous officer, who wouldn't argue. Within six weeks Lieut.-General Nobua Tanaka had taken over.

However, while Mutaguchi was talking to Yanagida, there were two other developments in the situation which were to have a considerable effect on the battle to come. At a meeting of the Combined Chiefs of Staff, General Arnold promised Mountbatten the loan of 400 transport aircraft, to reach S.E.A.C. in groups of 100 a month from the 1st July; and two brigades of the 5th Indian Division began their fly-in to the Imphal front.

On the 26th events continued to move steadily if unspectacularly. During the previous night the 50th Indian Parachute Brigade had pulled out of Sangshak, leaving 100 seriously wounded behind. In all, counting killed, wounded, and missing, the brigade had lost 500 men. Miyazaki had lost 220 killed and 350 wounded out of a total strength of 2,180; also the action had delayed him twice as long as he'd calculated. However, his line of communications was clear now, and he headed north-west towards Tuphema and the Imphal–Kohima road.

While Miyazaki advanced, Giffard flew into Comilla to see Slim, and there took a most important decision; this was that, pending the arrival of Stopford's headquarters, or a divisional headquarters, operational control of the Dimapur area, as far south as, but *excluding,* Kohima, should be handed to Major-General Ranking of the 202 Area. This was an emergency move, as Area commanders and their staffs are not equipped or trained to run operations, being purely administrative. But something had to be done, and this was apparently the best arrangement anyone could think of. The 2nd Burma Regiment, and the 161st Brigade, as it flew in, was to come under Ranking's command. The latter consisted of the 4th Royal West Kents, the 1st/1st Punjab, and the 4th/7th Rajputana Rifles; the commander was Brigadier D. F. W. Warren, and what he said when he heard that he was under the Area commander is neither repeatable nor printable.

At Kohima, Richards went out to Jessami to see Colonel Brown of the Assam Regiment, and about half-way there, at Chezumi, he ran into Pawsey who had just been up to Phek. Around him were hundreds of Naga families, all refugees from the country west of the Chindwin, and Pawsey was laying on food for them, calming them, listening to their troubles, and at the same time working out arrangements to have them sent on to Kohima. Richards began to realize the qualities of this remarkable man, and the complete faith that the Nagas had in him. As he says: 'They truly regarded him as their father who would solve all their troubles.' Richards also came to realize that the intelligence information passed on by Pawsey, from his Nagas, was always accurate—even when intelligence officers further back thought otherwise.

At Jessami Richards found 'an atmosphere of complete confidence and eager anticipation among the Assam Regiment... they were in great heart'. The whole defensive position was wired in, and included a command post, mortar positions, and a Regimental Aid Post. Also, a field of fire had been cleared. Now, as Richards had learned two days previously, the orders to the Assam Regiment from 4th Corps were that they were to fight 'to the last round and the last man'. This meant that the whole regiment must sacrifice itself to slow down the Japanese advance on Kohima, which, even for men of great courage, was a very stern task indeed. Just as Richards was about to leave, Brown took him on one side and asked if the order still stood. Obviously Brown's idea was that if there were to be any change *now* was the time to make it, as he added: 'I expect to be attacked by anything up to a battalion of Japs tomorrow morning.' Richards told him that the order must stand. Brown did not argue or dissent in any way and was obviously prepared to do his duty. However, on the way back to Kohima, Richards began worrying about the order and came to the conclusion that it wasn't justified. No one could fight indefinitely without an adequate source of water inside their perimeter, and this Brown lacked. Furthermore, the basic role of the battalion was now collecting information by patrolling. There was no intention to give battle to the Japs as far east as Jessami, and no intention either to reinforce Brown's positions. Once contact had been made the battalion should concentrate on harassing and delaying the enemy, which would obviously be much superior in strength. Richards, in the light of this reconsideration, decided to take the matter up as soon as he reached Kohima.

In fact, he did not reach there till the morning of the 27th. By then a signal had arrived informing him that the West Yorkshires must not be used in any forward role; and this was followed by a second signal saying that they should be sent to Imphal forthwith. So Richards was left with his 'odds and sods' again; and he had no troops for any delaying actions on the precipitous gullies along the Jessami track. The position was deteriorating fast. Then he learned that at 0600 hours Captain

Young, commanding the company of the Assam Regiment at Kharasom, south of Jessami, had phoned through to his C.O. to say that a column of Japs, a battalion strong, with mules, elephants, and artillery, was approaching his position. He had just opened fire. After this conversation, the telephone wire was cut, and no further news was received.

At S.E.A.C. headquarters Mountbatten received some good news: permission to keep twenty Commando aircraft, borrowed from the ferry over the Hump, for a further month. This meant that more troops could be flown in, which meant in turn an easing of the strain on the Assam railway line. Orders were therefore sent out that the 2nd Division should not be routed to the Arakan, as previously planned, but to Dimapur. 33rd Brigade of 7th Indian Division was also routed to Assam. Actually, the leading brigade of the 2nd Division, the 5th, had already entrained at Ahmednagar on the evening of the 26th, and the other two brigades were getting ready to follow it. So the paths of all the troops to fight at Kohima were now delineated; some, like the Assam Rifles and the Assam Regiment, were already in the area; some, like the 161st Brigade were on their way; some like the 33rd Brigade, were still in the Arakan, and others, like the brigades of the 2nd Division, were still strung out over fifteen hundred miles in India. Sato was only thirty miles away as the crow flies and sixty by jeep track; but every hour was to bring the two sides closer to their head-on collision. The pattern was set, irrevocably.

*

Stand-to in the Jessami box on the morning of the 28th was understandably somewhat tense, but no Japs could be seen, and eventually the men were allowed to stand down again. However, at 0855 hours Major Askew, a company commander, phoned Colonel Brown to say that twenty-four Japs with an officer at their head were marching towards him along the track from Kharasom.

'All right, old boy. Hold your fire.'

'Very good, sir.'

The Japs came on till they reached the wire across the road, then stood bunched round their officer, some forty yards from the forward Bren guns. For a moment there was silence. Then, after a curt order, the Brens started firing in bursts and all the Japs crumpled into a grotesque heap in the middle of the road. Two of them managed to crawl away into the undergrowth, but the remainder lay where they were. Again there was silence; and 'Bruno' Brown signalled back the news to Richards at Kohima. The result was an urgent request for any items of identification from the Japanese corpses, and a naik and a V Force scout volunteered to crawl forward to try and bring in one of them. The naik didn't get very far before he was killed, but the scout courageously went on alone. It was no use though, as Japanese reinforcements had arrived and any attempt at movement in the open was punished ruthlessly. Even a platoon was pinned down and further attempts had to be called off. The Japs didn't attack in daylight, however, despite their increasing numbers, and contented themselves with efforts to try and provoke the garrison into revealing their machine-gun and mortar positions. They were disappointed.

At Kohima things had livened up, too. Richards was sending away non-combatants, and useless mouths, back-loading stores to Dimapur, and making what arrangements he could for water storage. The latter were unsatisfactory, to say the least, as the water supply point was over on G.P.T. Ridge in a very exposed position, and the only receptacles for storage were two tarpaulins dug into the ground and six steel tanks which would obviously become riddled with holes once fighting began, and a large iron tank in the bungalow area. In the midst of these administrative problems, Richards learned that the 161st Brigade would be arriving with the immediate task of extricating the detachments of the Assam Regiment at Jessami and Kharasom. This was good news; and on the face of it transformed the whole situation. But by now Richards was cautious; things were far too fluid and might just as quickly deteriorate again.

At 10.30 a.m. Slim, Stopford, and a small group of staff officers flew from Comilla to Imphal for a conference with Scoones. Here they discussed the question of control and command, as between 4th Corps and 33rd Corps, and decided that, as Imphal was obviously about to be cut off, 4th Corps could not control the situation at Kohima. This was therefore to be added to Ranking's command. At 12.15 p.m. the party took off again and flew up the road, over Kohima, and touched down at Dimapur airstrip. Transport was waiting to take them to Ranking's headquarters and here they discussed with him the deployment of the troops now coming under his command. Concentration areas for the brigades of the 2nd Division were agreed, and for the 23rd L.R.P. Brigade which was now on its way from Hailakandi.

But a more immediate problem, which was thrashed out at a number of meetings in the afternoon and evening, was to decide on a policy for the defence of Dimapur and Kohima. Slim's view was that 'Kohima Ridge was an infinitely preferable defensive position to Dimapur'. Kohima, he considered, covered Dimapur, and 'as long as we clung to the ridge, we had some chance of concentrating our reinforcements as they arrived, without too much hostile interference'. Slim estimated that the Japanese would reach Kohima by the 3rd April—in six days' time. If they decided to split their forces and send a regimental group against Dimapur, he thought it would not arrive there before the 10th April, and by that date the 5th Brigade of the 2nd Division should be on the ground. Slim therefore gave Ranking three tasks: to prepare Dimapur for defence and when attacked to hold it, to reinforce Kohima and hold that to the last, and to make arrangements for the reception of reinforcements. These tasks were embodied in a written directive.

The only formation available to defend Kohima, apart from the fragmentary units of the garrison, was the 161st Indian Brigade which was now arriving. In the early evening its commander, 'Daddy' Warren, reported to 202 Area headquarters where Slim 'put him in the picture'. Warren (to quote Slim) was 'steady, unruffled, and slow speaking'. This is undoubtedly true; but he was also fast-thinking and fast-moving, and a very live wire indeed. His regiment was the 8th Punjab, and he spoke excellent Urdu and Punjabi, and was very good with the troops. He had been a staff officer in the Arakan during the heart-breaking battles of the previous year, and had few illusions about the business of fighting the Japanese. He had a strong temper; and a good deal of prejudice against the British service. But he was a fine soldier, and his moment was drawing near. On this hot, sticky evening in Dimapur, as Slim records: '... he heard me out, asked a few questions, and went quietly off to get on with the job. I hope I had as good an effect on him as he had on me.' Warren's job, of course, was to assemble his brigade and move it out to Kohima as soon as possible.

While Slim and Warren were talking, the advance guard of the 138th Regiment began their attack on the box at Jessami. Under covering fire from their machine-guns, the Japs rushed forward, hurling grenades and shouting their war cry—*Banzai! Banzai!* The men of the Assam Regiment held their fire till the attackers were close, then poured Bren and rifle fire into their ranks. The leading platoons were decimated and the assault was broken up, but time after time the Japs re-formed and came on again with fanatical courage. Often the pressure was so great that it seemed the defence must be over-run, but then attacks would be broken off just as suddenly as they had started. Crouching in their bunkers, the Nagas, the Kukis, the Karsis, and all the tribesmen that went to make the Assam Regiment, changed their red-hot Bren barrels, reloaded their magazines, then waited for the next attack. Sometimes in the silence they could hear the whimpering of the Japanese wounded lying just outside the wire. This sound would be swamped by the prelude to a new assault... and so the night wore on. Only a few enemy soldiers managed to infiltrate through the outer perimeter, and they were despatched by the men in the supporting bunkers. When daylight came their bodies were searched and a unit flag and items of equipment were discovered. Obviously, these had to be sent back to Kohima at once and, from several volunteers, Lance-Naik Jogendra Nath and a sepoy were selected. Choosing their moment, they slipped down the western escarpment, disappeared into the jungle, and headed west.

Meanwhile, the rest of the unit brewed up tea and ate their breakfast, while the Japs provided them with the morning's entertainment. This consisted of a strafe by the infantry gun, which did little damage, followed by appeals in English and Hindustani. 'O, Indian soldiers, stop fighting for the British and come and join us. We are freeing your country from domination.' Needless to say, there was no response to these invitations.

At Kharasom things were not so happy. The company there under Captain Young had now withstood an attack by vastly superior forces for two days and nights, and suffered a good many casualties. But all communication had been severed with battalion headquarters on the 27th so 'Bruno' Brown could only guess at the situation. And what worried him most of all was that he could do nothing to help.

During the morning there was a telephone call from General Scoones, who rang up from Imphal to ask what the situation was. Brown told him that it was under control at the moment, but his battalion could not be expected to hold out many days as the enemy forces increased. Scoones is said to have replied: 'Keep on hitting them and we will see what help we can give you from this end.' The incident is puzzling as, not only was Scoones himself about to be cut off in Imphal and therefore unable to help, but at the meeting with Slim the previous morning he had handed over responsibility for Jessami to General Ranking. Perhaps he merely meant that help would reach Brown from outside; or perhaps the line was indistinct and Brown misunderstood him; one cannot be certain. What was certain, however, as Brown realized only too well, was that the order to fight to the last man and the last round still stood; whatever happened, there could be no retreat.

As already mentioned, Colonel Richards was very concerned about the order, and when Warren arrived at Kohima on the morning of the 29th, with General Ranking, he raised the matter in discussion and pointed out that the Assam Regiment was being attacked by larger forces than had been imagined. Pawsey's information from his Nagas was that a whole division was advancing. Warren responded immediately and, with Ranking's agreement, laid on an operation to extricate all three garrisons from Phek, Jessami, and Kharasom. Briefly, the plan was that the 4th/7th Rajputs would deal with the first two positions, while the 1st/1st Punjab would look after the third. (The other battalion, the 4th Royal West Kents, were to remain in reserve at Kohima.) A major snag was that the telephone line to Brown's headquarters had now been cut and, as the radio set had gone out of operation, there was now no communication at all. So Richards suggested that he send an officer called Wemyss, who knew the lay-out of the position at Jessami, to Dimapur, with the idea that he should go up in an R.A.F. plane and guide it to the spot. A message in clear would then be dropped in the centre of the perimeter, ordering Brown to withdraw. Wemyss set off at once, and the next day he got aboard a plane and headed for Jessami; but the message fell in the battalion's old bivouac area instead of the perimeter, and Brown and his men fought on where they were. About this time some important news reached 4th Corps headquarters: the Japanese had reached the Kohima–Imphal road and established a block at milestone 72, near Maram. This was the leading battalion of the 58th Regiment, Miyazaki's advanced guard; although this energetic commander had been delayed four days at Sangshak he was still ahead of schedule.

When the sun came up on Jessami on the morning of the 30th March, it soon became evident that the Japanese had been considerably reinforced. Apart from small arms there was mortar fire and artillery, and the whole bunker position became thoroughly uncomfortable. In an effort to retaliate, 'Bruno' Brown ordered his battalion mortars into action, and for a while they put up a gallant show, breaking up several attacks. But by now the enemy was on the high ground to the south, overlooking the shallow weapon pits in which the mortars were sited, and one by one the detachments were knocked out. The men of the rifle companies, cramped and crouching in the bunkers, had repulsed more attacks than they could count and were palpably tiring; but their casualties had as yet been slight and they remained in good heart. Every post still held. No doubt the strain was greatest on Brown for he knew that the Japs wouldn't be satisfied until the position and the men in it had been obliterated; and, as they had artillery, apart from the small infantry gun, they would obviously succeed. But even Brown did not realize the true size of the column; that it contained the 138th Regiment, less one battalion, the whole of the 124th Regiment, a battalion of the 31st Mountain Artillery, and Sato's headquarters.

Some time that day, the R.A.F. plane came over the Jessami box again, guided by Wemyss, and a second message was dropped. This landed rather closer—about fifteen yards outside the perimeter. Immediately parties of men were sent out under covering fire to try and retrieve it, but the Japs had spotted the message too, and were trying to get it themselves. So a dog-fight started, both sides trying to get someone to the message; and in the end the Japs won. As it was in clear, they were able to read it and the plan was given away.

In fact, the plan didn't get very far. To begin with, the 1st/1st Punjab, who were moving along the track running from Tuphema to Kharasom, ran into a detachment of Miyazaki's columns and a sharp engagement followed in which about a hundred Japs were killed and the Punjabis suffered seventeen casualties. It was pretty obvious, however, that the Japanese were in considerable strength, and any advance on Kharasom by one battalion was out of the question. But, in the event, there was no need for it to try, as on the afternoon of the 30th General Ranking cancelled the whole operation and ordered the 161st Brigade back to the Nichugard Pass.

The circumstances which caused this extraordinary change of plan were as follows. As Stopford's staff arrived and he became operational, he naturally took command of the area, and Ranking therefore came under him. On the 29th, at Comilla Slim had asked Stopford to set down his appreciation of the situation. This he did and on the morning of the 30th handed it to Slim who approved it. Slim then asked him to draft a new directive to Ranking, 'telling him the lines on which to function', and it was agreed that Stopford should fly to Dimapur, hand this to Ranking personally, and presumably discuss any difficulties with him. Now, it is evident that Stopford saw the situation somewhat differently to Slim, and his directive set out Ranking's tasks in order of priority as follows:

1. The defence of Dimapur.
2. The protection of the railway.
3. The retention of a firm base and mobile striking force at Dimapur.
4. The defence of Kohima.

It followed logically from this that as Kohima had been given bottom priority, the 161st Brigade should be brought back from there and established in the Dimapur area.

Stopford left Comilla by air at 3.30 p.m., arriving at Dimapur ninety minutes later, but it would seem that he must have telephoned Ranking earlier, as the latter put through a call to Warren. During this he ordered him to break off the action his brigade was engaged in at once, and to concentrate at Nichugard, eight miles from Dimapur, by 1800 hours the following day. Warren protested angrily at this order and persuaded Ranking to go out to Kohima and discuss it. When Ranking arrived, he found Warren, Richards, and Pawsey waiting for him on the roadside, and they attacked him at once, asking what information the order had been based on. Ranking said that a column of Japanese had been seen by the R.A.F. moving northwards, round the left flank of Kohima, towards the railway. There was therefore some danger that, should Warren's brigade be left at Kohima, it would be cut off.

Warren and Richards had no faith in the R.A.F. report, and Pawsey would have none of it either. He said: 'If the Japs were there, my Nagas would have told me. What the pilot saw was a group of villagers returning home after their day's work.' Ranking saw the sense in this interpretation and promised to inform Stopford. Meanwhile, Warren impressed upon him the serious tactical repercussions of any withdrawal of his brigade. He argued: 'Once we are dug in here, the Japs wouldn't dare bypass us—they couldn't leave such a strong force in their rear.' Ranking listened to this argument, but insisted that the order to withdraw must be obeyed. At this Warren asked permission to fly to Comilla and put the case to Slim personally, but Ranking wouldn't agree. Finally, after some heated exchanges, he returned to Dimapur, leaving Warren, Richards, and Pawsey horrified and depressed. With their detailed knowledge of the ground, all their military instincts told them that the loss of Kohima Ridge would be a major disaster, jeopardizing the whole front. They knew that if the Japanese 31st Division occupied it from end to end, weeks, perhaps months, of action would be needed, with thousands of casualties before the position could be restored. They knew also that the only force which could deny the Ridge to the Japanese was Warren's brigade; that the garrison troops could not possibly hold out for more than a few days.

Apart from this major issue, there was the fate of the Assam Regiment. Warren considered that to abandon this unit would not only be inhuman, but dishonourable; such an action went against all his ideas of soldiering. Richards and Pawsey agreed with him, and after more argument on the telephone it was conceded that the Rajputs should be allowed an extra twenty-four hours to enable them to extricate the garrison from Jessami, the withdrawal being timed 'not before the night of the 31st March/1st April, and preferably on that night'. This was the only concession.

To Charles Pawsey the situation was especially ironic. Having spent twenty-two years in Assam, his knowledge of its terrain was immense; and ever since the Japanese invasion of Burma in 1942 he had tried to warn the Army (through his reports to the Governor) that Kohima was just as vulnerable as Imphal. Persistently he urged that it should be allocated first-class troops and be put into a state of defence. Though a Civil Servant by profession, Pawsey did not lack military knowledge, having served in the First World War where he won the Military Cross and bar. When the 4th Corps Sappers improved the old government bridle path, making it jeepable from the Chindwin to Kohima, he increased his representations, but without effect. And now what he had feared, what he had foretold, was coming to pass.

By one of those curious quirks of timing which punctuate this whole story, while Ranking was giving out his disastrous orders on the roadside at Kohima, 'the Auk' was making another speech, this time in the Indian Assembly. He said: 'We cannot stop every Japanese threat as soon as it makes itself apparent.... I am convinced, however, that the security of Assam has never been in any danger....' And a few hours later, Tokyo radio announced: 'Kohima has fallen.' It is difficult to say which of these statements was further from reality.

Things at Jessami that night were worse than ever. The Jap infantry showered the position with grenades, then came in furiously with the bayonet, wave after wave of them. The attacks were furious, but uncoordinated, and somehow the defenders were able to cling on. Whenever small parties of enemy infiltrated through the first ring of bunkers, they were exterminated by the second. The Assam Regiment had suffered remarkably few casualties, even now, which says a great deal for the siting and construction of the defensive positions. And the courage shown on all sides was magnificent. Peter Steyn wrote later:

> 'Young and inexperienced sepoys were fighting like veterans; red-hot machine-gun barrels would be ripped off, regardless of burns suffered in the process; Japanese grenades and cracker-bombs were picked up and thrown clear of the trenches with all the calmness in the world and there did not seem to be a man in the garrison afraid to carry out any task given to him.'

But everyone was getting very tired, and the odds were building up with each hour that passed. It was only a matter of time before the position would be over-run.

The next morning, the 31st, the enemy continued the pressure, though things were never quite so bad in daylight as at night. The R.A.F. flew over in an attempt to drop supplies, but the parachutes drifted across and fell outside the perimeter; and the men had the mortification of seeing Japs retrieve the precious packages. So the hours wore on... and darkness descended again. Towards ten o'clock there was a good deal of shooting at the southern end of the perimeter, and all posts were alerted to repel another attack. Then a man could be heard bellowing at the top of his voice:

'Stop firing, will you. It's John Corlett. Stop firing.'

Fortunately for its owner, the voice was immediately recognized, and Corlett was allowed to scramble through the perimeter and make his way to Brown's headquarters bunker. He was an officer of the regiment who had been with the detachment at Phek, and when orders came through to withdraw, he immediately inquired whether the rest of the battalion had been advised. Assured that messages had been dropped from the air, he remained somewhat sceptical, doubting whether the position could be accurately located, so made for Jessami with his orderly.

At first light, 'Bruno' Brown assembled all his officers and issued orders for a withdrawal the following evening. The battalion would be split up into two parties, the western sectors under Brown himself, slipping out by the west, while the eastern sectors would evacuate the position eastwards, skirt Jessami village, then strike westwards for Kohima, if possible linking up with Brown's party. This was a reasonable plan, and if the Japs hadn't read the message dropped by the R.A.F. it might have worked. But now they knew what the battalion was up to and renewed their efforts to destroy it before it could get away. In a whole series of savage attacks the perimeter was breached several times, and hand-to-hand fighting went on inside it. Bunkers were lost, retaken, lost, and won back again in fierce, deadly combat by small groups of men, friend and foe hopelessly jumbled. Somehow, despite the exhaustion, gaps in the defence were closed, but by 1700 hours, a large gap had appeared and there were no men left capable of putting in a counter-attack. For some reason, the Japanese did not pour any men through the gap, but it was clear that there was no point in continuing the struggle and, if the battalion was to get away at all, it must be now. Brown changed his orders, and the sections were told to move off as they were able to disengage themselves, after dark. The only hope now was to move in small parties and filter through the Jap positions. Documents were destroyed, and the men, having collected such possessions as they wished to take away, and some food and water, waited for their moment as darkness fell, and slipped into the jungle. Others were not so fortunate and could not disengage until it was almost too late. Some could not get away at all and fought to the end. Later that night, it is said, the Japanese ran howling and screaming through the empty bunkers, enraged that their prey should have eluded them. But not all the garrison who slipped away reached the temporary safety of Kohima; many bumped enemy detachments on the jungle tracks, and some parties, in panic, fired at each other.

The situation at Kharasom was even more tragic. No message to withdraw had reached Captain Young, but before dark he had seen a battalion of Japanese approaching his position, with mules and elephants, and he knew that he must soon be overwhelmed. His orders were to fight to the last round and last man, but increasingly he had come to the conclusion that they were senseless; that, having delayed the enemy with great gallantry for four days, his company had done enough. He therefore decided to disobey orders, and made plans for a withdrawal that evening. Unfortunately, however, as soon as the men learned of these they became restive and some of them slipped away before time, the company eventually becoming split up into three groups. But, though he refused to sacrifice his company, Young, perhaps wishing to demonstrate that this refusal wasn't motivated by fear, announced that he would stay to face the Japanese alone. This he did, and during the night the Nagas heard him destroying equipment. At first light when the enemy troops moved in to search the bunkers, Young took them on single-handed with grenades and his machine-gun, till riddled with bullets he could fight no more. He was a very gallant officer.*

The position at midnight on the 31st March therefore was that the road to Kohima was open to Sato's column, advancing from the east, and to Miyazaki's column, preparing to advance north up the road from Tuphema. Two battalions of 161st Brigade were now back at the Nichugard Pass, and the third was under orders to join them the next day. Ranking, who was becoming increasingly worried about the order he had been compelled to deliver to Warren, rang up Slim, who was at his headquarters in Comilla, and asked if he could leave the Royal West Kents at Kohima. The reasons he gave were not only military but political: in Pawsey's view, he said, the virtual abandonment of Kohima would be a great blow to the Nagas, who up to now had been doing such magnificent work. Slim replied that he would have to discuss the matter with Stopford, and with Brigadier Irwin, a staff officer, walked into his room. Stopford, however, remained adamant. 'I had to refuse to listen to these suggestions,' he wrote later. 'I had made my plan and must stick to it.... Slim eventually accepted this.'

Slim, it now appears, was in some difficulty. In agreeing to Stopford's appreciation and the directive to Ranking, he had

* Some very interesting information regarding the actions at Jessami and Kharasom has recently been revealed by Colonel Yamaki, Senior Intelligence Officer to 31st Division. He says that the reason why the Assam Regiment was attacked in such strength is that Major Shibasaki, commanding the troops on the extreme right flank of the Japanese advance, 'marched to the sound of the guns' and joined in the battle. When Sato came forward and heard this he was furious and reprimanded Colonel Torikai, the column commander. He said: 'Your correct course was to leave enough troops to contain the garrisons here and push on to Kohima.' Some months later, Sato remarked sorrowfully: 'If Miyazaki hadn't delayed at Sangshak, and Torikai at Jessami, the face of the Kohima battle might have been very different.' How right he was!

not appreciated that they entailed the withdrawal of the 161st Brigade. In his view, Kohima covered Dimapur. Stopford saw things differently; his view was that if—as Slim had agreed—the first task was to defend Dimapur, and the second to defend the railway, then the troops must come back. If Sato sent a column round the north of Kohima, as the R.A.F. report indicated he might be doing, then to have the only available striking force out on a limb would be to invite disaster. On the face of it, the case was unanswerable; and Slim, having given Stopford a job to do, had to let him do it in his own way. Perhaps the balance was tipped by the fact that Brigadier Irwin supported Stopford. So the fateful order remained; and Ranking was told that the 161st Brigade must be 'concentrated at Nichugard as soon as possible'. One historian has suggested that Ranking might have interpreted the phrase 'as soon as possible' more liberally, but this seems quite fatuous: as an officer holding a purely administrative appointment, he was in a most anomalous position as it was, commanding operations, and with Slim and Stopford on his neck he had no option but to do as he was told.

Stopford's recollection of this episode is slightly different from Slim's. He says: 'I don't think there was any misunderstanding between Slim and myself about the implication of his orders, but probably I was over-anxious about the likelihood of Japanese infiltration and he may not have realized the defenceless state of the Base.' Regarding Warren's argument, that Sato would not dare to leave a brigade in his rear, Stopford says: 'Admittedly, Kohima might be considered as covering Dimapur but it was a long way off and, from what I heard of the Jap tactics, I anticipated that they might try to seal off the frontier and infiltrate round it as the Base would be a most valuable prize.... Even a small attack on the Base during this interregnum [i.e. before the arrival of the 2nd Division] would have caused chaos.'

Both Stopford and Slim were working on imperfect information, with little knowledge of Sato's intentions; and there is no question of blaming either of them. But the historical fact is that Slim's instinct bowed before Stopford's hard logic; the last in a long chain of decisions was ratified, making a battle of attrition inevitable.

The tragedy was, though the British commanders could not know this, that Sato's objective was strictly confined to Kohima. Dimapur was in no danger.

Chapter Four

Green for Eastertide

At 1930 hours on the evening of Saturday, 1st April, a train pulled into Dimapur station, loaded with troops and kit. The first contingent of the 2nd Division had arrived—the 7th Worcestershires, and advance detachments from the other two units in the brigade, the Dorsetshires and the Cameron Highlanders. The Brigade Commander, Victor Hawkins, was already in Dimapur, and had reconnoitred a concentration area at Bokajan. This lay eight miles to the north, astride the track from Kohima, and was therefore the obvious place to go. Hawkins planned to build up a fortnight's supplies of food and ammunition, so that, if necessary, the concentration area could be used as a base for future operations. It cannot be said that Bokajan found great favour with the troops. Geoffrey White of the Dorsets has written:

> 'Of all the many jungles we have encountered, I would say unhesitatingly that the Bokajan species was the worst. It was wet and prickly, dank and gloomy, and it was not only rank but stank. By the grace of God and the Japanese, we were only there a very short time.'

If Bokajan didn't impress the 5th Brigade favourably,

Dimapur was even worse. The staff captain 5th Brigade wrote in his diary:

> 'The whole place is in one big flap. The L. of C. area are digging and wiring themselves in their offices, and gangs of pioneers are putting slit trenches round the Rest Camp. Transport with wild-eyed Indian drivers is speeding north along the Bokajan road with barely six inches between trucks. Haggard-looking coolies stagger on with loads and the number of refugees gets bigger every hour. They walk slowly along with their whole world on their heads; occasionally one collapses by the road and the others group round, blocking the traffic but doing nothing. Am told there are 80,000 men in this place, but only 10,000 rifles. Can quite believe it. Have never seen so many troops walking around unarmed.'

The 80,000 were coolies employed in the depots which lined the main roads, in areas cut out of the jungle. They could obviously not fight themselves, and would get in the way of anyone else who tried to. Some civilian labour had disappeared altogether. On the 2nd April an officer and his batman, just arrived with 5th Brigade, rode their motorbike into a large canteen issue depot. Walking up to the counter, they found themselves gazing at vast quantities of chocolate, food, toilet requisites, cigarettes, beer, and even whisky. There was not a soul to be seen and their shouts to be served failed to bring anyone. The whole stock was at their disposal. Debating for a moment what might be the most useful stores to take to war, they decided on chocolate, cigarettes, tinned pineapple, and a bottle of whisky, which were all stowed into the saddle bags. The officer then wrote his name and unit on the counter and offered to pay if a bill were sent him. Needless to say, it never was.

But the chaos wasn't only caused by the coolies and civilian labour. Large numbers of officers and troops who were on their way back to Imphal from leave when the road was cut were hanging around idly in the Rest Camps. Some of them, under the Area Staff, were formed into defensive companies and others were sent out on patrols. But they were very depressed and hated the whole business; if they were going to fight the Japs, they wanted to do so with their own units.

The chaos, understandably, extended into the Area offices; some people said it started there. The staff officers, like their commander, weren't trained or equipped to conduct operations, and their dealings with the staff of 5th Brigade who walked in, demanding transport, rations, defence stores, tarpaulins, ammunition, all in vast quantities on demand, were not very happy. One officer, being pressed for mortar ammunition, threw up his hands and declared piteously: 'Dear God, I didn't come here to fight a war!' As already mentioned, the whole of 2nd Division's transport was still on the road, including the R.A.S.C. transport trucks. This made the business of concentrating the brigade and building up supplies extremely difficult. The staff had to keep 'scrounging' trucks, then holding on to them in the face of angry demands for their return. For the first two days the staffs were even denied transport for themselves and had to walk from place to place. Eventually, Victor Hawkins got an issue of transport agreed with General Ranking, which improved matters a little. But the Division was still coming in at the rate of a train-load per day. There was no sign of any guns; and a group of staff officers and junior commanders, who had been sent ahead on a fast train, had vanished without trace. The frenzy and the fears of this time were expressed by an officer who wrote on the 2nd April: 'Couldn't sleep last night. My nerves are on edge. Not exactly through fear, but because I'm furious that our magnificent 2 Div. should be sent dribbling into this party without guns or tanks or workshops or transport. Lord, give us time and we'll ask for nothing else....'

But time, like tarpaulins and a good many other stores, was in short supply, both at Dimapur and Kohima.

*

On the afternoon of the 31st March, Richards watched the Royal West Kents get in their trucks and move down the road for Nichugard. All he could do now was shorten his line, set his men at work digging for dear life, and stock up the forward posts with food, water, and ammunition. The evacuation of non-fighting personnel was still going on—and would do till the road was cut—but it was under control of 253 Sub-Area, and Richards was neither advised nor consulted. How many men would be left to fight and how many still to be fed, he'd still no idea. His allocation of troops at this moment was as follows: G.P.T. (General Purposes Transport) Ridge, to the south, a composite company of Indian troops, with some V Force men, a company of Gurkha troops, and a few rear details of the Assam Regiment. A roadblock to the south of this position was manned by some Gurkhas under a British officer. On Jail Hill, there was a rifle company of the 5th Burma Regiment and a Garrison company of the same regiment. On D.I.S. and F.S.D., two platoons of Mahrattas, some V Force troops, a composite company of Indian infantry, some R.I.A.S.C. men, and a G.P.T. company under a regular Indian Army officer, Major Rawlley. Kuki Piquet, one of the hillocks on the ridge, between Garrison Hill and F.S.D., was held solely by some V Force men. The D.C.'s bungalow was held by a party of British troops, while the I.G.H. Spur was held by the Assam Rifles, commanded by Lieut.-Colonel Keene. On Summerhouse Hill there were some State troops, who also maintained a detachment on Naga Village, the high ground to the north. Five regimental aid posts were set up for the various sectors, and telephone lines were run out to the unit command posts round the perimeter. In the time available,

Richards also made his supply arrangements as comprehensive as possible. Fifteen days' rations were distributed, of which seven were the ordinary rations and the remainder were 'hard'. Two-inch and three-inch mortar ammunition was carried to the perimeter posts, together with smoke grenades, Mills bombs, and Verey light cartridges. As long as the men were alive, they would have something to fight with.

But water was a different matter. In the D.C.'s bungalow compound there was a large metal tank, filled by a pipe running from the Aradura Spur via G.P.T. Ridge. This pipe would obviously be cut very early in the battle. To help matters, the engineers had dug in two tarpaulin tanks, and there were six steel tanks at points between the bungalow and the F.S.D. How long these would remain unholed, once things got started, was very doubtful; and water would obviously be one of the main problems. The only hope, if things got really bad, was supply from the air.

Even more important than water was morale; fortunately the departure of the Royal West Kents had left this unimpaired, many of the troops being unaware of what had happened.

Some time during the 1st April, Richards received an operation order from Ranking which informed him that the garrison would be reinforced by the Assam Regiment 'if extracted from Jessami'. But, being an experienced soldier, Richards contained any optimism in this respect; he knew that the battalion must have been severely mauled, even if it escaped intact. The order continued: 'You will command the garrison of Kohima, and will deny Kohima to the enemy as long as possible without being destroyed yourselves.... The decision as to the precise moment when it will be necessary to withdraw from Kohima must be made by you.' This sentence revealed that Ranking wasn't subject to any false optimism either, and was obviously expecting the whole ridge to be taken. At the tail end of the document came detailed orders concerning the destruction of supplies, vehicles, secret documents, ciphers, and signal equipment. Richards was told to take action so that this could be carried out immediately, but refused. As he says: 'Nothing could be more unfortunate or undesirable than that there should get abroad any idea of the possibility of a withdrawal from Kohima, however remote. I therefore put the order in my pocket and neither showed it or mentioned it to anyone except Colonel Borrowman, my second-in-command.' One can't help remarking that Richards was wise in this decision, as in another. He had been told to ask Pawsey to inform the Nagas that if the British withdrew from Kohima, it was still their intention 'to return and destroy all the Japanese west of the Chindwin'. He decided that any premature announcement would be very dangerous indeed, and left the matter to be decided on the outcome of events.

On the 2nd April 33rd Corps headquarters opened at Jorhat and General Stopford assumed command of all troops in the Assam and Surma valleys. The tasks given him by Slim were: to prevent enemy penetration into those areas, to keep open the line of communications between Dimapur and Kohima, and to be prepared to move to the assistance of 4th Corps and help in all possible ways to destroy the Japanese forces west of the Chindwin. The speed with which these tasks could be accomplished depended very much on the speed with which his troops could be concentrated. Stopford's estimation was that by mid-April he would have the whole 2nd Division, 161st Brigade, 33rd Brigade (from 7th Indian Division), the Lushai Brigade, a regiment of armoured cars, a squadron of light tanks, and possibly a squadron of medium tanks. But the next ten days or so, while these units trundled over the ramshackle railway system of north-eastern India, were going to be anxious ones. As to the enemy, Stopford's information was that two regiments only were moving on Kohima, the 124th Regiment (which was moving at the rear of the Main Column) having been 'lost' by the Intelligence. What he was afraid of was that the lost regiment would move via Layshi into the Assam Valley, with Gologhat and Mariani as its objectives.

Meanwhile, another problem was raising its head. The 2nd Division was heavily mechanized and unequipped for fighting in mountainous country. Unless it were to be tied to the road during its advance towards Imphal, which would make tactical movement impossible, it would have to be found mule transport and instructed in its use. An urgent signal, therefore went to 14th Army for mule companies, though whether they could be spared seemed very doubtful.

Mountbatten, however, had good news this day. A signal from the Chiefs of Staff informed him that from Britain and the Mediterranean he would soon be receiving a total of ninety-nine transport aircraft. These would enable him to supply 4th Corps in Imphal by air, as planned—though not indefinitely. The signal added that seventy-nine of the aircraft must go back by the middle of May, as they were required for an operation in Italy.

In the afternoon of the 3rd April, there was a conference at Jorhat attended by Mountbatten, Slim, Stopford, and other commanders. Slim outlined the situation at Dimapur and Kohima, and said the latter must be held if possible, 'since it would be hard to recapture, and its loss would undermine Naga loyalty'. He added that he had told Stopford to reinforce the garrison, 'as soon as he could do so without endangering the safety of Dimapur'. Exactly when that moment would come, it was still impossible to say.

While the higher command was meeting at Jorhat, 'Bruno' Brown and a party of survivors from Jessami were climbing up the slope of Garrison Hill at Kohima, to report to Richards' headquarters. They were tired and foot-sore, but each man carried his weapon and was determined to fight on. The urgency of the situation precluded any courtesies, or any rest, and before long the troops were at their allotted sectors on the perimeter and hard at work improving them. Before dark, other small groups of men came streaming in, both from Jessami and Kharasom, some with officers and some without. Fortunately the Assam Rifles' Quartermaster was on hand to replace torn or blood-matted clothing and issue items of personal kit. He also saw to it that the men were fed. By the time the last stragglers had reported, 260 officers and men of the Regiment were available to help in the fight, some indication of the spirit of this young battalion.

Some time in the afternoon the Nagas brought in news of an enemy concentration at Mao Songsang, twenty miles to the south on the Imphal road. (This was part of Miyazaki's column, which was now preparing to move north.) In the evening, Richards sent out a fighting patrol, under Major Giles, with orders to get up into the high jungle on the Aradura Spur and harass the enemy. To their surprise, when darkness had fallen, the patrol heard the sound of digging close by, then movement behind them. Giles came to the conclusion that he was being surrounded, so collected his men together, ordered 'fix bayonets', and charged. After a number of Japs had been killed the patrol was able to extricate itself and streamed back into the perimeter. This was the first contact with the enemy at Kohima.

By the 4th April, Richards had moved his headquarters to its battle position in a dugout on the slope of Garrison Hill, facing Naga Village; and on the morning of that day he made a tour of the perimeter. Though food and ammunition was now in position in adequate quantities, one problem, he hadn't been able to solve was barbed wire. There was not a foot of it anywhere in the position. Why this should have been it is even now impossible to say; the depots in Dimapur were full of it, the Assam Regiment had drawn all they needed for Jessami and Kharasom, and the incoming units of 5th Brigade were collecting supplies without difficulty. But Richards' requests, more urgent with every day that went by, had been ignored by 202 Area; and personal pleas to Ranking had produced no action either. By the 3rd April it was obvious that no wire would ever come, so Pawsey collected his Nagas together and they made some sharp stakes, or panjies, which were rammed into the ground in rows to make some sort of obstacle. But the lack of wire still remained a great worry. The atmosphere at this time has been described by Peter Steyn: 'Tension mounted slowly and the question of whether Kohima could survive an attack was on everyone's lips. The answer lay in the realms of conjecture, but hopes and spirits were high. And so the last night of peace began....'

It lasted till just before midnight, when the Japanese attacked the lower slopes of the Aradura Spur, where an ambush had been prepared by a platoon of the State troops. Unfortunately, the latter weren't equal to the occasion and, after a bout of wild firing in all directions, they broke and ran. Some went right through the G.P.T. Ridge and Jail Hill positions, and a few kept going till Dimapur. Richards tried to stop the wild firing, knowing its effect on morale, but as soon as one sector had been dealt with, the jitters spread to another.

Earlier on the 4th, Stopford had flown to Dimapur for a conference with Grover and Ranking. On arrival, he found a 'very optimistic atmosphere', as reports from various sources indicated 'that 31st Jap Div. is of poor quality and demoralized'. Where these reports came from, it is now difficult to say, and all one can remark is that they were woefully inaccurate. However, it was at this meeting that Stopford came to an important decision, as he recorded: 'Everything indicates that no attack is now likely to develop in the Manipur Road base [i.e. Dimapur] and that we should withdraw troops from there in order to strengthen the garrison at Kohima.... Told Ranking to send forward one battalion 0f 161 Inf. Bde. to Kohima as quickly as possible.' In fact, after further discussion, it was decided to despatch the whole Brigade. This decision, a reversal of the one given a few days previously, was undoubtedly right; but unhappily it came twenty-four hours too late.

While Stopford was holding his conference, another important event was happening at Imphal: 4th Corps completed its withdrawal to the plain. The 17th, 20th, and 23rd Indian Divisions were now on their chosen ground, though encircled by the Japanese 15th and 33rd Divisions, and the I.N.A. forces. The 17th Division, which had already sustained heavy casualties was tired, but the 20th and 23rd Divisions had experienced an easier passage. All were now prepared for the onslaught to come. But as Scoones and his men all realized, the outcome of the battle depended not only on their own skill and gallantry, but on the success of the airlift and the length of time it could be maintained. They knew also that their own fate was now inextricably linked to the fate of their comrades at Kohima.

Mutaguchi, of course, knew this too, and Sato. By the night of the 4th, the latter had established his headquarters at Khanjang, south-east of Jessami; and his orders to Miyazaki and his regimental commanders were: ‘Capture Kohima—at once.’

On the morning of the 5th April, Richards carried out a tour of the perimeter to find that some Indian troops had come off the western end of G.P.T. Ridge (the southern end of the position) during the night. There was no alternative but to shorten the perimeter and dig new positions to close the gap. Tentage in front of these had to be struck, to provide a field of fire. The job was given to a company made up of Gurkhas from the reinforcement camp, and they hadn’t long started when sniping broke out, causing casualties. However, they behaved calmly, and went on till the ground was clear, then took over this sector on G.P.T. Ridge, helped by a platoon from the Assam Regiment.

In the afternoon, the 58th Regiment got ready to attack Kohima from the east. Apparently, unknown to the garrison, its advance guard had entered Naga Village the previous night. Captain Tsuneo Sanukawae of the 11th Company has written:

> 'We entered Naga Village at 4 a.m. on the 5th. The town was fast asleep. After dealing with the sentries we occupied seven depots and took about thirty trucks. The enemy had not noticed our advance and at 9 a.m. came to the depots to draw their rations. We got them and made them prisoner. At 10 a.m. I was prepared to attack the town, but at that moment we were fired on by artillery.* At 1300 hours we informed our main body that we had occupied Kohima Village, and an hour later they arrived. We could not say we had won Kohima until we had gained the hill beyond the road junction, so we attacked.... Praying to God, we rushed into action, under cover of light machine-gun fire, throwing grenades as we went.'

Naoje Koboyashi, another member of the Company, has written in similar vein:

> 'When we reached Kohima we were all tired out after the ceaseless advance day and night, and the troops fell asleep where they were. At first light I looked across towards the Hill [i.e. Garrison Hill] and could see the enemy soldiers walking about... they still seemed not to realize we were there.'

At this point it may be worth mentioning that the 58th Regiment was the crack formation of the Division, with a proud tradition and a long series of victories behind it. The Regimental depot was at Echigo, in the Niigato Prefecture, 150 miles north of Tokyo, on the west coast. This is an area famous for its rice harvest, and most of the men were of farming stock. They were, therefore, tough, self-reliant, and accustomed to hardship. Most of them had seven or eight years service behind

* In fact, by the one 25-pounder in the garrison.

them. The 58th considered themselves superior to the 138th, and had no great opinion of the 124th at all. However, they had been somewhat shaken by the action at Sangshak and by the ferocious defence put up by Hope-Thompson's brigade. Many good officers and N.C.O.s had gone down leading attacks, and the Regiment arrived at Kohima somewhat mauled, and temporarily exhausted. However, its fighting spirit and morale still remained unimpaired; and in a matter of hours it was launched into the attack.

This was led by Captain Nageie of the 2nd Battalion, but it was broken up, largely thanks to the mortars of the Assam Regiment, operating from Jail Hill. Unfortunately, however, they were knocked out and there was no choice but to evacuate the whole of G.P.T. Ridge. It was while this operation was being carried out that the 4th Royal West Kents arrived, under their commanding officer, Lieut.-Colonel Laverty. Warned that the unit would be coming, Richards had laid on guides for each company and went down to the road to welcome Laverty in person. As Richards records, the meeting was not a happy one: 'Laverty merely asked, "Where's Kuki Piquet?" I told him and he went off without speaking further.' Fortunately, the battalion got into position without being shelled and occupied the D.I.S., Kuki Piquet and sectors of the perimeter on Garrison Hill and I.G.H. Spur. With it came a troop of the 20th Mountain Battery, a platoon of sappers and a detachment of 75 Indian Field Ambulance.

As the troops of the Royal West Kents sorted themselves out and slid into their weapon pits, Richards had a talk with Major Dick Yeo, the gunner, who was digging in his 3.7 howitzers in the garden by the D.C.'s bungalow. He had not got out many words, however, when the Jap artillery began plastering the area. Moving over to Laverty's headquarters, Richards was in time to see the enemy launch an attack on Jail Hill. The defenders replied with rifle and Bren fire, and all the grenades they could lay their hands on; but, unsupported by artillery or mortar fire, they obviously couldn't hold out long, and as the enemy mortars took their toll and casualties mounted, gaps began to appear. Soon the Japs got a foothold on the near side of the road, and it became clear that, if Jail Hill was to be held, a counter-attack must go in at once. This was organized by Lieutenant Brown and Subadar Kapthuama Lushai, of the Assam Regiment, but it made no headway and, when Brown was killed, immediately broke up. So within twenty-four hours the perimeter was shortened for the second time.

To say that the Royal West Kents were displeased to be pushed back into Kohima, and invited to fight alongside the motley collection of detachments which formed the bulk of its garrison, was an understatement. They were horrified; and one cannot blame them. Troops in the field like to fight alongside their sister units which they have grown to know and trust; and under their own commanders. They like their own gunners to support them, their own R.A.S.C. or I.A.S.C. to supply them, and their own doctors to look after them. They tend to despise base or L. of C. troops, and prefer to have as little to do with them as possible. The idea of going into battle with them is anathema.

But to understand the feeling of the Royal West Kents is not to uphold their prejudices. In fact, the Assam Regiment and the Assam Rifles had already fought the Japanese with great gallantry; and the scratch companies of British and Gurkhas possessed great fighting quality too. Some officers of the Royal West Kents began to appreciate this; but, on the whole, mistrust dispersed very slowly and in some quarters not at all.

The man who bore the brunt of this mistrust and suspicion was undoubtedly Colonel Richards. Many accusations were made about him at the time, and many have been since; but all have proved entirely without basis or fact, though only now is the record being put straight. Richards, as must be evident, had a most unenviable task. He had been trying to plan the defence of Kohima without any idea as to the troops he would have allocated, and his administration was of necessity hasty and improvised. As the Royal West Kents observed caustically, the defences were badly dug; but they had mostly been completed by civilian labour before Richards arrived. The arrangements for water supply, as they observed also, were quite inadequate; but Richards had had no time to institute engineering works, even if there had been men to carry them out. The medical arrangements were unsatisfactory too; but until it was known which medical units would be in the siege, more advanced arrangements were out of the question. However, Richards was the commander; and unjustly took the blame.

It cannot be said that Brigadier Warren helped the situation either. As already mentioned, he was very pro-Indian and very anti-British service; and he resented the fact that Richards, whose experience lay solely with British and West African troops, should be in command of a garrison containing Indians and Gurkhas. From the first day of the siege, Warren refused to deal with Richards and spoke to Laverty direct. In his own phrase, he regarded Laverty as 'the tactical commander of the Kohima box'.

However, in his major decision, perhaps the most important of his whole career, Warren did more than any one man to save Kohima. This decision was to form a second box with the other two battalions and eight of his guns at Jotsoma, two miles along the road towards Dimapur. Pushed forward again on the 5th, his orders had been to put the whole brigade into Kohima, but with the perimeter shortened and the enemy already attacking it, he realized that the situation had changed completely. There was no longer enough room for three battalions and, not less important, there was no position from which to fire his guns. With his excellent eye for ground, Warren at once appreciated the dominant position of Naga Village, to the north of the perimeter, but it was very doubtful if he could reach it; and the tactical situation demanded that he should be on the north-west, that is the Dimapur side of Kohima, so that he could link up with the 2nd Division when they advanced along the road. After a quick reconnaissance, he decided on an area near the village of Jotsoma, just over two miles from Kohima. It was not an ideal defensive position by any means, but it commanded an excellent view of Kohima Ridge, and was near enough for the guns to give close support to the garrison. There was another point in its favour: Warren had a good deal of transport, which had to be brought into the defended area, and, by a stroke of luck, Jotsoma was on a loop road running up to the high ground, from milestone 43 ½, and descending three miles later. The road junctions were dubbed 'Lancaster Gate' and 'Paternoster Row', and so they were known throughout the campaign. All day during the 6th April, Warren's men moved up to Jotsoma, and quickly prepared their defensive position. The Rajputs* (less one company which had succeeded in joining the garrison of Kohima) occupied the south-eastern sector, and the Punjabs closed the box to the north and east. Meanwhile, the guns of the 2nd Battery, waiting on the road at milestone 42, provided a sitting target for the Jap mountain gunners, now established over the valley to the north, on Merema Ridge. Shells rained down among the hastily scooped-out gun pits, but by some miracle did no damage; and when the 2nd Battery began returning the fire, the Japs immediately took their guns out of action. Major John Nettlefield records: 'Shortly afterwards, an elephant carrying what our binoculars seemed to indicate was another mountain gun, was spotted ambling along the Bokajan track. Our first round landed very close and the elephant was seen to charge, apparently out of

* The Rajputs are a tall, martial race from Rajputana, a province in North-West India.

control, into the nearby cover. We followed up with a few more rounds for luck—we were sorry about the elephant, but it was war...' By the late afternoon the eight guns were in position on a reverse slope in the Jotsoma box, and radio contact was made with Major Yeo in the garrison. Immediately the guns began registering, and laying on defensive fire tasks, which could be called for as required by the garrison. They were required at once, and at short intervals for many days. At the peak of their activity these Indian mountain gunners were firing at the rate of 400 rounds per gun per day; and despite the pressure, the infantry recorded that they had never seen such accurate shooting in their lives.

The night of the 5th April had been a quiet one for the Kohima Garrison; but Colonel Fukunaga, commanding the 58th Japanese Regiment, had been at work planning an attack on Jail Hill for the next morning. Soon after first light, heralded by a heavy mortar barrage, it went in and the defenders were driven off. The Japanese suffered heavily in this engagement, and Captain Nageie was killed at the head of his men.* (In Japanese accounts, incidentally, Jail Hill is known as 'Uma Hill' and Garrison Hill is usually called 'Deputy Commissioner's Hill'.) An incorrect report reached Laverty that only a platoon of Japanese had been involved in the action, so he at once ordered a company to stage a counter-attack. Preparations were at once put in hand, but it soon became evident that there was something like two companies of Japanese on the hill, firmly established in defensive positions. Any assault would have involved the garrison in a large number of casualties which it hadn't the faculties to handle, so the operation was called off. The loss of Jail Hill was serious, however, as it dominated the D.I.S. and F.S.D.,

* The 2nd Battalion, 58th Regiment was to lose no less than four commanding officers at Kohima: Nageie, Shiro Sato, Takeo Igawa, and Torao Ishida.

though fortunately the woods still gave the men on the perimeter a good deal of cover.

Right through the 6th there was intermittent shelling and mortaring, which made movement within the perimeter increasingly dangerous. Troops had to keep in or near their trenches and the business of distributing food and water became almost impossible in the hours of daylight. But some movement had to take place: as obviously the D.I.S. and F.S.D. would be the enemy's next objectives, all non-combatants had to be cleared out and found a place on I.G.H. Spur.

*

At Maymyo General Mutaguchi was not displeased with the march of events. His 33rd and 15th Divisions were now battering at the gates of Imphal, while his fellow member of the 'Cherry Society', General Sato, had reached Kohima at the appointed time, and signals indicated that he had already secured two-thirds of the objective.

It was not mere chance that Sato hit the jeep track running from the Chindwin to Jessami and Kohima. Since December 1943 a Lieutenant Masa Nishida and a mixed party of Japanese troops and Indians (all disguised as natives) had been operating in the country between the Chindwin and Kohima with orders to reconnoitre five routes for the 31st Division. All the men had been specially selected and trained at the Nakana School for espionage in Tokyo, and they accomplished their mission brilliantly, though not without some hair-raising escapes and adventures. The fact that the track had been built at all by his enemies was, of course, a slice of luck for Sato; but, as Clausewitz remarks, 'War is the province of chance' and, with an operation as daring as the advance on Kohima, Sato was surely entitled to any luck that was going.

In general, the situation looked so promising that Mutaguchi permitted himself a few moments of his 'private speculations'. Interpreting the intelligence reports which came flooding in from Assam, he suddenly realized that there was a ripe plum ready for picking: the base of Dimapur. This had not figured largely in the initial planning of the campaign, the generals probably assuming that it would be heavily defended; but now it was at his mercy. If Sato took it, which he should be able to do with a regimental group, the British could neither reinforce their beleaguered troops in Kohima and the Imphal Plain, nor use the railway to retreat to India. The whole central front would be paralysed, then smashed. Mutaguchi sent off two signals, the first to Sato ordering him to advance on Dimapur at once, cut the railway, and secure food and supplies for his troops; and the second to General Kawabe, commander of the Southern Area Army, asking him to signal Count Terauchi to request the air cover to Dimapur. Once this request had been agreed, so Mutaguchi calculated, Sato could reach Dimapur in three days. But it was not agreed; Kawabe replied immediately that 'Dimapur is not within the strategic objectives of the 15th Army'. Mutaguchi protested, giving his own interpretation of the order, but Kawabe remained adamant.

The reason for the difference in interpretation was this. The Japanese generals had argued so bitterly among themselves during 1943 that the final orders for the Burma offensive were something of a compromise. The instructions sent to Kawabe by Imperial Army in Headquarters on the 7th January 1944 ran as follows: 'C.-in-C. Southern Army will break the enemy on his front at the opportune time, and will capture and secure the strategic areas near Imphal and in North-East India for the defence of Burma.' But what were 'the strategic areas' and how far did they extend? The phrase was a vague one, capable of many interpretations; Kawabe interpreted it strictly, and Mutaguchi more liberally, stretching it to accommodate his daydreams. Mutaguchi was right, there could be no doubt whatsoever; this was what Napoleon called 'the favourable moment', and Sato had only to hold Dimapur for a month to bring the British to the brink of disaster. But Mutaguchi dared not disobey Kawabe; and the moment passed. Sato's troops were called back, to join in the fight for Kohima.

On the night of the 6th April, Lieut.-Colonel John Young, commander of the 75th Field Ambulance, made his way into the perimeter and took charge of all the medical arrangements. Deciding that the five aid posts should be amalgamated into an A.D.S. (Advanced Dressing Station), he sited this on the reverse slopes of Summerhouse Hill, not far from the Royal West Kents' command post. Men of the Pioneer Corps dug trenches for the wounded, and Young designed a large pit, covered by a tarpaulin, for an operating theatre. Though this was the most sheltered spot to be found, it was by no means ideal, and the condition of the wounded, lying out in the slit trenches, was pitiable in the extreme. The whole area was shelled and mortared day and night, and some of the men were wounded a second time, and others killed. The officers kept their revolvers loaded under the blankets, ready to shoot themselves if the Japanese broke through the perimeter. Young was quite tireless, and an inspiration to all the medical staff and stretcher-bearers. He attended the wounded in the open, quite regardless of his own personal safety, and on one occasion led a party outside the box to retrieve some medical supplies from a lorry on the road.

On the night of the 6th, the 2nd and 5th Companies of the 58th launched their attack on the D.I.S. and F.S.D., coming in two columns from Jail Hill. Both these features were protected on the western flank by steep banks and the Japanese had to cross the road to reach them. It was here that the guns of Jotsoma caught them, firing on a prearranged defence task. Dozens of the attackers went down on the tarmac, and many more, having survived this curtain of fire, were destroyed by the rifle and Bren gun fire which poured down at them from the defence posts, and by the grenades which came rolling down the banks. The first attack faltered, stopped, then broke up; but a second wave came on, then a third, then a fourth. But the covering fire from the Japanese mortars was accurate, and as time went on gaps appeared in the forward rifle pits. Small parties of Japanese streamed through these gaps and made for the bashas and huts on the hilltop. Here they found a good store of grenades, which they began using with good effect against 'C' Company of the Royal West Kents, who had to throw out a protective flank. Nothing could be done about these insurgents till daylight, however, as any action within the box might result in casualties to friend as well as foe.

*

When daylight came, Laverty soon saw the Japanese intruders were concentrated in the bakery area, where ovens were dotted over the hillside, and he ordered his 'D' Company to destroy them. The job was tricky, not only because the trees obscured observation, but because the enemy now had some 75-mm. guns on G.P.T. Ridge, which were able to shoot up the advancing company in the flank. However, the attack went in; the Royal West Kents poured small arms fire into the bashas and the vehicles which were parked among them, then gave covering fire for the sappers, who rushed forward with pole charges. A series of explosions shook the hill, then the whole area became a sheet of flame through which a number of figures could be seen running. The first of these turned out to be Indian troops the Japanese had captured, and they were followed by the Japanese themselves. Fire was already belching from many of them, but others, rather than face the encircling guns, fried to death where they were. And some, perhaps the most foolish party of all, took refuge in the ovens, thinking perhaps that the brickwork would save them. But unfortunately for them, the basha containing the ovens attracted the attention of Lance-Corporal John Harman, a brilliant soldier who was soon to win the V.C. As he approached the basha, one of the Japs let off some shots which missed him, and Harman ran back to his section post for a box of grenades. Dragging this along behind him, he returned to the basha, went inside, and took cover behind the nearest oven. Here he took a grenade out of the box, removed the pin and let the safety lever fly, then counted three seconds. Quickly, before the grenade blew up on the fourth, he lifted the steel lid and popped it into the oven. There was an explosion and the Jap inside was killed; and Harman dragged his box of grenades along to the next oven. In the end, he had dealt with all ten. Curiously enough, when he went to inspect the insides of the ovens, two of the Japs were still alive, though badly wounded. These he dragged out into the open, then, putting one under each arm, carried them across to his section post. The men began cheering, and soon the excitement spread from post to post. In all, forty-four Japanese bodies were counted in the bakery area. Later, so it was realized, one of the men brought across by Harman was an officer of the 58th Regiment, and in his haversack was discovered a panorama of Kohima, indicating Japanese artillery positions. He also had a survey map, from which it appeared that his regiment was deployed with a battalion on Naga Village, whose objectives were the Treasury and the D.C.'s bungalow, at the northern end of the perimeter, a battalion on Jail Hill and G.P.T. Ridge, and a battalion in reserve on the Imphal road. The regiment's supply base was marked at Khangjang, where also was located Sato's divisional headquarters.

According to accounts written by Japanese soldiers after the battle, this attack was led by Captain Shiro Sato (no relation to the General), who took over the 2nd Battalion on the death of Captain Nageie. Their attacks were broken up, they say, 'by heavy artillery fire, and when daylight came we had over sixty casualties. Then the artillery fire became so deadly that Sato decided it was better to attack than to be killed where we were, and ordered the advance.'

The Battalion Commander, Major Shimanoe, described this action as 'a crushing defeat for the 58th Regiment'. Never in its history had it encountered such determination in defence. Some of the men could be heard complaining: 'This is even worse than Sangshak.'

Another notable event happened this day: a Company of the 4th/7th Rajputana Rifles from the Jotsoma Box, managed to slip into the perimeter. They made a very welcome addition to the garrison.

Richards was now very much occupied with administrative problems.

The Japanese had cut the water supply on G.P.T. Ridge and only a trickle was coming through the pipe. Orders had therefore to be issued, rationing each man to a pint a day, a pitiable amount in the warm climate, and in the heat of battle. Fighting is the most dehydrating occupation known to man. Lieut.-Colonel Borrowman, now Richards's second-in-command, worked hard at the administrative arrangements, as did Major Franklin, second-in-command of the Royal West Kents. A large number of chagals (canvas water containers) were available, and using these, and anything else they could improvise, the troops showed great ingenuity in dodging snipers and mortar fire, to brew up 'char'. The constant shelling and mortaring, however, was ripping the leaves off the branches and the branches off the trees, so that each day the position became more exposed. Even the luxuriant growth of rhododendrons surrounding the D.C.'s bungalow and the Club area was ravaged, though some hardy bushes blossomed unconcerned. The sniping grew so bad that all movement in the daytime in the neighbourhood of Richards's headquarters became extremely hazardous. His wireless set had failed on the morning of the

5th, as the batteries were exhausted and his charging engine had not arrived. He mentioned the matter to Laverty, to be told that the Royal West Kents' engine had all it could do recharging their own batteries. So Richards was now cut off from the outside world, and all signals from Warren or anyone else had to go to Laverty.

The number of walking wounded was beginning to mount up; and Colonel Young considered that, as they'd been able to walk in, they should be able to walk out. So a party was organized, the guide being Lieutenant Corlett (the Assam Regiment subaltern who had taken the withdrawal message through to Jessami), helped by a Naga detailed by Charles Pawsey. The commander of the party was Major Franklin, and a platoon of the 4th/7th Rajputana Rifles, from the company just arrived, acted as escort. When evening came, and there was a lull in the fighting, the party, which now totalled some 100 wounded, plus some non-combatants, slipped out of the perimeter by I.G.H. Spur with the escort, and made its way down the precipitous slopes into the Zubza nala. The risks were great, as everyone knew, and if they bumped anything but a small patrol they'd be lucky to survive the journey. However, all went well; no Japs were encountered and for once the guides didn't lose the way. By daylight the party were safe in Zubza, without a wounded man being lost.

On the night of the 7th, the garrison expected a heavy attack, but it didn't materialize. When the Japs were heard forming up on the slopes of Jail Hill for an attack on the D.I.S., Major Yeo called for defensive fire from the guns at Jotsoma, which was brought down in a matter of seconds. An attack came in, but it had obviously been broken up and disorganized by the shell fire and wasn't pressed home. Later that night, there was an attack on the D.C.'s bungalow area, but the British troops there were never in any trouble and the action petered out. Despite these minor successes, however, Richards kept any signs of optimism well under control; just after dark, he had seen a column of lanterns moving into Naga Village, obviously carried by reinforcements moving up from Jessami. He pointed out the column to Yeo, hoping that it might just be in range of the guns at Jotsoma, but unhappily it wasn't. More frustrating still, the guns Yeo had manhandled on to Summerhouse Hill couldn't be used against the target either; the only possible site for them, on a reverse slope, was now full of wounded. So the Japs were allowed to settle into their new position unmolested. And next morning Richards saw five elephants moving along the track, carrying more guns.

During periods of silence during the night, the Japs had brought another weapon into action: the loudspeaker. It had been set up near the Treasury, and an Indian of the I.N.A. came on, speaking in Urdu: 'Hindustan ki jawan!' he called, 'Soldiers of India, the Japanese army has surrounded you. Bring your rifle and come over to us. We are liberating India from the iniquities and tyrannies of British rule.' Someone let off a burst of Bren towards the speaker, but the voice still went on, repeating the same message over and over again. What the Indian troops thought of it, it's hard to say. But certainly none of them moved from their weapon pits.

During this period, as more companies and platoons of the 58th came to join their comrades investing Kohima, there were inevitably men who were going into action for the first time. Naturally, their officers and N.C.O.s tried to relieve the tension by various means, some of them rather crude as in this story told by Lieutenant Seisaku Kameyama of the 2nd Battalion:

> '"You see," I said to my soldiers, "keep your heads, keep cool. If you want to find out just how cool you are feeling, put your hands inside your trousers and feel your penis—if it is hanging down, it is good." I tested mine, but it was shrunk up so hard I could hardly grasp it. More than thirty

soldiers did the same thing, then looked at me curiously, but I kept a poker-face. I said, "Well, mine's down all right. If yours is shrunk up, it's because you're scared."

Then a young soldier said to me: "Sir, I can't find mine at all. What's happening to it?" With this everyone burst out laughing and I knew I had got the confidence of the men.'

The platoon went into action, and by nightfall only eighteen men out of thirty were left.

On the 7th, Stopford had passed an order to Warren via General Ranking, that he must get on and stage a counter-attack to regain the ground that had been lost on G.P.T. Ridge and Jail Hill. Warren replied that he was collecting information 'to make sure that my attack goes in at the right place'. What he didn't appreciate was that Miyazaki and the 58th Regiment were steadily working round his western flank and would soon be cutting him off.

Meanwhile, Stopford was hard at work on the plans for his counter-offensive. Though he had a great respect for Slim, his admiration for the 14th Army staff was minimal; and with the considerable verbal equipment at his command, urged them to get a move on. 'I don't think,' he said, 'they realize the administrative implications of attacking through this awful country... with the rains only a month away, they are terrific' It would be fair to add that 14th Army staff weren't the only people not to realize the difficulties; no one did.

On the 8th April the pressure on the Kohima garrison increased steadily. The enemy had now hauled some quick-firing anti-tank guns up on to G.P.T. Ridge, and these were cunningly sited so that the battery from Jotsoma couldn't touch them. The shells from these came so fast that there was no time to duck or slide into a trench. The shell, in fact, arrived before the noise. The trees, though they gave cover from view, made the situation worse on the whole. If a shell lands on the ground a soldier in his trench is unharmed, but if the shell hits a tree its fragments explode into the trenches. It soon became evident, therefore, that head cover must be provided, though the snag about this was that it limited the soldiers' field of fire and constricted them in the use of their weapons. Eventually the answer proved to be the construction of covered trenches besides the weapon pits; but this took time and meanwhile a good many men were lost.

It was on the 8th that John Harman won his V.C. During the night, so it was discovered, the enemy had established a machine-gun post covering the D.I.S. This meant that if an attack were made, the men of the Royal West Kents could not defend themselves and would be slaughtered if they withdrew. So, ordering the rest of his section to give him covering fire with the Bren, Harman worked his way round to a position from which he could attack the post. Moving forward slowly between the trees, he brought up his rifle and shot one Jap, then another. There were still three of them left, with automatics, but with immense courage Harman fixed his bayonet, then ran up the ridge towards them. By some miracle the Japs all missed him, and then within seconds he was leaping down on them with his bayonet. Watching from a distance, the rest of his section could see his rifle rising and falling as the bayonet went in and came out again. Then there was a scream and a single shot, and the astonished soldiers saw Harman hold up the machine-gun for them to see, then fling it away among the trees. A burst of cheering broke out, and Harman came down from the ridge to start walking back to his section post. Seeing this the men shouted to him to run, to get back into cover, to stop being a bloody fool, but for some unknown reason Harman ignored their entreaties and walked on till the inevitable happened. A machine-gun post further along the ridge that no one had spotted opened up and shot him through the spine.

Altogether, the 8th wasn't a happy day, either inside the perimeter or outside it. A patrol from the Jotsoma box, moving back along the Dimapur road to mend a telephone wire, found the road blocked by milestone 36, just to the north of Zubza. The troops manning the block were from Colonel Torikai's 138th Regiment, and they had come across from the Merema Ridge with the object of stopping reinforcements from reaching Kohima. Reconnoitring, they found a spur running across the road and out into the valley, with two pimples on it which would make a most effective defensive position. Immediately they began digging in. So Warren's force was now besieged just as surely as the garrison he'd set out to relieve, and already Miyazaki was exerting pressure on his right flank. Warren, however, took things calmly. He'd acquired some chickens from the local village, and got his men to construct a chicken run just near the mess. Ian McKillop, a liaison officer from the 5th Brigade, was amazed to see him calmly eating his breakfast eggs, while the guns thundered away in the dell outside and the birds flapped and squawked excitedly. The eggs were supplemented by wild raspberries, which a bihisti (a water carrier) collected on the hillside and brought in for Warren, Grimshaw, his brigade-major, and the other members of the staff. In the evenings, the demands of war were not allowed to interfere with Warren's favourite game of cards and many enjoyable hands of 'vingt-et-un' were played.

There was no time to play cards in Kohima. At dusk the enemy artillery opened up from the east, the south, and the west, then an attack came in on 53 I.G.H. Spur. It was held in the main, but some of the Japanese succeeded in establishing themselves across the road and began digging in on the lower slopes of the spur. It was impossible to deal with them in the confusion and darkness; a counter-attack had to wait till the morning. Meanwhile, another attack came in on the D.C.'s bungalow at the eastern end of the perimeter. This was helped by a heavy mortar barrage, but the troops in this sector, who were well dug in, weathered it without serious casualties.

But the Japanese kept on coming on, wave after wave of them streaming over the road, scrambling up the steep slopes, and pushing on through the undergrowth. Eventually the garrison troops had to withdraw, and take up a position behind the bungalow. Here our troops were dug in along the banks at the western end of the tennis court and fought back with grenades; the Japs replied by hurling their own grenades from the other end of the tennis court. So this small rectangular area became the 'No Man's Land' between the garrison and the Japanese and was to remain so for some weeks, the focus of some of the bloodiest fighting in the whole battle. To restore the situation, Richards ordered a counter-attack by platoons of the Assam Regiment and the Burma Regiment, and later the Royal West Kents attacked. These had only limited success, and most of the area the Japs had captured they were able to retain. A man who distinguished himself again in this night of bloody and confused fighting was the gunner, Dick Yeo. As Richards records: 'He controlled the defensive fire with great accuracy, and was able to bring it down on call at an incredibly short distance in front of our troops. There is no doubt that this fire resulted time and again in breaking up the Japanese attacks. We could hear their screams as it fell among them.'

On the morning of the 9th, the Japanese still went on attacking to extend their gains on I.G.H. Spur; but the attacks were held. Then the ground lost the previous night was heavily mortared and Colonel Keene put in a counter-attack with two platoons of the Assam Rifles to recover most of the area. In the afternoon the enemy began mortaring the F.S.D. area, though no attack developed. Intermittent shelling continued all day. Inevitably, some shells fell among the wounded lying in the open around the A.D.S., and it was learned that forty had been killed.

Water was becoming a pressing problem, as nothing came through the pipes any more and the tanks were holed by shell-fire. Fortunately, Colonel Keene had discovered a spring in a re-entrant running into the side of I.G.H. Spur and, as news of this got round, men came scrambling over the hill to fill chagals and water-bottles. It was obvious, however, that if this practice went on there'd be far too many casualties, so water parties were organized which crawled forward at night. The ration was fixed at three-quarters of a pint per man per day—enough to sustain life but not much more.

The 9th April was Easter Sunday. It was impossible to bring men together in the Kohima box to celebrate this great day in the Christian calendar, but at Bokajan the padres of all denominations put on their jungle-green surplices, set up their mobile altars, and celebrated Holy Communion on the fringes of the jungle. Many officers and men attended these services, kneeling on the muddy jungle floor with their weapons by their side. There was no music and little singing, and very often the voices of the padres were drowned by the roar of trucks, which came slithering along the tracks, and punctuated by the chatter of the refugees streaming by, or of the stragglers from the detachment which had bolted from G.P.T. Ridge, who were now being questioned at the Field Security Collecting Post. But the services were very real, and to some men unbearably moving, as they realized they might well be hearing the familiar words of the service for the last time. For many this was the case.

While the services were going on at Bokajan, and Colonel Keene was launching his counter-attack on I.G.H. Spur, Stopford and Grover were in conference with Ranking at Dimapur. The 124th Regiment had now been identified, so it was clear that a whole Japanese Division was now operating in the area, and plans had to be laid on that basis. As Grover had nearly half of his division now concentrated, it was agreed that he should take operational control of all the area forward of Dimapur, while Ranking should remain responsible for the railway. Grover's orders (which were later formalized at a meeting in the evening) were to open the road to Kohima, clear it of the enemy before the monsoon, and secure it as a firm base for further offensive operations. Operations were to start at once.

At this stage, Grover, who had only arrived on the 1st April, had not seen Kohima nor any of the mountainous country beyond Nichugard. He appreciated, however, that Kohima would be the stage for his first major battle and studied it carefully on the map. He noticed that on the right flank the high ground ran up towards Mount Pulebadze and Mount Japvo, and came to the immediate conclusion that the best way to deal with the situation was to put in a left hook with two brigades via the Merema Ridge. The importance of this latter feature struck him forcibly: it overlooked the whole length of the road from Zubza to Kohima; and if the Japs got astride it with any considerable force of artillery, they could paralyse the movement of both men and supplies. But when he made this early plan, Grover still imagined that there would only be a Jap regiment at Kohima; and he could not know that in Assam maps can only give a very feeble impression of the ground.

It was an uncomfortable night both at Jotsoma and Kohima. The sky was covered by black clouds and then the rain came down, soaking the men in the slit trenches and the wounded lying out in the open. At Jotsoma there were sporadic attacks, and forward positions in the Punjabis' area changed hands time and again, as desperate, hand-to-hand fighting blurred the edges of the perimeter. At 2200 hours the Japanese at Kohima put in an attack across the tennis court, and kept it going for an hour and a half; but automatic fire, well directed and controlled, supported by a liberal use of hand grenades kept them at bay. On the far side of the tennis court, the shells brought down by Major Yeo's orders were forming a curtain, cutting off the movement of reinforcements, and for long periods it was only twenty-five yards in front of the perimeter. The second attack came against the Assam Rifles on the I.G.H. Spur, but they held it without trouble. It was put in by companies of the 138th Regiment, and an identification was obtained. The garrison had for some days suspected that they had three regiments against them and now they had proof of two at least. The third attack came in against the Royal West Kents in the D.I.S. area, and was preceded by a shower of grenades, fired from discharger cups. The Japs could not break the line, but some took refuge in trenches evacuated by the wounded, and from these they were able to make life very uncomfortable for the section posts near them.

By now, after five days of siege, corpses, Japanese, Indian and British, were littering the hillside; the smell was obnoxious and the flies were a constant torment. Unfortunately, there was an acute shortage of shovels and entrenching tools and some units, like the Assam Rifles, had none at all, as they weren't on their establishment. The Royal West Kents, quite understandably, were unwilling to lend their entrenching tools, so the corpses lay where they were, black and swelling. To make matters worse, the garrison were now beginning to realize that Warren and the two remaining battalions of 161st Brigade wouldn't be able to help them, except with their guns; and the 2nd Division in Dimapur seemed a long, long way away. All they could do was go on fighting and hoping; they'd no illusions as to what would happen if the position were over-run.

But the situation was changing, if slowly and painfully. On the 10th April, Victor Hawkins summoned his battalion commanders and gave out his orders. His staff were to work all night laying on transport for the whole brigade, which at first light the following morning was to leave the hot, humid, flea-ridden atmosphere of Dimapur and move forward into battle. The brigade's orders were to open the road, make contact with the 161st Brigade, and be prepared to capture Kohima.

Chapter Five

A Phase is Ended

Grover had made his first contact with Warren by radio at 1115 hours on the 10th April, after jeeping forward to milestone 32. The most pressing job was to clear the roadblock separating them, and Warren thought he could tackle this. If he failed, however, the job would obviously have to wait for the 5th Brigade, when they advanced up the road. Regarding the situation in Kohima, Warren seemed pessimistic and put forward the idea that the whole garrison, including the Royal West Kents, should be withdrawn to an area by milestone 43 that night. Grover forbade any such move, as it would open the road to the enemy and might interfere with 5th Brigade's move forward. There would also be grave political consequences. However, Grover could see some sense in Warren's suggestion and decided to discuss it with Stopford. It was clear even now that once a road had been blasted into Kohima the garrison would have to be relieved—an operation which would tie up a brigade of the 2nd Division, so making it unavailable for movement. Later on, Grover discussed the matter with Stopford, who, having referred to Slim, gave him discretion to act as he saw fit.

By the afternoon a further message had come from Warren, indicating that he couldn't move the road block, so two companies of the Worcesters were ordered forward. Grover's appreciation was that the Japs were abandoning frontal attacks on Kohima and working their way along the flanks. His policy to counter this was to build up a strong force forward, to keep the road open to Dimapur by armoured car patrols, and to protect Dimapur from a position at Nichugard.

Early on the 11th the Brigade moved forward to join the Worcestershires, who were already in action in the Zubza area. One company had moved off at 0200 hours with the object of making a flanking move above the road, then getting into a position to protect the sappers who were to mend a blown bridge. Unfortunately, the company came down on to the road short of the bridge, so was ordered to keep going along in the open to a bend. Here the road disappeared round a knoll, and a spur jutted out to the left. When the leading troops were about fifteen yards from the bend, the Japanese opened up from a position on the spur, and the company, sustained some casualties before it could extricate itself. Major Elliott put in an attack against the Japanese on the spur (which commanded the blown bridge, as well as the road), but, owing to lack of supporting fire, his company made little progress.

Meanwhile the Brigadier had ordered Jack Stocker, the commanding officer of the Worcestershires, to form a perimeter in Zubza, and his men began working their way up from the road towards the jungle-covered hills behind. Here a platoon of Japs was found digging in and, having no weapons with them, bolted to another position already completed, from which they began sniping. Fortunately a gunner officer had gone up to join the Worcestershires and a quick shoot was put in, after which the infantry went in with the bayonet. This little operation was the brigade's first success.

But things on the whole were unsatisfactory, the brigade having surged forward and got itself rather disorganized. Brigadier Hawkins recorded: 'As I looked around it dawned on me that everyone was acting as if they were on an exercise. I suppose we had done so many exercises, and made them as real as we could, that the chaps were finding it difficult to realize that they were up against the real thing at last.' It was at this precise moment that the Japanese chose to administer a stern reminder. Seeing the Worcestershires gaily moving around in Zubza village, a 75-mm. gun opened up from Merema Ridge, killing the padre and a sapper subaltern, and wounding a company commander, apart from some N.C.O.s and men. After chis, things began to settle down.

The obvious thing now was to get to grips with the main Jap position to the left of the road, so Hawkins went forward with Stocker to carry out a reconnaissance. His immediate decision was that the position was a fairly strong one and 'it was no use pecking at it... we had got to find out all about it first, and then hit it hard.' This meant waiting till the guns could be got into position off the road in a 'shootable' position, the tanks brought up, and an air-strike laid on with the R.A.F., but Hawkins considered the delay was worth it. If the brigade could kick off with a solid success morale would be boosted enormously; and the brigade would then be ready for the sterner tasks that lay immediately ahead.

It was at this moment that Grover arrived, heard what had happened, and urged Hawkins to get on. But, standing his ground, Hawkins said: 'Please don't make me put in an attack before I'm ready.' Grover just had time to agree when the Jap 75-mm. opened up again. Brigadier Burke, the divisional C.R.A. who was with him, became furious that the gunners of the 10th Field Regiment who were just moving in made no attempt to reply, and upbraided the nearest officer he could find. The latter replied that the guns supporting the Worcestershires were in no position to answer, and this produced such an explosion from Burke that a couple of them were moved in a matter of minutes and went into action. To do them justice, the gunners were never caught with their trousers down again.

In between these alarms and excursions Hawkins found time to take a look at the country towards Kohima, and 'was a bit worried' by what he saw. The vast size of the hills, the valleys, the spurs, the re-entrants suddenly rendered his original order 'to prepare to take Kohima' somewhat unrealistic. The valley between the road and Merema Ridge was over two miles wide and 1,500 feet deep, and Kohima Ridge, which formed a great concave bastion at the far end of it, looked the most formidable defensive obstacle he'd ever seen. In view of this, he asked Pat Burke to have a word with Grover to see if the orders could be modified, which he did. But there was no need for any prolonged discussion; Grover had realized instantly that 'Orders off the map' would be somewhat useless in this campaign. As he put it: 'The country is very big... it rapidly absorbs large numbers of troops.'

Faced with this situation, Grover took Hawkins with him and they went forward to nave a good look at the ground ahead of them. After some discussion, Grover laid down that the orders to clear the ground and link up with 161st Brigade should still stand, but that after this had been accomplished Hawkins should work out a plan with Warren for an operation by both brigades. Here the matter was left.

That night the Worcestershires stayed in Zubza village, while the Cameron Highlanders established a position at milestone 32, four miles back. Overlooking the latter was a village called Khabvuma, and Hawkins suggested to Grover that the Camerons should be told to occupy it. Grover thought that it wasn't necessary, that he should take a risk, but the situation kept worrying Hawkins, and eventually he ordered the Camerons to send out a patrol. That night, the duty officer recorded:

> 'The Brigadier is lying by my side, trying to sleep, but he is worried and the slightest noise wakes him. An aeroplane flies

> overhead. He sits up suddenly and says: "Make a note of that." Soon after midnight a message comes to say that the Camerons have got their patrol up on the hill unopposed. He sighs with relief, turns over, and sleeps.'

Hawkins' fears were only too well founded. When the Dorsets came up to relieve the Camerons next morning, the Japs were just moving forward to occupy the village.

Hawkins was a tall, lean man, with an eager, somewhat tense manner. He'd fought long and hard in France, and had thought hard, too, about the fundamentals of his profession. Though no one could ever accuse him of being unaggressive in the face of the enemy (or indeed any opponent) he detested the waste of a single life. 'You can build a gun in two days, or a tank in a week,' he once said, 'but it takes twenty years to breed an infantry soldier.' He was immensely keen on physical fitness, believing that without it his men could neither beat the enemy nor survive an arduous campaign. Every week the whole brigade would be taken out for a three-mile run, Hawkins in the lead for the first two miles, after which he would give the 'advance' signal and three thousand men would go tearing over the brown, sun-baked hills. Sometimes, if he felt in need of further exercise, he'd look round the mess after tea, and say: 'I think I'll go for a run. What about it?' There would then be a horrified silence, till his eye lit on the officer of his choice, and he added: 'Come on, Bill [or whoever it was]. Let's get cracking.' But, despite such peccadilloes and the occasional splenetic outburst, the whole brigade had a great affection for him. Certainly no commander since Lord Hill ever cared more for his men.

In the confusion of this first day of action, the brigade, or at least its staff, had made their first acquaintance with mules, 400 of them arriving with their Pathan muleteers under the command of Captain Horton, a brisk individual with waxed moustaches. He'd no great worries, he said, except that his animals needed 2,500 gallons of water a day.... Luckily, there was a small wooded area below the road with a trickle of water, and the company descended happily towards it.

Another arrival was a bulldozer section from the Royal Engineers, which began cutting away at the banks to make standing places for vehicles and tracks for the guns. This was the first time that the troops had seen such a machine and gazed at it in amazement. Before long units were on the phone to brigade asking if they could borrow it; the bulldozer had immediately established itself as an important weapon of war.

On the morning of the 12th, Grover spoke to Warren on the radio, to learn that the garrison had had a fairly quiet night, during which a company of the Royal West Kents had taken over the D.C.'s bungalow area. Like patients after a serious operation, the troops in general were described 'to be quite comfortable and in very good heart'. But medical supplies were running short, and the situation of the wounded, who were increasing every day, was becoming critical. An air-drop of water, medical supplies, grenades and mortar ammunition was urgently called for. Warren was also running low on 3.7 ammunition himself, and this was particularly serious as, if the guns were reduced to impotence, even for a matter of hours, Kohima would fall. Grover promised to set matters in hand.

At mid-day General Stopford came forward to see Grover. He'd already expressed his opinion that Warren had been slow to get into Kohima and relieve the garrison, and naturally he wanted to know what was holding up 5th Brigade. However, he accepted the explanations given and concentrated on forward planning.

It might be mentioned here, that if Stopford thought Warren was slow, Warren thought Hawkins was slow; and this was the pattern that was to repeat itself at all levels, right through the battle. Until one was confronted with a particular problem oneself, it took a major act of the imagination to conceive the difficulties; and as the physical conditions rapidly deteriorated, any such mental effort was severely curtailed.

All day during the 12th April, 5th Brigade manœuvred itself into an attacking position. The Camerons came forward, then sent two companies to occupy Sachema, a village two miles to the south of Zubza, and about a mile from the road. From here they began patrolling forward towards the Jap position across the road, which was now known as 'Bunker Hill'. With immense physical effort, the guns of 10th Field Regiment were manhandled on to a patch of fairly flat ground, on the southern face of Zubza, where they were lined up, almost wheel to wheel. Nettlefield, the gunner in the Jotsoma box, had no information as to code words or wave-lengths in the 2nd Division, so a set was put on the job of interception. Soon the headquarters of 10th Field was contacted, normal radio communications were established, and it wasn't long after this that the regiment was able to join in the D.F. (Defensive Fire) tasks to help the garrison. At any hour of the day or night, the cry would ring out: 'Troop target!' and in a matter of seconds the twenty-four guns would be roaring away. Though 25-pounders aren't so accurate as 3.7 howitzers, only on one occasion, when there was confused fighting inside the perimeter, did they have to be silenced.

On the 13th, the Camerons moved down from Sachema to occupy two features behind the Jap positions on Bunker Hill. Hearing this, Grover, who had gone forward to Hawkins's headquarters at Zubza, urged him to get on with the attack. But the guns hadn't yet registered, so it was agreed that zero should be at noon the following day. Again the Jap gunners on Merema Ridge seemed to sense John Grover's presence and began 'browning the perimeter', so the two commanders took refuge in a slit trench and continued their discussions there. Some shells fell around them, but did no damage, and when Grover left the shelling stopped again. As it soon became apparent, the Japanese were somewhat regular in their habits, resembling the Germans in the First World War. An officer at Zubza on this day recorded:

> 'The box is sited on the uphill side of the road, just before the country starts falling away to form an oval-shaped bowl, with the road winding along just below the rim, and the white bungalows of Kohima at the far end. Dotted along the front edge of the box were the infantry posts, reinforced on the flanks by M.M.G. The broken ground in the middle was occupied by the guns, spaced in lines by troops, every twelve yards or so. Down in a nala the mules were being led to water, rather too bunched for safety, I thought. From the cook house, men were bringing their dinner in mess tins and sitting down to eat on the boxes strewn around. Everything and everyone out in the open; and 500 yards away on a small hill like a lump of jelly left over in the bowl, you could see the Jap bunker. But everything was peaceful as both they and we had lunch. However, at 1330 hours, they finished theirs just ahead of us and began mortaring. I had to nip back and stop a convoy of twenty 3-t0nners who were corning along the road with gunner ammunition. Five minutes earlier and they'd have copped it.'

In Kohima itself things were not quite so peaceful, even at lunch-time, and this day came to be known by the garrison as 'the black 13th'. Richards records: 'There was continual shelling, and movement had become difficult as snipers gave us so much trouble. The trees by this time were bare and there was no cover. The air-drop was a great disappointment too...' What happened was that the first flight, by the United States Army Air Force, mistook the dropping zone and delivered their loads on to the Treasury area, right outside the perimeter. Later, the R.A.F. came along and spotted the zone correctly—the signs had been laid out by the Royal West Kents in a dip between Garrison Hill and Kuki Piquet—but by some mistake dropped 3.7 howitzer ammunition intended for Jotsoma. However, some medical supplies came down, which by now were needed desperately. Later it was discovered that the loads which fell on the Treasury included 3-inch mortar ammunition and, as the Japs had already captured some mortars, this came back again with devastating effect.

But, apart from the supply position, the tactical position was getting serious too. The enemy had infiltrated into the garrison's positions in the F.S.D. area, which was being defended by a company of Laverty's men, aided by some Rajputs, and a platoon of the Assam Rifles. In the morning they put in a counter-attack, and managed to restore the perimeter, but before they could clear the hill overlooking it a Jap heavy machine-gun opened up from G.P.T. Ridge, caught them in the open, and the assault withered away. The result was that the D.I.S. had to be abandoned; and the enemy could now snipe the whole Royal West Kents' area. The business of living became harder than ever.

Another factor began to operate too: the troops knew that if they became wounded, however, seriously their chances of being treated properly and evacuated to a place of even relative safety were nil. This knowledge did not seem to impair their fighting spirit, but it increased the mental strain enormously.

Sensing that a crisis of morale was being approached, Richards realized he must do something positive to stiffen the troops' resolution and give them hope. He therefore published a Special Order of the Day:

1. I wish to acknowledge with pride the magnificent effort which has been made by all officers, N.C.O.s and men and followers* of this garrison in the successful defence of Kohima.
2. By your efforts you have prevented the Japanese from attaining this object. All his attempts to overrun the Garrison have been frustrated by your determination and devotion to duty. Your efforts have been in accordance with the highest traditions of British Arms.
3. It seems clear that the enemy has been forced to draw off to meet the threat of the incoming relief force and this in itself has provided us with a measure of relief. His action now is directed to contain us by harassing fire, while he seeks to occupy odd posts under cover of that fire.
4. The relief force is on its way and all that is necessary for the Garrison now is to stand firm, hold its fire and beat off any attempt to infiltrate among us.
5. By your acts you have shown what you can do. Stand firm, deny him every inch of the ground.
6. I deplore the sufferings of the wounded; every effort is being made to alleviate them at the first opportunity.
7. Put your trust in God and continue to hit the enemy hard wherever he may show himself. If you do that, his defeat is sure.
8. I congratulate you on your magnificent effort and am confident that it will be sustained.

Richards is a spare, conventional, and reserved Englishman, and this Order of the Day may well be the most emotional document he has penned in a whole lifetime. Even after many years, it is difficult to read the order without being moved; to observe how, even after long danger and privation, the basic character

* Non-combatants.

of the man still shone in his words, with their deep echoes of the Psalms. All mention of this document has been omitted from some accounts of the siege; and its general effect is hard to assess. But it is difficult not to believe that for any man with a love for the English language its impact would have been great.

It was also on this black day that the main pit of the A.D.S. was hit by a mortar bomb; two doctors were killed and a number of patients were wounded. According to Richards, the only good news to reach him was that Colonel Lander, the C.R.E., had been to inspect the trickle of water, first discovered by the Assam Rifles. Being close to the road, it could only be used at night by organized water parties, bringing over chagals, but until the R.A.F. succeeded in dropping water supplies it would save the situation.

The night of the 13th saw bitter fighting at both ends of the perimeter. The Royal West Kent companies holding the F.S.D. were attacked by wave after wave of Japanese. Fortunately the light was enough to see their figures advancing through the trees, and the Bren gunners waited till they were only fifteen yards away, then let go in long bursts. Great numbers of the attackers went down, but some got through to the trenches to start fighting hand-to-hand. One soldier is said to have shot three Japs, one after the other, as they dropped down into his trench; another was laid out and came round later to find a Japanese officer sharing his slit-trench. Unable to find his rifle in the darkness, he attacked the officer with his bare hands. Around the D.C.'s bungalow the attacks were held without great difficulty, though there was one nasty moment when a Bren gun jammed. Its gunner was bayoneted but his No. 2, Private Williams, fought things out with a shovel, killing one Jap and driving off the others. However, while this was going on, a party of Japs had poured through the hole and occupied a hut on a small knoll inside the perimeter. Fortunately, the platoon commander was on hand with a section of men, and after some hard fighting the insurgents were all killed. The attacks went on most of the night, but the Brens all behaved themselves and the line held. But the men were getting desperately tired and how long they could keep going it was impossible to say.

The Camerons were in action that night too. An officer and a sergeant had got right on top of Bunker Hill, having shot up the bunkers all the way, to find the whole position apparently deserted. News was radioed back to Victor Hawkins, who gave orders that a platoon, then a company should occupy the position. But he warned the Jocks to go carefully, as the Japs might be up to their tricks and laying on a carefully prepared ambush. He was right. The first platoon reached the top of the spur without trouble, but just as they were settling into their positions the whole feature came alive. Fire was directed at them from every side, even from the bunkers that had been blitzed on the way up. The platoon came down in a big hurry. But at least, as Hawkins put it, 'we knew where we were. There was anything up to a company of Japs dug in on that position. So we'd give them everything we'd got, and make a job of it the next day.'

But the excitement wasn't over for the night. A company of Japs from the 138th Regiment worked their way up a nala just before dawn with the object of occupying Zubza and to their amazement found it occupied already. They first bumped the sappers of the Field Company and shot through them towards the tanks, the crews of which were asleep in the open. Luckily the sapper sentries began loosing off their Stens and, as the Japs came towards them, the tank crews clambered inside their vehicles, closed hatches, and began firing with their 75 mms. at point-blank range. The Japs who managed to escape this barrage got into some bashas on the hills above the village where they began squealing and yelling at the tops of their voices. When daylight came Hawkins told the Worcestershires to organize 'a grouse drive', which they did most successfully.

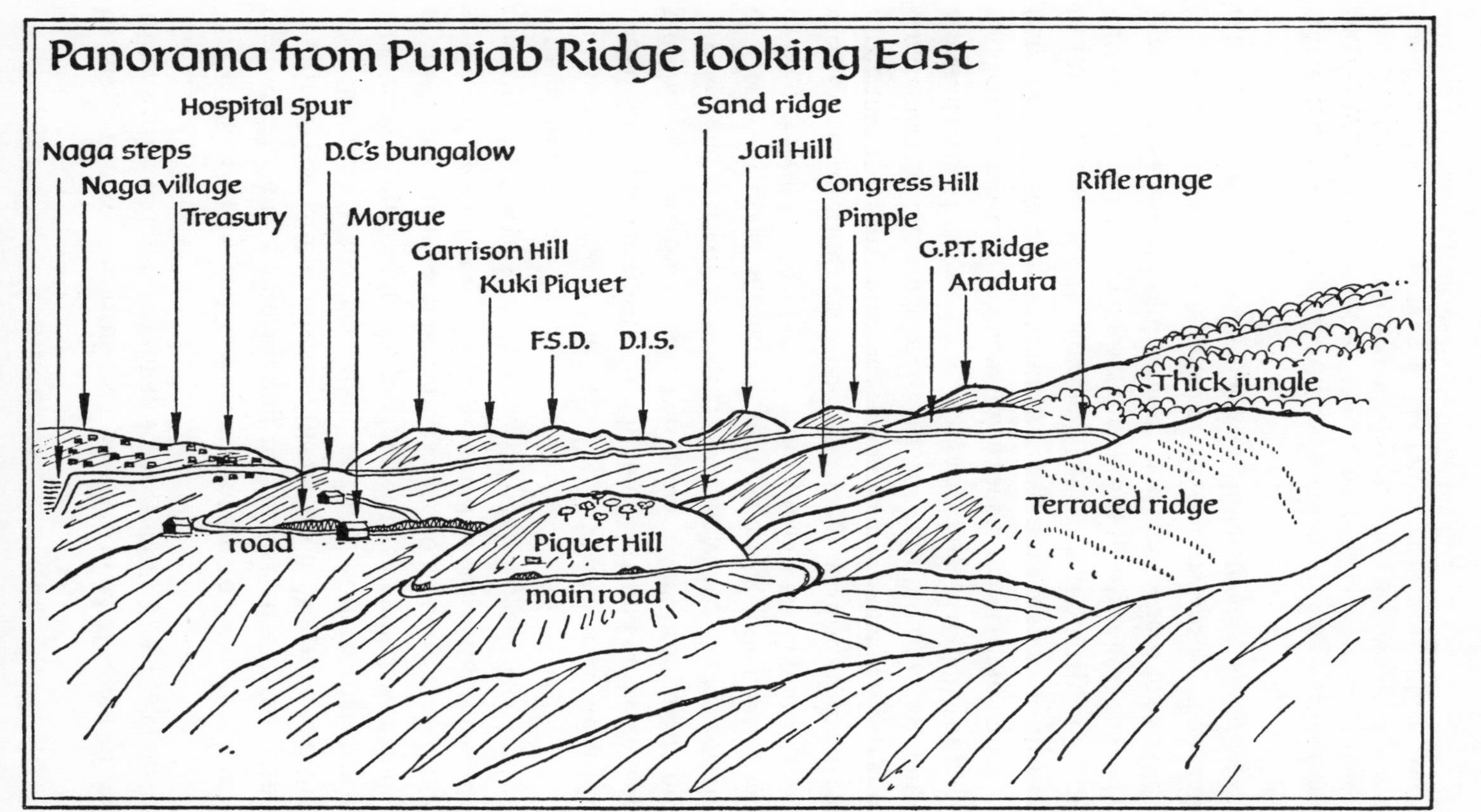
Panorama from Punjab Ridge looking East
Hospital Spur
Naga steps
Naga village
Treasury
D.C's bungalow
Morgue
Garrison Hill
Kuki Piquet
F.S.D.
D.I.S.
Sand ridge
Jail Hill
Congress Hill
Pimple
G.P.T. Ridge
Aradura
Rifle range
Thick jungle
Terraced ridge
Piquet Hill
road
main road

By the time it was over only six Japs remained alive out of the 100; and the company commander was shot trying to get away across the road.*

On the 14th when Richards went up to Laverty's headquarters, he found him talking to Warren on the radio and describing the serious plight of the garrison. When he had finished Richards spoke personally and told Warren that unless relief came soon it would be too late. Warren replied: 'I'm doing my best, but intend to make a proper job of it.' Later that day he sent word that relief might be expected in two days' time—on the 16th. By the time of this message 5th Brigade had broken through to him.

On the morning of the 14th Victor Hawkins sat on a hill overlooking the Jap position on Bunker Hill, and pushed ahead with his plans for the attack. The mortars were brought up into position and started registering, then the M.M.G.s of the Manchesters were dragged forward, and the tanks came up the road to their start-line. With growing impatience Hawkins watched the guns registering, each one separately because of the close range and the proximity of the Cameron companies carrying out the attack. The angle of fire was awkward too. Occasionally Hawkins would ring up Lieut.-Colonel Harry Grenfell, the gunners' commander, to ask how much longer he was going to take; but Grenfell, like Hawkins himself, was not a man to be hurried or flustered, and the registering went on methodically. Not till 1200 hours did Grenfell give any clue as to when he'd be ready. Then he rang up and said simply: 'You can fix zero for 1230.'

By now it was raining hard and Hawkins was on edge. The tanks had rubber tracks which were liable to start skidding on

* The Japanese soon identified the 2nd Division. 'It was very strong and very well disciplined,' Colonel Yamaki records, 'and we heard that it came from Yorkshire.' The second observation is interesting: the Divisional sign, the 'Cross Keys', was taken from the keys of York, but there were no Yorkshire regiments in the formation.

the road, and this meant that some of them might go over the bank before they'd even got into action. Also, the back of the hill worried him as, owing to the slope, his guns couldn't touch it. There'd been no signs of earthworks on this slope, but the Jap could have concealed them, in which case the Jocks—who were attacking from the rear—would 'catch a bloody nose'.

However, precisely on time the guns opened fire and went on for fifteen minutes, putting down 1,500 shells onto the Jap position. As they finished, the mortars began their barrage, and as they finished the tanks came into action. At least, they should have done. But, in fact, there was no sign of them. Hawkins was just worrying how on earth he would cover the advance of the Camerons when the tanks appeared, moved up to a position some 200 yards from the objective, and began firing over open sights. Then it was time for the Jocks to appear. At first Hawkins couldn't see them, but then they came, moving forward slowly over the broken ground. One of the company commanders, David Graham, could be seen moving about controlling his men, as if on an exercise. There were no Japs on the near slope of the hill, but those towards the crest were alive by some miracle and still ready to fight. One of them flung a grenade at Graham and, as he threw himself down, a Jock lay on top of him till it became evident that the grenade was a dud. Then remarking 'its okay, sir', he got up and continued his advance. However, a few minutes later, Graham got hit in the shoulder and was put out of action. C.S.M. Cook, an ex-Army boxing champion, went into the fight with great spirit; coming across an officer with a sword, he wrested it from him, killed him, then used the sword on any other Japs that came his way.

By 1400 hours it was all over and the Jocks were in full possession of the hill. The sappers went forward to mend the broken bridge. Captain Watari, the Battalion Commander, was later informed that an entire company had been wiped out.

Victories solve one set of problems only to bring the next set a stage nearer. As soon as he'd reported to Grover and given the news about Bunker Hill, Hawkins went on to point out that by the time he'd picketed the increased length of road he'd have no troops left to recapture Kohima. Grover, however, realized already that the initial orders were no longer viable and, in fact, had discussed the matter with Brigadier Stevens, and asked him to put his position to the Corps Commander: to explain that it was simply impossible to build a striking force forward, while protecting forty miles of road back to Dimapur. Stopford's reply was that he should stop worrying about his L. of C. and take a risk, but this he couldn't regard as satisfactory. By no means all his division had arrived; there were R.A.S.C. personnel, gunners, sappers, and all kinds of specialist units still on the road. There were officers and men returning from leave and from courses. And there were still vast stocks of food and ammunition to ferry forward—hundreds of tons of it every day.

Nevertheless, despite his own worries, Grover agreed to relieve the two companies of Dorsets, who were tethered back along the road, so that at least Hawkins should have his whole brigade under control. But when the detachments of Worcestershires and Camerons protecting the divisional artillery could be relieved it was still impossible to say.

On the whole, the 14th was a quieter day at Kohima, though there were too odd incidents. In the morning a reconnaissance patrol from the F.S.D. found four Japs seated in a bunker, chatting. They seemed quite friendly, for some reason, and called out 'Come here.' Needless to say, the patrol did nothing of the sort but went back to their platoon for a Bren gun and shot the Japs dead. The second incident came at noon—just as the Camerons were waiting to go into action. A thick mist sprang up which mingled with the smoke and orders went out for all men to stand-to. Then, through the smoke came forty Japs armed with gelignite with which, under the cover of grenades, they tried to blow up some trenches manned by one of the composite companies. There was a series of explosions, and through the smoke the section under attack could be seen running, but when it reached the safety of the next line of trenches it got into fire positions and engaged the Japs with rifles and Brens. The two flanking sections joined in, and then the mortars brought down fire on the captured trenches. The Japs retreated again, leaving their dead strewn over the area.

There were no major attacks for the first night in a week, a relief for which the garrison were profoundly thankful.

On the 15th, the sappers of 208 Field Company, attached to 5th Brigade, were out on Bunker Hill at first light, removing booby traps and collecting up arms, equipment, and personal possessions off the bodies. The staff captain, seeing this assorted junk, wrote:

> 'There were piles of photographs, curiously enough not of wives or families but of military groups and mass parades; also small parties of men in civilian clothes, big, leering and evil... some with such a lack of brow as to seem sub-human. The odd geisha girl smiled up at us too; expensively gowned, groomed, and painted à la Max Factor.... The sappers looked through the photographs with great curiosity, bursting with laughter when they found a "filthy" one. There were diaries, pamphlets, and English phrase books. I saw: "Is this water fit to drink?" and "Have you any cattle in the village?" opposite Japanese translations. There were soldiers' pay-books too, surprisingly like ours in character. One sapper, seeing a figure entered in red, exclaimed: "My God, the little bugger's in debt!"'

The Intelligence people and translators couldn't take quite such a frivolous view of this material. As John Grover wrote: 'It includes a tremendous amount of valuable maps, documents, and equipment... more than the "I" staff can handle.' One thing was established immediately, however: the troops on Bunker Hill were from the 1st Battalion 138th Regiment. This, so the Intelligence Staff told Grover, accounted for their great size, as the unit came from the northern islands. Some were over six feet, which fact had very much surprised the wee Jocks. A corporal was heard asking his company commander with some indignation: 'What's all this about *little* Japs? This lot are bastard big ones!'

At 1100 hours on the 15th the Dorsets made contact with 161st Brigade and, soon afterwards, Hawkins went up to Jotsoma to see Warren. Any criticisms of 5th Brigade's lack of speed were left unexpressed for the moment, and Warren gave a description of the battle for Bunker Hill, as seen from his viewpoint. He had a grandstand seat and was very impressed with the weight of the artillery concentration. He then went on to speak of the plight of the Kohima garrison. Hawkins writes: 'He was deeply anxious about the Royal West Kents who all this time had been hanging on to Garrison Hill... they now had something like 250 wounded men inside the perimeter.' Hawkins couldn't help Warren with his own brigade as it was now committed to other tasks. However, at 1500 hours John Grover arrived and discussions immediately began to devise a plan to clear up the whole situation in the centre of Kohima. The 1st Royal Welch Fusiliers (it was agreed) would be put under Warren's command, with a view to carrying out a relief operation with the 1st/1st Punjab the following day, 2nd Division Artillery giving support. Once the relief had been accomplished, 6th Brigade, under Brigadier Shapland, would be responsible 'for re-establishing the Kohima area'. Grover then departed, leaving Warren to work out his plan in detail.

The 15th was a fairly quiet day so far as the Kohima Garrison was concerned; but in the Jotsoma box things got quite hilarious when the R.A.F. air-drop started about four o'clock. Gaily coloured parachutes came floating down, bringing 3.7

howitzer ammunition right on to the gun positions. The Indian troops thought this was a great lark and went scampering about happily, retrieving the ammunition and stacking it by the guns. And when another load came down by Brigade headquarters, causing the 2nd Division recce party to scatter in all directions, they roared with laughter.

All this day the regiments of the 2nd Division were moving forward to Zubza; the Royal Norfolk, the Royal Berkshires, the Durham Light Infantry. The Royal Welch Fusiliers were already established there and engaged in minor actions with parties of Japanese, who were still filtering down the division's right flank. After dark, a patrol under Lieutenant Hill bumped a party of the 138th Regiment on the road. The Japanese officer went for Hill with his sword, but the subaltern was ready for him and killed him with a burst from his Sten. Later it was found that the officer had been decapitated and his head removed.

On the whole, the 15th April marked a change of atmosphere so far as the 2nd Division was concerned. The party feeling was over—but so was the 'flap'. 'There is a new air of confidence abroad today,' an officer noted. 'The troops feel that their General has got the situation in hand. Instead of shooting us off in penny packets, he can use us as a striking force.'

The 16th didn't open so happily. To begin with, captured Jap documents indicated an intention to hold the ridge running north of Kohima, through Merema and Cheswema. This meant that he would be overlooking the road all the way from Kohima to Zubza, across the river valley, and therefore that Grover's L. of C. had now become his front line. This was, of course, an absurd tactical situation which would obviously have to be countered as soon as possible. If the Japs managed to get any considerable strength of artillery on Merema Ridge, the whole forward build-up would be jeopardized.

When he'd heard Warren's plan for the relief of the Kohima Garrison, Grover didn't like it. As he said: 'I found several flaws in the plan, particularly as regards time for the recce by the units of 6th Brigade involved, and the lack of adequate provision for the security of the right flank of the brigade....' An excellent tactician himself, Warren could see these flaws, and appreciated the risks involved, but he considered that the plight of the garrison was such that the latter must be accepted. For a while he argued strongly, urging Grover to let the relief go ahead that day, but Grover was adamant, and so it was postponed till the 17th.

This news came to Richards, Laverty, and the garrison as a bitter disappointment. Though they'd had a short respite from major attacks, and the R.A.F. were dropping water and supplies, some of which fell inside the perimeter, the troops were exhausted; and the plight of the wounded, still lying in the open, still suffering the ordeal of shell-fire and mortar fire, was almost beyond describing. All eyes had been focused on the road, searching for a glimpse of the relieving column, and when, in the afternoon, the sun began dipping towards Mount Pulebadze, and it became obvious that no one would come that day and another night of torment must be endured, the tension (to quote Peter Steyn) 'had reached such a pitch that an outlet had to be found'. This was organized by Major Callistan who now held the D.C.'s bungalow sector, with a composite company of Assam Rifles and Assam Regiment men, and took the form of a grenade raid across the tennis court. On the far side of this the Japs had established a machine-gun post amongst the trees, which had been harassing the forward troops for some time, and if it could be wiped out life would be somewhat easier. As the light failed, Sepoy Wellington Massar climbed on to the billiard-table in the club to give himself a good field of fire and began firing bursts with his Bren. As a second Bren joined in from the flank, four men, led by Naik Dilhu Angami, rushed forward holding grenades with the pins extracted. Covering some thirty yards before the Japs realized what was happening, they hurled their grenades into the machine-gun pit, then sprinted back again. But, unfortunately, the enemy in surrounding posts recovered rapidly and returned Sepoy Wellington's fire. Then his Bren jammed, and as he struggled to free it he was hit and fell from the billiard-table on to the floor. But with great courage he cleared the fault and went on firing through window till the grenade party were back again. For this action he was awarded the Indian Distinguished Service Medal, but unfortunately died of his wounds a month later.

The night of the 16th was dark and later turned to rain. Having attacked unsuccessfully in the D.C.'s bungalow area, the enemy switched his attention to the F.S.D., at the southern end of the perimeter. Here two companies of the Royal West Kents were attacked by wave after wave of Japs and, completely out-numbered, gave ground after heavy hand-to-hand fighting. It was obvious to Richards that some of the Royal West Kents would have to be relieved, so he sent up two platoons of the Assam Rifles and one from the Assam Regiment. They were very tired, like the Royal West Kents, but had not been shelled and mortared to the same extent. With these troops 'Bruno' Brown put in a counter-attack and some of the lost position was reoccupied, but the Japs remained dangerously near the top. While possession of the F.S.D. was being disputed, Colonel Keene and the Assam Rifles on I.G.H. Spur were attacked, but they held their line without great difficulty and when daylight came twenty-four bodies were counted in front of the perimeter. Somehow, the garrison had survived another night. Fervently they prayed it would be the last of the siege.

But it wasn't to be. While the Royal West Kents and the Assam Rifles were under fire, the Royal Welch Fusiliers of 6th Brigade, who had relieved the Rajputs on the high ground to the south of the road junction at Lancaster Gate, were attacked and two sections were overrun, the men in these being taken prisoner. Fortunately, a subaltern called Callaghan was on hand and, using a covered way round the left flank, he staged a counter-attack which completely surprised the enemy, who were all killed. To their immense relief, the prisoners found themselves free again. However, some confusion remained on the ridge during the night, and when Grover saw Warren on the morning of the 17th it was obvious that the latter was now worried about his right flank, and had decided 'to modify his plan for the relief of Kohima, by limiting offensive action to the close picketing of the road'. He was still, of course, desperately anxious about the garrison and had great fears that they might be overrun that corning night. Grover was less anxious, having received a misleading message that the garrison 'was firm and in good heart'. So the relief was put off another day.

This was another blow to the garrison and far worse than the previous postponement. Many of the men were almost at their last gasp, their morale was sapped by constant shelling and lack of sleep, apart from the desperate fighting each night. They may even have come to the conclusion that what Richards and their officers had told them was lies, that help would never come. As an officer of the Royal West Kents has recorded: 'No one had had an opportunity to wash or shave since the 5th April and very little chance of sleep since then….' Peter Steyn of the Assam Regiment says: 'Many were the anxious questions being asked. "Sahib, how long do you think we will have to stay here? Do you think we can hold out?"' The officers had been answering these questions with a bland certainty, but now even *they* were beginning to doubt. 'Courage,' as Slim has said, 'is expendable'; and so far as the garrison of Kohima was concerned, the reservoir was nearly empty.

If the situation was critical for the British and Indians it was difficult also for the Japanese. Sato was somewhat surprised at the tenacity of the Kohima garrison and at the failure of his men to subdue it. Already his losses were large, and steadily mounting each day, which meant that the longer Kohima defied him the fewer men he'd have to capture it with. Also he was feeling the pressure of Warren's brigade on his flank and knew that another formation was entering the field against him. According to his intelligence reports it was 'arriving at the rate of a battalion a day'; and he could assess the growing weight of artillery himself. Another problem Sato was having to face was that his long, tenuous supply line from the Chindwin seemed to be drying up. Ammunition, food, supplies were coming through fitfully and in smaller quantities; and protests to Mutaguchi at 15th Army headquarters had so far produced no coherent explanations, nor any action. Already units were beginning to kill off their mules for food. Altogether then the situation was that if he were to succeed in taking Kohima at all, it must be now. The next attack must be the last.

Mutaguchi, though still confident, realized that the attack had lost its initial impetus both at Kohima and Imphal, and the battle had settled down to a hard slogging match. The cool withdrawal of the British and Indian forces and their defence of Imphal had impressed him; since 1942 they had improved beyond measure. Nevertheless they were fighting in their last ditch; and only eight miles separated his men from Imphal. Pondering the problem as to how he could achieve a breakthrough with maximum speed, Mutaguchi considered the idea of robbing Sato of a regiment. This would undoubtedly render Sato's task much more difficult; but, on the other hand, he had already captured over three-quarters of Kohima Ridge, and the garrison were penned in an ever-shrinking circle. Whether their collapse came in two days' time or in ten, it didn't matter; the British would still not be able to reinforce Imphal. But if Miyazaki were to fling a regimental group at the northern tip of the Imphal perimeter, this might make all the difference. The scales, now evenly balanced, might suddenly swing to the Japanese advantage. Sending for a staff officer, Mutaguchi ordered him to draft the necessary signal.

On the night of the 17th a heavy artillery barrage came down on the F.S.D., and the perimeter in that sector disintegrated. Suffering heavy casualties, the Indian troops evacuated the positions and the Japanese began feeling their way forward, in small parties at first, then in strength. Running back, the Indians had gone through the positions of the Royal West Kents and some of their men began to panic. But their N.C.O.s soon had them in hand, and as the Japanese came on they were met by a murderous small arms fire, and went to ground. After a short pause they began sending over a shower of grenades and fired phosphorus bombs at the huts on Kuki Piquet to set them alight. Then, leaping to their feet, and screaming at the top of their voices, they surged on again, but the defenders still held firm. As the noise of battle raged, and the hill was covered with a baleful light, C.S.M. Haines of the Royal West Kents, though blinded by a shell burst, stayed with his men shouting encouragement and urging them to hold fast. When the fighting died down in one sector, he would ask to be led to another, and so he went on with fantastic heroism till a burst of machine-gun fire caught him in the face and he fell back dead. Meanwhile, the company commanders were plugging holes wherever they appeared, sending a section here and a section there. The situation was more desperate than it had ever been, and men were not only watching their front but listening to the firing on their flanks, praying the Japs hadn't broken through there. Several times that night Colonel Keene on I.G.H. Spur thought the game was up and expected to see the Japanese come running over Garrison Hill to take his positions in the rear. But though the roar of guns and grenades was deafening, and the glare kept sweeping across the shrinking area of ground, somehow the perimeter still held.

Then, at 0230 hours, an attack came in on Kuki Piquet and that was lost. The troops, who had stood so much, could apparently stand no more, and no officers, no N.C.O.s could hold them to their posts. As Richards realized at once, the garrison was now within a millimetre of defeat; from Kuki Piquet the Japanese could launch a thrust on Garrison Hill. Luckily, the Mortar Sergeant of the Royal West Kents realized the danger too. Though wounded in the jaw, he obtained Laverty's permission to move his mortar platoon to a new site, then assembled the necessary ammunition, and brought down a concentration on Kuki Piquet. But this took time, and at any moment it seemed that the Japanese must come screaming down the hill, and it would all be over. For some reason, however, perhaps amazed at their own success, they stayed where they were; and then the mortars opened up and the situation was saved. But it had been a horrible night. Richards wrote: 'The shelling was the heaviest and most concentrated we'd had. How my own headquarters and the Royal West Kents' headquarters escaped direct hits, I don't know, but they did.' When he walked out next morning to find what was left of his command, he found trench after trench filled with British and Indian dead. He knew without any shadow of doubt that unless relief came within twelve hours it would be too late.

Fortunately, things soon began to happen. At 0800 hours the guns of the 2nd Division opened up on the Japanese positions encircling the garrison and hammered them for the next half-hour. Then, supported by tanks, the 1st/1st Punjab began attacking along the road, and dropping off pickets on the high ground as they advanced. Peter Steyn wrote of this moment: 'To the garrison, it seemed unbelievable that the nightmare of the past few weeks could be drawing to a close. Tired eyes watched as fighter-bombers of the R.A.F. roared overhead to strafe G.P.T. Ridge and the surrounding areas.... Weary faces smiled as news of the attack came through.' There was not a great deal of opposition, but Warren did not want any slip-up and his units felt their way forward slowly. At milestone 45 the Japs had established a road block and, before this could be cleared, the tanks had to be brought into action and the infantry put in a right hook. This took an hour and it was almost noon before the column reached I.G.H. Spur. All this time Major Yeo had been directing the fire of the artillery against the enemy batteries, keeping them quiet; if they were allowed to bring down a concentration on the re-entrant where the relieving troops were entering the perimeter the slaughter would be great. But by now Yeo knew every inch of the ground, and as the 25-pounders at Zubza kept roaring away and the shells shrieked over, the Japs were too occupied to think of offensive action. The Punjabis made their way into the perimeter without difficulty.

After the leading infantry there came the transport; ambulances, three-tonners, and carriers. For some hours Colonel Young had been making arrangements for the evacuation of the wounded, collecting walking cases into groups under leaders, getting non-combatants to help carry the rest of the wounded down to the ambulances. This was a tricky job and had to be done a few cases at a time, as snipers were still active. Some men, having endured days and nights of pain, were wounded again as they went down to the trucks, and others were killed. Several non-combatants, who understandably lost their heads and charged down in groups, were picked off too. The process of evacuation went on till evening.

The commanding officer of the 1st/1st Punjab was Lieut.-Colonel Grimshaw, and as he followed the guide who was to take him to Laverty's headquarters, he noticed the scene of utter devastation around him, and particularly the black, swollen corpses of the Japanese. His meeting with Laverty was short and confined to the business on hand; the deployment of the Punjabis to give the maximum support to the garrison. In general, agreement was soon reached, but then the position of the D.C.'s bungalow sector was discussed, and Laverty appears to have been in some doubt as to whether the troops should be relieved or merely withdrawn. The matter was referred to Richards who insisted that the sector must be held, so a company of

Punjabis moved down to take over from the Royal West Kents. Later events proved Richards to be right.

Though they were still in their slit trenches, still under shell fire, and facing yet another night of attack, the garrison were now in much better heart. The sight of fresh troops arriving had produced a great psychological effect. No longer did they feel isolated and abandoned. They knew it would only be a matter of time now before they were taken out of the perimeter and given a long rest; and this new hope brought new courage.

*

After watching the start of the relief operations, John Grover returned to his headquarters to meet Stopford, who had come forward from Jorhat. Immediately discussions began on the subject of the L. of C. which was causing Grover a good deal of concern. Stopford, it will be remembered, had advised taking a risk, but with the threat to his right flank increasing, Grover begged to differ. The road, he argued, must be kept open until all the road parties of his Division had arrived from India, during the next ten days. Till they were all through, Grover considered, he must hold strong defended areas at Zubza and Priphema, five miles further back.

Stopford agreed to Grover's appreciation and the discussion moved on to Grover's plan for future operations. The main features of this were to establish the right flank, to extend the area now held to Kohima, and to carry out forward reconnaissances in anticipation of the major operation of wresting Kohima Ridge from the enemy. Also it was agreed that the 2nd Division should get a footing on Merema Ridge. No timing was mentioned for the operation, but both commanders understood that it must be carried out just as soon as possible. Already it was known by Mountbatten and Slim that the transport aircraft supplying 4th Corps at Imphal had failed so far to achieve their target number of sorties, even in fine weather. The pressure was on.

*

While Stopford was conferring with Grover, Sato was studying a signal from Mutaguchi ordering him to send a regimental group to Kanglatongbi, with a view to reinforcing 15th Division's attack on Imphal. Apparently intending to comply with the order, he asked Miyazaki to concentrate the 124th Regiment (less its third battalion), the 1st Battalion 138th Regiment, and a battalion of the 31st Mountain Artillery, on the Aradura Spur, to the west of Kohima. He also gave orders for the 138th Regiment to hold the Cheswema-Merema ridge, with the task of harassing the Dimapur road, and for the 3rd Battalion 124th Regiment to hold Naga Village. Meanwhile the 58th Regiment were to continue their efforts to capture Garrison Hill. Sato's plan was a sound one; if he could hold both ridges, and the Kohima Ridge which joined them, the 2nd Division and the formations under its command would be attacking into a deep salient, harassed on their right flank, shelled from their left, and blocked by the almost im pregnable positions ahead. (As Grover put it: 'It's like trying to force yourself out of a bottle.') It is sometimes said that, like Marshal Soult, Sato was better at bringing his troops into battle than manœuvring them afterwards; that his mind was rigid and inelastic. This may be so, though when judging him one should remember that his orders were very limiting; but in defence he was undoubtedly brilliant—a fact that the 2nd Division were soon to discover.

To turn for a moment to Mutaguchi's order to send the three battalions to help in the attack on Imphal, it now appears that having originally intended to obey the order Sato began to have doubts. About the 19th he signalled Mutaguchi: 'It will take six or seven days for these troops to arrive on foot, so please send transport.' To this Mutaguchi signalled: 'Carry out this order immediately without fail. Use the transport you captured at Kohima.' This signal (like so many missives from Mutaguchi) enraged Sato; it appears, however, that he did not reject the order but decided to keep stalling and watch events. Why Sato had no transport of his own to use is not clear, as, from reports of the 58th Regiment, they captured some thirty vehicles. It may be that these had all been immobilized, or the Japanese troops, in their enthusiasm, had destroyed them.

On the night of the 18th, after some minor scares, the Japs attacked the Punjabis in the D.C.'s bungalow sector, and a brisk battle developed on the tennis court. Grenades were hurled from end to end, some reaching their objectives but others exploding around the base line. The Punjabis fought gallantly but were outnumbered, and eventually the Japanese were able to move forward on a flank. In the noise and confusion it was impossible to organize a counter-attack that night; all the company could do was hold on till daylight. Then Jemadar Mohammed Rafiq, though all his three section commanders had been killed, put in a platoon attack to regain the lost trenches, and succeeded brilliantly. Sixteen Japanese were killed and the Jemadar was awarded the M.C.

While the Punjabis were engaged at the northern end of the perimeter, 'A' Company of the Royal West Kents were trying to beat off an attack from the south-west. A platoon of Indian troops had retired through their lines and the Japs, following up, had occupied their old positions, which included one bunker only a few yards away. From here the Japs attacked again, infiltrated between two sections, then, using the cover of some bushes, began wriggling their way forward. By now they were only forty yards from the Battalion Command Post and the situation looked very ugly indeed. No troops were available for a counter-attack and the only way to stop further penetration was by individual stalking, in the flickering light a game of hide-and-seek was played, dozens of minor clashes and individual actions being fought. Time went on, and soon it became evident that the Japanese effort had spent itself. The perimeter was torn, but at least the only Japanese inside it were dead ones. At first light, Grimshaw put in a counter-attack to gain the lost ground, using smoke liberally to blanket the objective from Japanese positions on the flanks. The action was completely successful and nineteen of the enemy were killed.

But if the perimeter was still intact, it was by now too small to deploy the troops ready to come into it and Warren decided that Kuki Piquet must be retaken. The whole of the 2nd Division artillery (seventy-two guns) put down a concentration, and then the Punjabis went into the attack. Watching the action, Richards thought that none of the enemy on Kuki Piquet could have survived the concentration, but no sooner had the Indians got on to the feature than all the bunkers came alive and machine-gun fire poured out of them. The attack was therefore broken off. This pattern was to repeat itself over and over again in the weeks to come.

But to go back some hours: at 0630 hours Grover had held a conference at Jotsoma with Warren and Shapland, commander of 6th Brigade. A new situation had arisen. Warren, who up to now had been asking that his brigade should complete the relief and re-garrisoning of Kohima, now said it was too tired and should be withdrawn for a rest. Grover, who was short of troops, couldn't agree to this request entirely; but he did concede that the troops who had been in the siege should go back to Dimapur and that the remainder of the brigade should be withdrawn to a quiet sector. This meant that units of the 2nd Division must take over, and it was decided that the Royal Berkshires should go into Kohima. But first there was a tricky situation, as news had come through that a company of the 4th Rajputs who were occupying a feature called Terrace Hill, commanding the road into Kohima, had been overrun. Two attacks had been repelled with the aid of the artillery, firing on D.F. tasks, but the third was successful and very few Rajputs managed to get away. Lieutenant Loudon, the gunner officer who had been calling down the fire, suddenly found himself surrounded by the enemy. But he was able to shoot his way through, killing eight Japs with his Sten before he was blown into a nala by the blast from a grenade. It was quite obvious that Terrace Hill must be retaken before any relief column could venture along the road, and the job was given to the Durham Light Infantry.

This was a fine fighting unit, which had already seen action in the Arakan. The artillery fire, the mortars, and the infantry were all co-ordinated like clockwork and soon the men were prodding among the bunkers, hurling grenades, and engaging with the bayonet any Japs who came out to fight. Over fifty of them were killed and the company began to organize itself for defence. Unfortunately, at this moment the company commander, Robert Allen, was caught by a burst of machine-gun fire in the chest. In the few seconds of life left to him he found the energy to whisper congratulations to his men.

All this day wounded were evacuated from Kohima and stores, ammunition and food were taken in. By now there had been more air-drops and the whole ridge was covered with gaily coloured parachutes, many of them unfortunately caught in the trees and their precious cargoes hanging well out of reach.

In the evening Grover received a report from the Camerons that an officer called Carbonell had gone right up to Merema Ridge and found a complete enemy position unoccupied. Grover immediately told Hawkins to send a strong company patrol over, supported by another the next day. Their object should be to establish themselves astride the Merema–Kohima road. Once they had done this plans could go ahead for Victor Hawkins's left hook.

During this period the regiments stationed along the road running back to Zubza, and beyond, fought a whole string of small actions, too many to enumerate. Most of them were sharp and bloody, life or death dependent on the speed of reaction. For example, on the 14th the Royal Norfolk, who had been given the job of protecting the tank laager at Zubza, were attacked by a company of Japanese, and a brilliant action led by Sergeant Hazell killed thirty of them. Some were grotesque and others comic. On the night of the 16th, a sentry of the Royal Welch Fusiliers, at Zubza, thought he heard some Japanese crawling along a nala bed towards his position and threw a grenade into it. As it happened, some barrels of tar dumped by the road-menders had been rolled into the nala and these exploded, sending burning jets of tar high into the air. Cries of amazement came from all the trenches in the neighbourhood and a man in the Worcestershires was heard to exclaim: 'Bloody hell! They've got a secret weapon!' About this time, Major Elliott of the Worcestershires fought an action against a Japanese company in which one of their officers was wounded and lay in the open, moaning. Neither side would let the other approach to recover him, and the officer took out a phosphorus grenade, pulled out the pin, and held the grenade to his chest. A column of smoke spiralled into the air and there was the foul smell of burning flesh. But till the moment of his death the officer did not take the grenade away from his chest. A few nights later there was the sound of hoof-beats on the northern edge of the Zubza perimeter, and the cry went up: 'They're driving elephants through us.' Firing broke out all round the box and nothing could control it. The mule company nearest to the point where the sound was heard blazed off most of its small arms ammunition. In the morning a dozen cows were found shot to pieces a few yards in front of the wire. The mule company commander, carpeted by Victor Hawkins, swore that two of his posts had been attacked and one of his men wounded. He was told angrily that if his men ever fired again he'd be expected to produce the bodies. On the 19th the Royal Scots fought their first action, in the Zubza valley, a company attacking two small pimples. Unfortunately the company commander sent his men in without adequate supporting fire and several were killed before the action was broken off. ('This is the first time I've done this,' he remarked, 'and the last.') The wounded were carried into the houses of a nearby Naga village where they weren't impressed by 'the evil-smelling cow-dung floors and the gruesome decorations of tiny skulls strung along the walls'. The regiment was annoyed, however, 'at having lost some good men to no purpose', not being able to swear that they'd killed a single Jap. The commanding officer therefore asked the 16th Field Regiment to have a go at the forward slopes of the hill with their guns—the rear slopes being too steep to reach. The gunners went into action, then the mortars, and some Hurribombers, after which the Scots imagined that there couldn't be a Jap alive, and put a company into the attack. But it was the old story; no sooner had the infantry got on to the position than it became alive. A left hook was impossible because the Jap position was sited on the edge of a precipice, and a right hook failed because of a well-sited machine-gun. So the Royal Scots kept hammering at the position with their mortars and machine-guns, and in the morning it was observed that the Japs had gone. Twenty bodies were found, all beheaded and the heads taken away. Among them, though the Royal Scots couldn't know this, was the corpse of Major Shibasaki, commanding the 1st Battalion, 138th Regiment.

On the night of the 19th the Japanese put in some routine attacks on the Kohima garrison, but they were not pressed home with the usual ferocity and the perimeter was not in any great danger.

At 0900 hours on the 20th, John Grover went forward to his command post to watch the final relief of Kohima, with his C.R.A., Pat Burke, and a radio, ready to call up artillery as required. 'We sat side by side,' Grover has recalled, 'able to see the whole operation in panorama before us, and switching on artillery support to any required area like playing a hose.' The operation was prefaced by a strike from the Hurribombers, which attacked Japanese positions on G.P.T. Ridge and Jail Hill, then the artillery took over, pounding all the positions from which interference might come. Soon after nine o'clock the men of the Royal Berkshire Regiment debussed at Picket Hill, half a mile beyond milestone 44, and took up their position behind the tanks. Then the column slowly moved forward, winding its way uphill towards the re-entrant on I.G.H. Spur. The Japs were so inactive that Grover even began to wonder whether they had started to pull out of Kohima, and by 0945 hours the Royal Berkshires were climbing up into the perimeter, and the relief of the garrison began.

The contrast between the troops of the Royal Berkshires and the Royal West Kents could hardly be imagined. While the former looked clean and fresh, the latter were filthy, bearded and bedraggled. Their eyes were bleary and deep in their sockets, their figures were thin, and their shoulders drooped. Some of them looked more like scarecrows than soldiers, and there was some good-natured twitting from the Royal Berkshires about 'standing closer to the razor'. It is said that the men of Kent were too tired to reply, but some jawans* of the Assam Regiment raised a cheer. They could hardly believe that it was time to go.

Like everyone else who saw Kohima Ridge for the first time, the Royal Berkshires were utterly appalled by the scene around them. Their giant commanding officer, Wilbur Bickford, said later:

> 'We were most profoundly shocked by the conditions which prevailed on Garrison Hill.... The stench of festering corpses—Japanese, British and Indian—was overpowering.

* Indian soldiers.

There were no sanitary arrangements and stores of all descriptions were lying about. It was possible to pick up anything from a Tommy-gun to a pair of ladies' shoes, and the place was a veritable paradise for flies.'

Major John Nettlefield, the gunner, has written in similar vein:

'When we first saw Kohima it was beautifully fresh and green—an attractive town perched on the hills.... Now... the place stank. The ground everywhere was ploughed up with shell-fire and human remains lay rotting as the battle raged over them. Flies swarmed everywhere and multiplied with incredible speed. Men retched as they dug in... the stink hung in the air and permeated one's clothes and hair.'

All day the garrison, once their sectors had been taken over, collected in small groups and made their way downhill towards the waiting transport. Many of the jawans of the Assam Regiment, according to Peter Steyn, took a last glance 'at the battle-scarred hill, festooned with dangling parachutes caught up on blackened and blasted trees, and wondered by what miracle they had been spared'. As Major Yeo walked down the hill with his Indian gunners a Jap gun opened up from G.P.T. Ridge. It is said that Yeo, even at this moment, paused, took out his binoculars on the Ridge to spot the flashes, then wrote a message on his pad for the gunner attached to the Royal Berkshires. This he gave to a runner and, his final duty done, made his way towards the trucks. Even before he'd driven away the 25-pounders from Zubza were opening up and the enemy gun was silenced.

Of his last hours in Kohima, Richards has written:

'I made my way up the hill for the last time and on to I.G.H. Spur from where I watched the relief going on. Then about four in the afternoon I went down to the bottom of the spur where the trucks were waiting. I'd had a message from Major-General Grover telling me to call at his headquarters.... Up to the night of the 17th–18th when we lost F.S.D. and Kuki Piquet I had always thought we should be able to hold out and I think this feeling was largely shared. There was certainly no atmosphere of gloom or despondency. After the loss of those positions, however, it was obvious that nothing less than the prompt arrival of the relieving troops could save us.... I have always thought that the tremendous concentration of shell fire put down by the whole of the 2 Div. artillery on Kuki Piquet on the afternoon of the 18th saved us that night. The Japs must have suffered heavy casualties from this.... But regarding the night of the 17th–18th, it seemed to be nothing less than *providential* that the Jap did not follow up his capture of Kuki Piquet with a further attack on Summerhouse Hill. Had he done so in strength, I think it is almost certain that we should have been overrun....'

Richards was desperately tired, but at least had the great satisfaction of knowing that he had done his job. The garrison had suffered 600 casualties, but Sato's losses had been many more; and he had still not taken his objective. By nightfall Richards was away to Dimapur.

On Kohima Ridge the Royal Berkshires manned their weapon pits at evening stand-to. The first phase of the battle was over.

Chapter Six

Left Hook; Right Hook

At 1030 hours on 20th April, Slim arrived at Stopford's headquarters in Jorhat to acquaint him with the political repercussions of the Japanese invasion. Chiang Kai-shek, it appeared, considered that the British 'had mucked up the Assam campaign and would not play until it was tidied up'. By that he meant that his eleven divisions, now hovering on the northern borders of Burma, would take no part in the campaign. Slim added that Washington—no doubt prompted by 'Vinegar Joe' Stilwell—shared Chiang's views, and were taking the line that 'the British weren't even trying to open the Imphal road, as they could supply it easily with the American aircraft on loan'. The result of all this political activity was that Mountbatten was being pressed to get a move on, and he had pressed Slim, who had now arrived to press Stopford. No doubt the question of transport aircraft was mentioned at this meeting, too; the time limit for their return to the Americans was running out and without them Imphal must surrender or starve.

As it happened, Stopford had sent one of his staff to sit in on Grover's morning conference and, after Slim had left Jorhat, he arrived to inform Stopford that in his view plans for 2nd Division's build-up were too slow and methodical. 'At this rate,' he said, 'we shall never capture Kohima.' Stopford therefore wrote to Grover impressing on him the need for speed, and asked his own chief of staff, Brigadier Wood, to take the letter the following day.

Meanwhile, two events happened which considerably affected the situation. On the Imphal Plain a copy of Mutaguchi's order to Sato to send a regiment to Kanglatongbi had been captured and rushed to the translators. Before they could deal with it, however, Carbonell, the Cameron subaltern, who was still up on Merema Ridge with his patrol, saw a Jap sergeant-major come cycling down from the village with a despatch-case. Some Japs were dug in not far away on the other side of the road, but Carbonell managed to shoot the sergeant-major, snatch his case, and disappear into cover before a shot was fired, in the case was found a copy of Sato's operation order and this, too, was rushed to the translators. By 1630 hours they were on the telephone to Stopford, who sent messages to Slim and to Grover. Later that evening Slim came on to say that so much pressure should be exerted at Kohima that Sato couldn't send troops away. Stopford naturally felt that his letter to John Grover should have taken care of things, but at 2200 hours Brigadier Wood came on the line to say that in his view 2nd Division's programme was still too slow. So just before midnight Stopford sent off a further signal, repeating the orders of the Army Commander.

Actually, Grover's programme, which Stopford's staff considered too slow, was as follows:

24th April Clear D.C.'s bungalow
25th April Put another half-battalion into Kohima
26th April Clear up F.S.D. area
27th April First part of relief of Kohima Garrison
30th April (approx.) Major operations.

At this stage in time one can only wonder how carefully the

staff had observed the ground; in the event, the programme proved wildly optimistic.

Early on the 21st Grover had given orders to Shapland, commanding 6th Brigade, to start clearing the foothills of Kohima Ridge. And 5th Brigade, under previous orders, were already poised for their move on to Merema Ridge.

This would obviously be a tricky operation. As Victor Hawkins wrote :

> 'The country has to be seen to understand the full implications of this task.... And to add to my difficulties I was told that the Brigade would get very little artillery support, if any, and that we were to try and do everything by "infiltration" methods.'

However, things started off well. Two Cameron companies left Zubza, skirted Bunker Hill, the scene of their first battle, climbed down to the bottom of the valley, then scaled the steep hills at the far side. The journey took four hours and it was hard slogging all the way. When darkness fell, Peter Saunders, the commanding officer, went off with the rest of the battalion and by next morning they were firmly established. Victor Hawkins therefore summoned his 'O' Group (which included Jack Stocker, commanding the 7th Worcestershires, and Lieut.-Colonel West, commanding the Lancashire Fusiliers, who had temporarily replaced the Dorsets) and gave orders that the rest of the brigade should follow at 1900 hours on the 22nd. Hawkins didn't minimize the risks of moving in single file across the enemy's front. 'If anything goes wrong,' he said, 'we shall catch a packet.' Then added with a wry laugh: 'I wonder what they'd say at the Staff College if I suggested a move like this... probably send me back to my unit as unfit for command.' But if Hawkins was worried, no one else was. The whole brigade had complete faith in their commander; they knew that he was always at his best on an independent show. Perhaps they hadn't realized the implications of the operation, though they could at least guess the probable lack of comfort. Though the nights were chilly in Assam, no blankets were to be taken, no cookers, no comforts, no messes at all. Just the men, their weapons, such ammunition as they could carry, and a few medical stores. It was hoped that for the first three days the brigade could be maintained by coolie columns, and after that by air-drops.

There were no questions, and the 'O' Group dispersed. During the next few hours the Brigadier kept looking at the sky, which was steadily becoming more overcast. He knew that if rain fell his brigade might find itself trapped in the valley.

In Kohima, the Royal Berkshires were settling down to the unpleasant existence which was to be their lot for some time to come. An officer noted:

> 'Garrison Hill was conical in shape, with a small flat top. In consequence, the defence posts were sited on the forward slopes where they were exposed to Japanese observation. No one stirred without being shot at, and whenever they moved men ran swiftly from cover to cover.... A tedious agony of nights and days followed. The individual water ration was a pint a day for all purposes. Shaving and washing were forbidden. Some supplies arrived by air; others were delivered, in guarded convoys, to the Morgue [below I.G.H. Spur] from where fatigue parties humped them up the steep slopes of Hospital Hill. It was a dangerous and wearisome business. Throughout the period no one enjoyed more than two consecutive hours' sleep. The give-and-take of positional warfare continued unabatingly. Mortar and artillery fire were constantly exchanged, and snipers' bullets flicked everywhere.'

In short, the physical conditions were no better than those

endured by the garrison; and only when the Japanese could be knocked off the surrounding heights would they improve.

But when would this happen? At 1300 hours on the 21st, Brigadier Wood reached Grover's headquarters with the Corps Commander's letter, urging him to get on. While accepting the urgency, Grover tried to point out some of the difficulties: the fact, for example, that the Jap had been able to dig himself in on the high ground for some time. Also that even now the Division's tail was still arriving, which meant that a large part of his effort was engaged in keeping the road open. He then took Wood forward to look at the ground. Part of Stopford's impatience—apart from the natural reaction to the pressure exerted by Slim—was his belief that the 2nd Division was faced by only five enemy battalions. The reality, as Grover was well aware, was that a whole division of nine battalions was blocking his path, dug into some of the finest defensive country in the world. A B.B.C. news correspondent arriving about this time was heard to remark: 'I'd no idea this is what you were up against... I've seen nothing like it since Keren.'*

Early on the following morning (22nd April), Grover went forward to Brigadier Shapland's headquarters, and gave him verbal orders to launch an attack at once on the D.C.'s bungalow, supported by artillery and mortar fire and tanks. He was also to try and occupy the F.S.D. and clear the Japs from the high ground to the right of the road forward from Jotsoma, known as Shrewsbury. As Shapland bustled off to carry out these orders, a message came through from Stopford saying: 'Two brigades must be freed for the urgent clearing of the Kohima area. All reasonable risks must be taken as regards road protection.' Faced with this, Grover decided to send Warren's brigade back to Zubza and to bring 4th Brigade forward to Jotsoma, where it could hold the defended area and be ready

* The great mountain stronghold in Eritrea, taken in 1942.

for operations as required. He also gave Victor Hawkins final orders for his move across to Merema. These decisions were communicated to Stopford who agreed them.

Neither of Shapland's actions that day was a great success. The Royal Welch Fusiliers attacked Shrewsbury with great spirit, but came under such a heavy fire that they could make little progress, and eventually the commanding officer, Lieut.-Colonel Braithwaite, called off the attack. The assault on the D.C.'s bungalow was carried out by three platoons of the Royal Berkshires, supported by medium tanks of the 149th Regiment R.A.C. and light tanks of the 45th Cavalry. These rounded the I.G.H. Spur, went on past the Jap positions at the road junction beyond the bungalow, then turned the corner and drove down the far side of it. A few yards along the road a drive was cut into the bank, and the object of the tank commander was to negotiate this and get right up to the bungalow. This was to be done—according to the plan worked out with Shapland—before the artillery concentration came down. But things went wrong. The Japs had blocked the road, and by the time the tanks were able to burst through, the guns had already begun firing and shells began bursting all around. Fortunately none of the tanks received a direct hit and not much damage was done, but one tank went over the khud and was lost. Then it was found that the drive up to the bungalow was too steep for the tanks. The Squadron Commander of the 149th R.A.C. was directing operations out of his tank, exposed to heavy fire, and showed very considerable courage. He tried everything he knew to get his tanks on to their objective, but it was no use. They had to content themselves in shooting up some of the smaller bunkers along the road, and the main bunker at the back of the tennis court was left untouched. Despite the mechanism of the attack having obviously gone wrong, the men of the Royal Berkshires still went in. They destroyed four bunkers and all the Japs in them—eight corpses were counted in one bunker alone. But when it became clear that the tanks could not help them with the large bunker at the back of the tennis court they had to give up.

Learning this news, Grover decided that there should be no more attacks on the D.C.'s bungalow 'until the area has been thoroughly softened up'. He also asked his C.R.E. to examine the possibility of bulldozing a way up through I.G.H. Spur. As he noted, 'A single tank on the crest of the hill would completely dominate any position from the D.C.'s bungalow, but the problem is how to get it there.' It was a problem indeed; and many devices had to be tried and discarded, and many men had to die before it was solved.

It may be worth mentioning here how the drive up to the D.C.'s bungalow came to be so unmanageable. Charles Pawsey (who arrived in 1922) was the first Deputy-Commissioner at Kohima to own a car, and as there was no drive capable of taking a vehicle up to the bungalow, he got the local Nagas to construct one. As the job had to be paid for out of his own pocket, it was done somewhat roughly, and the corner of the drive, just before it reached the bungalow, was so sharp that even a saloon car could not negotiate it without reversing once. It is extraordinary how, twenty-two years later, this small domestic incident was to prove such an important factor in a great battle.

At 1900 hours on the 22nd, 5th Brigade moved off for its Merema adventure. An officer wrote in his diary: 'After dusk the Brigade got under arms and led off down the road in single file. It was dark and cold and no one was very happy. But discipline tells and the troops moved in good order, silently, and with barely a word spoken.' The Worcestershires were in the van, followed by Victor Hawkins and his tactical headquarters, then the machine-gunners of the Manchester Regiment (a tough, magnificent body of men), the 5th Field Ambulance, then the Lancashire Fusiliers. It was slow, difficult going, even at the start, and then, in the black darkness, the rain came down. Also the guides—like nearly all guides in this campaign—lost their way. Hawkins writes: 'As a result, at about 10.0 p.m. we found ourselves on a precipitous slope, on very slippery going. Eventually, after one or two men had slipped down, I considered that it was impossible to continue on that route in the rain and dark.... I therefore ordered the column to halt and wait till either the rain stopped and we could see something of where we were going, or till daylight.'

At this moment Hawkins and his headquarters were in no little danger, and the only way the men could prevent themselves from going over the cliff was 'by straddling the trunks of trees'. And there they remained for five hours till the rain stopped and it was possible to see a little. The mental strain on Hawkins at this moment is not difficult to imagine; apart from the Camerons, his whole brigade was strung out along a single track, and if a Jap patrol happened to appear and report his position the whole formation could be destroyed. But even as it grew lighter things didn't really improve. Taking Ian Thorburn, his brigade-major, with him, Hawkins moved forward to contact the Worcestershires, whom he found lying on the track, waiting for orders to move. Passing them, Hawkins went on to try and find their battalion headquarters, but without guides it was impossible to discern the correct route. However, by four o'clock, when daylight came, Hawkins identified the track and got the brigade moving again. By this time the men were wet, tired, and hungry; but heavily laden they toiled up the slopes. Time after time they would imagine they'd reached the top, only to find there was a false crest and the jungle-mountain still towered way above them. It wasn't till eight o'clock that Hawkins joined up with the Camerons and met Peter Saunders. Saunders was astonished to see him at all. He said:

'Didn't you get my signal, sir? I sent word that it was absolutely impossible to cross that valley by night. We had a hell of a time by daylight.'

Hawkins smiled wearily. 'Yes, I got your message, Peter,' he replied, 'but after we'd left. And I was damned if I'd turn back then.' The rest of the column were struggling in for another four hours. But Hawkins's reputation for being lucky still held; not a Jap was seen and not a man was lost.

A mile away the Camerons were already in contact with the Japs near Merema village, and Hawkins went forward to take a quick look at the situation. Then he returned to his own headquarters and, having seen that the brigade was deploying in good order, did as a wise commander should and 'took the rest of the morning for sleep'.

While the 5th Brigade were struggling across the Zubza valley, things were hotting up at Kohima. General Sato had decided that before the 138th Regiment left him for Imphal it should join in a final attack on the perimeter. As he probably knew, the Royal Berkshires had now been joined by the Durham Light Infantry, and the longer they were in the position the harder it would be to dislodge them. He therefore laid on a two-pronged attack, three companies from Colonel Fukunaga's 58th Regiment being ordered to advance through the D.C.'s bungalow area and attack the Royal Berkshires on the northern end of the perimeter, while Captain Watari's battalion of the 138th Regiment hit the Durham Light Infantry, from Kuki Piquet.

All was quiet till 0130 hours and then a rain of mortar bombs and spring grenades came down on 'C. Company of the D.L.I. The company commander, Major 'Tank' Waterhouse, ignored it, as he'd been told by his C.O. 'to get a good night's rest'. However, sleep was impossible, as (to quote his own words) 'the noise and the shit increased', so he decided to move forward and see what was happening. His platoon on the forward slope was taking a hammering and losing men fast, as the Japs had each Bren position pinpointed. By now it was light, as several trees had been set on fire, and an ammunition dump hit 'and the place looked like Blackpool during a firework display'. Lengthening their range, the Japs mixed smoke and high explosives, then came in at the forward platoon in great strength. In the glaring light Waterhouse could see them coming up the hill, shoulder to shoulder, the leading wave wearing respirators and throwing phosphorus grenades. In a roar of small arms fire, great gaps appeared in the ranks, but there were always more men to come up from behind and maintain the momentum of the attack. Inevitably, as the pressure was maintained, they broke through and the position on both flanks became very confused. Frantically, Waterhouse tried to get his company into something resembling a line about 'C Company headquarters, which he succeeded in doing, and here the enemy was held. Whenever an opportunity offered itself, groups of men would rush forward to carry out a minor advance, but each time this happened the losses were heavy. For the most part, all Waterhouse's men could do was lie down shoulder to shoulder and keep pouring bullets into the mass confronting them. Unfortunately they were vulnerable to the Jap spring-grenades which kept coming over and exploding among them, and every minute more men were being killed or wounded. But still, by some miracle, they were able to hold on. Below them they could hear the Jap officers and N.C.O.'s shouting at their men, urging them on to yet another assault: General Sato had told them they must capture the position that night and they dared not fail him. So up the hill they went again. Unfortunately Waterhouse had no line communication by now and his gunner O.P. officer had been killed. It therefore took two hours before any D.F. fire could be brought down from the guns. But still the D.L.I., held out. At 1400 hours Waterhouse launched 'D' company into a counter-attack on the right flank of the Japs, and as their fire went in the enemy could be heard shouting and screaming. A company commander went along urging them into another attack, but for the moment they seemed to have had enough, and for the first time in nearly three hours there was a lull. Roger Stock, commanding 'C' company, and Waterhouse sat back for a moment and had a cigarette. They talked of Teesdale and wondered when on earth they'd see it again… when they'd get some more leave. Then the screaming started from down the hill and the Japs came on again for a last effort. Roger Stock went back to his company and a few minutes later was killed. It was getting lighter now and the battle died down again, but the Japs were obviously determined to hold every inch they had gained. 'Tank' Waterhouse went across to the commanding officer to tell him what had happened, and it was decided that a platoon of 'A' company should go in at five o'clock to restore the situation. Led by the company commander, Captain Sean Kelly, the men fixed bayonets, crawled forward to an agreed position, then charged with great dash and spirit. The scene that followed was macabre, horrific:

> 'Lying on top of each other all over the hilltop were the bodies of friend and foe, all intermingled, and half of them had been set alight by the spreading blaze of the ammunition dump which in the darkness ht up the whole grisly scene. The platoon commander and his sergeant were wounded right at the start; but the platoon went forward amid a welter of fire and grenades and began to clear the Japs from what were originally "C" company's trenches. One section set about them with Sten guns and grenades.'

A diminutive Scot called McLellan, carrying a Bren gun, fell bottom first into a foxhole and stuck there, his arms and feet pointing skywards. Swearing horribly, he saw the company commander come past and demanded to be pulled out. When this was done he immediately reloaded his gun and went back into the fight. Every moment it got lighter and the Japs on Kuki Piquet now came into action and began pouring down machine-gun fire. Captain Kelly, who had been hit in the shoulder, went back to order another platoon into action, commanded by a subaltern called Stockton. He showed them the ground and laid on covering fire, then Stockton led his men into action. But the volume of fire coming off Kuki Piquet rendered the whole situation untenable; Stockton was killed and so were his batman, his sergeant, and two section leaders. His right-hand section ceased to exist. There was nothing for it but to withdraw the remnants of the company back up the hill, where they occupied a position already in existence. This consisted mostly of dug-outs without fire-slits and the men worked energetically to improve things. While they dug, two volunteers called Wood and Ward lay out in front, putting down covering fire. This made things a little more comfortable, but as Kelly remembers: 'It was difficult to stop the snipers. Every now and then there would be a crack and nearly always a groan or cry for help and the stretcher-bearers would rush forward and kneel where the man had been hit, dress him, and carry him off. What cold-blooded courage! It's nothing to charge in hot blood, but to kneel and do your job where a man has just been hit, and where you must be hit too, if another comes, is the bravest thing I know.' Altogether, it had been a savage night's fighting for the Durham Light Infantry. Out of fifteen officers in the three forward companies only five remained; and 'A' company alone lost seventy-six men. 'D' and 'C companies fared little better.

Though heavily attacked, the Royal Berkshires had an easier time. Through the light of the phosphorus bombs they obtained a good view of Fukunaga's men as the latter advanced past the D.C.'s bungalow and, holding their fire till the last moment, decimated them. Not a single post was overrun. At daybreak, Sergeant Kemble was amazed to find two platoons of Japs putting scaling ladders up the steep banks on the near side of the road. Quietly warning his men, Kemble waited till the Japs were on the ladders then poured fire into them. Not a man escaped.

Later that morning Sato was informed that, apart from gaining a few yards of ground at the southern end of the perimeter, his men had achieved nothing. He was also informed that out of seven companies taking part in the attack the equivalent of four had been slaughtered. It may be that this was the moment when he decided that, if he were to obey Mutaguchi's orders and send a third of his strength to Imphal, he never would take his objective.

The resolute defence of the Durham Light Infantry had another important effect on the tactical development of the battle. According to Japanese accounts, it was Miyazaki who broke the bad news to his Divisional commander. Sato took it calmly, remarking: 'Major Shimanoe has lost almost two companies? That's a great blow for him.... But don't let this reverse discourage you, Miyazaki. If the troops can hold the positions they have gained tonight, we may still get Garrison Hill tomorrow.' When Miyazaki reacted pessimistically to this suggestion, and asked what had happened to the companies of Colonel Torikai's 138th Regiment at Khabvuma, Sato replied: 'I'll try and get in touch with them.... Meanwhile, don't worry too much about Garrison Hill. Our main task is to make sure that the road remains cut, and no enemy troops go down it to Imphal.'*

From this date, the 23rd April, Japanese attacks dwindled in scale and increasingly they concentrated on their defensive role. The tactical importance of this development can only be realized when it is viewed in conjunction with events at Imphal. Here, on the 19th April, that is four days earlier, the 15th Division had broken off its attacks on the northern end of the perimeter and dug in. Mutaguchi was evidently awaiting the arrival of Miyazaki and his regimental group from Kohima before resum-

* An observation by Colonel Yamaki is interesting in this connection. He records that Sato and Miyazaki disagreed strongly on the subject of night attacks. About this time Sato gave orders that they should be abandoned 'in favour of more orthodox tactics'. He added: 'We're losing so many troops this way, before long we'll be too thin on the ground to achieve anything.'

ing the offensive. The vital question now—both for Kohima and Imphal—was, therefore: would Sato obey Mutaguchi's order?

Grover was getting increasingly worried about the high ground a mile to the south-west of the main Kohima position running up towards the foothills of Mount Pulebadze, where the Japs were increasingly active. This was known at the time as Pimple Ridge. He therefore decided that what was needed was an artillery O.P. right on top of the mountain. On the 23rd he had sent Henry Conder, second-in-command of the Royal Norfolk, to go up on to the hill above Pimple Ridge and have a look. Unfortunately, the Naga guides took Conder over an open route; they first saw signs of Jap occupation and then bumped a patrol. A Naga was shot in the leg and the whole party came downhill in record time. It was obvious that any operations between Mount Pulebadze and the road would need a great deal of preparation, and for the moment the O.P. was impossible.

Another project of Grover's turned out disappointing; on the 24th April, Colonel Garwood, the C.R.E., reported that the business of bulldozing a tank track up I.G.H. Spur would take eight hours, and a working party of 100. This, Grover thought, condemned the whole idea, as the bulldozer would attract sniping and mortar fire and the working party would be shot to pieces. Another way must be found.

The only good news came from 5th Brigade, in the form of a message from Victor Hawkins, to say that he was firmly established below the road near Merema. He asked if he should make a frontal attack on the Jap position facing him, or by-pass it, and press on towards Kohima. Grover ordered him to do the latter and establish a road block about a mile north of Naga Village. This would obviously be a complicated operation, unorthodox and dangerous too; but Hawkins made no complaint and set in hand the necessary reconnaissances.

But meanwhile, till air-drops could be organized, his brigade was out on a limb and almost at the end of its rations.

Hawkins had, however, made a plan for the use of coolies, with Lieut.-Colonel Simpson, the A.Q. at Divisional Headquarters, and the latter asked Eric Lambert to produce 250 Nagas for the morning of the 24th. They were to leave Zubza at 1030 hours, and (so it was hoped) arrive at the Brigade position on Merema Ridge four hours later. In theory, the arrangement seemed good and simple; but like most things in this campaign it required a good deal of improvisation. The staff captain, 5th Brigade, noted:

> 'I'd waited from 1030 hours till 1115 with two trucks full of light scale rations, and four grinning Nagas beside me. I looked at them and they looked at me... and I wondered what the hell the Brigadier would say when the brigade went hungry. Then, hearing some chattering behind me, I turned to see Nagas tumbling off the bonnets of jeeps, leaping out of trucks, degorging from ambulances and any vehicle that would give them a lift. And in the distance a colourful stream was flowing down the road towards me. This was better; but where was the interpreter? From a Dodge 15-cwt. jumped a smart-looking gentleman in khaki shorts and a red sweater. "Good morning," he said. "I am Mr Kevichusa. I will get the coolies organized for you." I thanked him politely, but doubted if the Lord himself could bring order from this chaos. But Mr Kevichusa had faith; he also had some sturdy lieutenants. These gentry flung themselves bodily into the mob with a reckless abandon, uttering angry words in an ugly language. They pushed some men here, pulled others there, whispered sweetly to one, and roared at another. Slowly the crowd began to move in a confused pattern, rather like a Sir Roger de Coverley gone wrong. Five minutes went by... The lieutenants were now producing notebooks and making entries with short grimy stubs of pencil, and I began wondering whether they were writing up the show for the

local paper. Then a pattern began to emerge. Each group of Nagas—they were in groups now, some even formed into ranks—was numbered, and more entries were made in the notebooks. The lieutenants reported to Mr Kevichusa who then reported to me that there were 220 coolies. Then he added: "What is the load, please?" "Two tins per coolie," I said firmly. "They weigh about 23 lbs. each." More shouting as the lieutenants spread the bad news, then a deadly hush, or at least a roar pianissimo. After a few seconds a single Naga stepped forward, grabbed two tins, and attempted to tie his lash round them. It wouldn't go. So he wriggled it, retied it, and this time it did. Next came the problem of adjusting the flat band to fit against his forehead, and there was no shortage of advice as to how this should be done. The village groups had now merged into one swarming mass and the Naga and the tins had disappeared completely. Sorrowfully I found myself thinking that this wasn't war; that if this was the best system the Division had to supply its troops, once off the roads, it had better pack up and go home. But then there was a moment's silence, after which the crowd parted and the Naga came towards me with the tins on his back, uttering a loud cry of triumph. This did it. The remaining 219 Nagas grabbed their loads and began moving forward. Quickly I pushed the armed escort into position, pulled the guides from their char mugs, and the whole column was on the move. Later, Brigade came on happily to say that the Nagas had reached them in *two* hours instead of the estimated four. I was amazed and relieved.'

The work of the Nagas in the earlier stages of the campaign has already been touched on, but it may be profitable to mention here the arrangements made between Grover and Eric Lambert of the Indian Police. Though willing to continue their Intelligence activities, the Nagas were naturally worried about the fate of their villages, and Grover undertook that these would not be shelled or bombed except by prior arrangement with Lambert, for example when it was believed that the Japanese were in them. In return, the Nagas undertook to provide 300 levies from Kohima which would provide escorts for patrols, and also harass the enemy. (Some shotguns had already been issued which didn't impress them at all, and they requested rifles.) Though the Nagas didn't ask for payment for any work they undertook, Grover insisted that they should be paid. He also laid on a canteen so that they could have a cup of tea and something to eat on return from their missions. As he put it: 'All the troops are filled with admiration for these stout-hearted, cheery hill men.... They are doing us so very proud that I feel we must at least show our gratitude....' As the battle went on, the Nagas added another field to their activities: the evacuation of the wounded down the slippery hills, a job they carried out with great endurance and courage. If it weren't for them, hundreds of men must have died; no European could possibly have taken stretchers over that country. All the troops knew, when they first encountered the Nagas, was that they were head-hunters, who had been forcibly restrained from this practice by the Indian Government. But soon they were struck not only by their cheeriness and eagerness to help but by their intelligence. Most officers have to be trained to 'read' air photos, but when Grover showed a set to some Nagas they understood them immediately, exclaiming: 'Yes, d'you see—that's our village.'

It is doubtful, however, if the Nagas would have undertaken any of this difficult and dangerous work if it had not been for the extraordinary character of Charles Pawsey, the Deputy-Commissioner of Kohima. A rather quiet, modest man, he had a burning sincerity and a selfless love of the people whom fate had decided he should serve. He was just, incorruptible, but at the same time merciful and with limitless understanding. The Nagas were his children and regarded him as their father. They trusted him completely; they knew that in no circumstances whatsoever would his word be broken. When the Japanese invaded Burma and the Nagas found themselves in the front line, they looked to Pawsey for their salvation; and knew that he would fight for them to the limit of his powers. So, when Mutaguchi's thrust against Kohima began, the Nagas remained loyal to the British cause, despite the loss of their homes and territory, despite danger and death. Among the records of the 58th Japanese Regiment several stories have come to light showing how staunch these hillmen were. In the initial stages of the campaign, when the Japanese were willing to pay for food, the Nagas would lure their men in ones and twos to lonely places up the hillside and kill them. The result was that the Japanese had to send larger and larger bodies of troops out foraging, which meant that their positions were correspondingly weakened. Altogether, the part played by Charles Pawsey, both directly through his courage and indirectly through his influence on the Nagas, was an important one. It should never be forgotten.

But to return to the main story: at 1245 hours on the 24th April, Stopford came forward to see Grover and urge him to set things moving as soon as possible. There was now no question of letting the central position in Kohima go, which meant that 6th Brigade would be increasingly tied up there and so unavailable for movement. Also the Dorsets were to go in to reinforce the troops there. 5th Brigade, however, were ordered to advance south on Kohima as fast as possible: and it was agreed that the Royal Scots, the Royal Norfolk, with 143rd S.S. Company, should do a right hook *round the back* of Pulebadze, and cut the Imphal Road below the Aradura Ridge, some two miles to the south of Kohima.

The disadvantages of such a manœuvre were immediately obvious. The country was wild and mountainous, and the altitude was considerable, Pulebadze running up to 7,522 feet. The slopes were steep, the gulleys were wide, and the jungle, or such of it as had been explored, was very thick. The Nagas were very sceptical about the whole operation and said that, should the rains come on, even *they* couldn't get over the ground. Nevertheless, they offered to accompany the column as porters, and pressed some of their womenfolk into service to make up the numbers. It was obvious, however, that the Nagas could not carry sufficient supplies to maintain the column for four days, the time it was estimated the hook would take, and Grover hoped to deliver the remainder of the supplies by air-drop.

The great advantage of the move was surprise. The Japs were obviously ready for a shallow hook, that is one between the mountain and the road, but long conferences with the Nagas and patrol reports convinced Grover that the country west of the mountain was clear of the enemy, and the wide hook would solve his problems on this flank. Also, if he could establish 4th Brigade beyond Kohima, there was a good chance that the Japs might start pulling back.

Tactically speaking, the hook obviously meant the final demolition of Grover's plan to put two brigades round the left flank; it also meant the wide dispersal of his Division. But the plan had been eroded already, 6th Brigade being tied up in Kohima itself, and supply problems limiting any reinforcement of the left flank. Also, the sole reserve now consisted of a weakened 161st Brigade. However, the orders were: Get on... get on! So there was nothing for it but to launch the 4th Brigade column just as soon as possible.

The commander of 4th Brigade and so of the column was Brigadier Willie Goschen, probably the only Grenadier Guards officer within several thousand miles. His courteous but somewhat elaborate manners sometimes seemed out of place in the wild regions in which 2nd Division had been serving, but his quiet way of doing things and his obvious command of the job made him very much liked and respected in the brigade. In the afternoon he was summoned to Grover's headquarters, to be told of the impending move, and got down to studying the route. This (so it was eventually decided) was to be from the iron bridge at milestone 39½, to the west of Jotsoma, up the Druza nala, to the old fortified village of Khonoma (where Lieutenant Ridgeway of the 43rd Bengal Infantry had died winning the V.C. in 1879 during General Nation's campaign against the Angami Nagas), then along the Khuri Nala in a wide sweep to a spur a mile and a half due south of Pulebadze, and finally north-west to Aradura. By the map the whole journey was just over seven miles and on the ground would probably be two or three times that distance; but even then, four days' march seemed reasonable. What didn't seem reasonable was the timing, as the operation had to start the following evening and the administrative work to be carried out by Goschen's staff, the battalion commander, Robert Scott of the Royal Norfolk, and A. G. Mackenzie-Kennedy of the Royal Scots, was immnese. Scott, who was away on reconnaissance for an attack on 'Shrewsbury', one of the features above Jotsoma, had only a few hours' notice. Every man was to carry 100 rounds, two days' light-scale rations, half a blanket, a gas cape, water-sterilizing tablets, a dah, his weapon, and two Mills grenades, and there would be an entrenching tool to every third man. So far as the Royal Norfolk was concerned, Robert Scott wanted to wear bush hats, as steel helmets were so hot and uncomfortable in the jungle and tended to fall off as men scrambled up and down the steep cliffs. The chief medical officer, however, got to hear of this and, worried about head wounds, ordered that helmets must be taken. This edict provoked an immediate row with Robert Scott, and things got somewhat turbulent, till John Grover stepped in and said that helmets it must be. So the men, who'd already unpacked and packed their kits, wearily began to unpack them again.

Robert Scott was one of the great characters in the 2nd Division, a huge man with a great personality and corresponding appetites for food and drink. But he also had a great knowledge and love of music, and in action he always carried a pocket edition of Shakespeare. His occasional rages and bursts of violence annoyed the troops, but like most soldiers they would forgive a 'character' almost anything. Scott was something of an Elizabethan, and larger than life. He was also one of the few men to whom great violence and danger were natural elements; he trod the battlefield like a great actor treads the stage.

The Japanese could overlook the approach to Khonoma, so the operation began just before dark. Henry Conder had gone ahead with guides and porters, an escort from 143 S.S. Company under Major McGeorge, and an officer called Stewart Liberty manning an O.P. for the 99th Field Regiment R. A. (This was a T.A. unit from Buckinghamshire, and its officers were mostly men of some wealth. When Mountbatten, during an inspection, asked Liberty what he did the reply was 'I'm a draper, sir.' Mountbatten gave a puzzled frown and passed on down the line.) 'The going,' according to Captain Hornor, 'was slow and tedious, and Khonoma has many and steep entrances. In the pitch dark guides could not be found, and time and tempers were lost on all sides.' Robert Scott, on arrival, cursed Henry Conder, and Conder cursed the guides and it was dawn before the last company reached the village, and much later before they'd been sorted out. The Mortar Platoon, the machine-gunners of the Manchester Regiment, and the Signallers had been carrying tremendously heavy loads and were whacked. And the Royal Scots were still to come.

However, the morning of the 26th saw things sorted out somewhat, and everyone had great praise for Major Lloyd, the 4th Brigade D.A. A. and Q.M.G. (that is, the senior administrative staff officer), who worked tirelessly, sorting out stores, allocating porters, and generally bringing order out of chaos. As everyone realized by now, the operation had been launched too quickly and without adequate preparation. But there was no use bellyaching; things would have to shake down as the column moved forward. By 1300 hours, orders had been given out to company commanders, and by them to their platoons, and the milling throng of troops and Nagas had dissolved into something like military order. Major McGeorge fell in the S.S. Company and ordered it to advance, and wearily the troops got to their feet and followed.

The way continued hard. To quote Hornor again: 'It was a case of up one steep khud and down the other side, then up a steeper and down again.... Parties of Naga porters were interspersed in the column for their protection and they were quite unable to understand why the troops were out of breath when they reached the top of a hill.' Out of breath.... To anyone who hasn't soldiered in Assam the physical hammering one takes is difficult to understand. The heat, the humidity, the altitude, and the slope of almost every foot of ground, combine to knock hell out of the stoutest constitution. You gasp for air which doesn't seem to come, you drag your legs upwards till they seem reduced to the strength of matchsticks, you wipe the salt sweat out of your eyes. Then you feel your heart pounding so violently you think it must burst its cage; it sounds as loud as a drum, even above the swearing and cursing going on around you. So you stop, horrified, to be prodded by the man behind or cursed by an officer or N.C.O. in front. Eventually, long after everything tells you you should have died of heart failure, you reach what you imagine is the top of the hill... to find it is a false crest, and the path still lies upwards. And when you do finally get to the top, there is the hellish climb down. You forget the Japs, you forget time, you forget hunger and thirst. All you can think of is the next halt.'

Goschen, with Guardee precision, had ordered that the regular ten-minute halts should be observed on the hour, but in practice this turned out to be impossible. Soon the columns took more frequent short halts which suited the men much better.

But the Nagas hated them and complained bitterly; what they wanted to do was travel for some hours without pause, then rest for several hours; and eventually they were allowed to do this. Though how they were able to continue for so long with 80 to 100 lbs. on their backs the troops could never understand.

Out in front, McGeorge and his men of the S.S. Company had, if anything, a worse time, for they not only had to find the way but very often *make* it too. For hours on end they would hack through virgin jungle, and cut paths on the sides of hills when the tracks were too steep. (Naga tracks invariably run straight up and down even the steepest hills.) Also, they had to patrol forward and to the flanks. Whatever happened, the column must not let itself be surprised.

All movement was by day and at night the column bivouacked. It was cold and the jungle was wet that first night. Half a blanket and a gas cape was almost no protection at all, and the discomfort experienced by all ranks was acute. The men of the Royal Norfolk, unfortunately, hadn't been issued with 'Tommy Cookers', so many of them tried to light fires to brew up tea. The result of this was a flood of curses from officers and N.C.O.s who reminded them that they were behind the Jap lines… that for all anyone knew the Jap was engaged on a 'hook' himself and might not be far away. Moaning and cursing the whole operation, the troops put out their fires and looked for some other way of producing their beloved char. Then an unnamed genius discovered that if you shaved bamboo very fine it made a smokeless fire, and the word spread happily down the whole column. Hornor records: 'All cooking was in mess tins, and the general menu was: breakfast—porridge of crushed biscuits, with a little salt and powdered milk added; and, of course, char, made with boiling water if possible, and if not, stewed up to some degree of warmth, painfully, and with much blowing and blasphemy. Tiffin would be a biscuit and a bit of cheese munched on the march, and for dinner a bully stew with selected leaves to add flavour. The monotony was hardly noticed as everyone was so tired....' This was on the first day while the light-scale rations were in use; by the third, things were even worse.

While 4th Brigade were moving on the right flank, things were happening in the centre and on the left with 5th Brigade. The latter, it will be remembered, had received orders to press on towards Kohima and secure a road junction at a point about one and a half miles from the town, that is about the same distance south of Merema. Hawkins immediately started active patrolling and when the route had been thoroughly reconnoitred sent a company of the Worcestershires to occupy a dominating feature *en route*. Their orders were to lie doggo during the 24th and cover the advance of the Brigade during the following night. Meanwhile, the Camerons were to watch the Japs in Merema and follow on when ordered.

To begin with things went well. The Japs left the brigade alone all day, and at 1900 hours Hawkins ordered the column to move. The distance of the advance was only three miles, but the country was intersected by deep nalas and, as time went on and the jungle thickened, it got very dark. When the moon came up that helped a bit, but parties of men kept losing touch, and there was halting and bunching, until the whole advance was a nightmare—just like the crossing of the Zubza valley. Eight hours after starting, that is at three in the morning, the brigade was still a mile from its objective, and the track rose steeply. Then the real troubles began. Lieut.-Colonel John Bunting, who commanded the Field Ambulance, had overloaded his men, and now they couldn't keep up with the column. Hawkins had warned him before they set out that this would happen, and there was some fierce argument; but Bunting was a strong-minded character and had his way. And now the whole brigade were paying for it. As Hawkins found when he moved forward, after a prolonged halt, the column had broken in two, the leading men of the second half being lost and having no clue as to the way. The guides, of course, were way ahead with the first half of the column. Eventually, Hawkins put his brigade-major, Ian Thorburn, in the lead, positioning himself some way back, and they made some progress. But then Private Hill, Hawkins' gunman, called to him:

'Brigadier, sir.'

'Yes?'

'There's only ten men behind us.'

Hawkins looked back and found that this was so. Though he'd been moving very slowly, the remainder of the ambulance men still couldn't keep up, so the column had fragmented again. The Brigadier was left in front of the Japanese position with ten unarmed men.

It was almost daylight now. Hawkins couldn't be certain where they were or how much further they had to go. Eventually he decided that the only sensible thing was to keep moving and hope that everyone else would do likewise and join up again. This is what happened, and within a quarter of a mile Hawkins' group caught up Thorburn's which in turn had caught up the leading group. But then there was another halt and, going forward, Hawkins discovered that they were on the wrong track, and the guides from the Worcestershires were nowhere to be seen. Hawkins therefore went right to the head of the column to try and find Jack Stocker, the CO. of the Worcestershires, but was told here that he was out looking for Major Burrell, whose company was providing the guides. So the only thing to do was sit down and wait—and hope that as daylight came the column wouldn't find itself slap in the middle of a Jap position.

At first things didn't look too hopeful. A patrol from the Worcestershires came along and the subaltern informed the Brigadier that he'd just bumped the Japs not far away. More alarming news could hardly be imagined and, as Hawkins put it: 'If just one patrol of Japs in any strength should find us and proceed to start trouble, anything might happen....' Then, just as dramatically, the situation changed. A runner arrived from Jack Stocker to say that he had found their objective and was ordering the Worcestershires up to him. Hawkins went with them 'and with Herculean labour on the part of the Brigade staff and the commanding officers, the battalions were got into position just as day broke, solidly astride the Jap lines of communication'. Curiously enough, Frank Burrell and his company had not heard the brigade go by in the darkness, though they were in the right place. And the Japs obviously heard nothing either.

The main jobs on the 25th were to dig in and prospect for water. Burrell had found a pond below the hill and offered to take a patrol along and see that the country around it was clear. To his amazement, however, he found a Japanese company commander sitting comfortably at a table outside his tent, paying out a platoon. Burrell signalled to his men and they eased forward into position. Then the Bren opened up and the officer and the entire platoon were wiped out. Quickly Burrell's patrol went in, to strip the bodies of documents, maps, money, and personal possessions. They also took the cash box and led away five horses and some mules. No reaction came from any Japanese units in the neighbourhood so the water point was secured.

Later in the day the Camerons were ordered forward and made the journey in three hours without trouble.

That night, apart from a small attack on the Lancashire Fusiliers, everything was quiet. And the following day the Japanese 'Q' staff in Kohima kept sending their supply convoys out to Merema as ordered; and these were dealt with.

The brigade was still, however, about a mile from the road junction, its immediate objective, so Hawkins set things moving again. Reconnoitring forward, he found two distinct features ahead and quickly worked out a plan for attacking them. The Worcestershires were put on to the first feature, which they occupied without opposition; and the Lancashire Fusiliers then went forward to deal with the second. This proved to be held, however, and intermittent scrapping went on for an hour before it was taken. Once the troops had consolidated, Hawkins again went forward to reconnoitre and saw a large wooded hill which, he decided, would demand a set-piece attack which would take some while to lay on. In the meantime, the brigade would be halted.

On the 26th, after an air-drop had been requested, the R.A.F. planes came over and circled the dropping zone, and the whole drop was deposited on target. This was the brigade's first experience of air supply and they were rather delighted with it, as rations were running short. Another surprise that day was the arrival of a Naga column with ammunition, more rations, medical supplies, and those basic necessities of war—rifle oil and flannelette.

*

While the Royal Norfolk and the Royal Scots were carrying out their right hook round Pulebadze, and 5th Brigade were pushing south from Merema, the 2nd Dorsetshires were installing themselves in the northern sector of the Kohima perimeter. Their second-in-command, Geoffrey White, seemed to realize instinctively that this would be the scene of their operations for some time to come and he began examining the complex structure of the land in great detail. The Allied and Japanese positions were now so close, and locked in such a complicated jigsaw, that only a detailed study of this kind, he reasoned, could provide the key to further operation. So, he noted:

'The Deputy-Commissioner's bungalow spur was divided

into four terraces, each separated by a steep bank varying in height from ten to forty feet. Starting from the top, there was the Club square on which in happier days the members had played badminton. Ten feet below the club lay the tennis court. On the south side, the tennis court was bounded by a large iron tank and a long tin building which appeared to be the servants' quarters. These themselves were sunk so that only the roofs appeared level with the tennis court.

The next drop was a very steep one of about thirty to forty feet to the terrace on which was situated the bungalow itself in its own compound.

Finally, below the bungalow, there was another drop which brought us to the lower garden, which overlooked the important road junction twenty feet below.

On the south side of the spur lay various ornamental gardens, a drive in to the Deputy-Commissioner's bungalow, and the bungalow of the Commandant of the Assam Rifles.

One further feature is of interest. On the south side of the club (topmost) terrace rose a small pimple about thirty yards long, fifteen feet broad and twenty feet high.'

As Geoffrey White found, the most extraordinary feature of this whole spur 'was the impossibility of being able to see what was happening on the terrace next below'. The conformity of the ground, aided by the trees and bushes, also prevented any reconnaissance from the flanks. When Jock McNaught, the commanding officer of the Dorsets, asked Wilbur Bickford of the Royal Berkshires, who'd been there some days, about the ground outside the perimeter, the reply was that his knowledge was still somewhat scanty. The exact location of the tennis court even wasn't known.

However, an attack had to go in without delay, and it was agreed that the Royal Berkshires should clear the club square, and the Pimple (which they were now sharing with the Japanese).

'C. Company of the Dorsetshires should attack the tennis court, while 'A' Company on the left should use a nala to get round to the north side of Bungalow Spur. The object of the operation was to secure a knoll covering the road junction, so that the tanks could get by and fight their way up to join 5th Brigade. Zero hour was fixed for 0300 hours and the tortuous route was traced with parachute cords. Though the company commanders concerned spent hours peering through the bushes they could see very little; the attack was obviously going to be a tricky one, and needed a good deal of luck.

However, at 0200 hours, the leading company ('A' Company of the Dorsetshires) set off on their approach march along the nala, relying on silence and surprise to get them past the Jap positions by the nala edge. It only needed someone to catch their foot on a tin can and the grenades would come showering down. However, for an hour nothing was heard and Jock McNaught and Geoffrey White waited anxiously at their command post, on the northern edge of the perimeter, where at first light it was hoped they could glimpse a corner of the tennis court. 'C. Company had by now moved off in the centre, towards the tennis court, and there was no news from them either.

Then at 0300 hours automatic fire started up, and grenades could be heard bursting around 'A' Company's objective. Once they'd attacked, a whole group of inter-supporting bunkers came alive, and the company went in with the bayonet. Confused, desperate hand-to-hand fighting followed, in the darkness. One platoon under Lieutenant Murrill succeeded in getting into a position overlooking the road junction, and some of his men slid down the steep bank on to the road, to start mopping up the bunkers dug into the side. Men crawled along, sometimes under the muzzles of the Jap guns, to throw in grenades, often letting the lever fly off and counting two seconds before letting go. Meanwhile, the other two platoons of 'A' Company had turned right and advanced towards the tennis court from the north. Here, in the broken terrain, they pressed home their attack with great spirit, searching out the Jap positions, whether in banks or bunkers or buildings, and going for them without hesitation. By first light they'd even got a foothold in the bungalow itself, but then heavy fire came down from the Japs dug into the bank below the tennis court, and they had to withdraw.

'C' Company had enjoyed a limited success, destroying a large bunker on the north-east corner of the tennis court, from which the Japanese had sniped anyone approaching the perimeter in daytime. On the club square the situation was now an extraordinary one, the two sides facing each other only fifteen yards apart. The slightest movement brought a burst of fire, and grenades came hurling across. The attack had cost the company heavily, its commander being wounded and a platoon leader killed. At one point, the Company Sergeant-Major had to take over, till the C.O. called forward Captain Morice, the company second-in-command. He ordered the men, with some of the Royal Berkshires, to organize around the club square and Pimple. Like all the actions this night, this one was desperate, confused, and bloody.

The Royal Berkshires had cleared the Pimple, which was a mercy as it was an ideal spot for snipers; but whether they could hang on to it was another matter. It was doubtful, too, whether John Bowles and 'A' Company could hang on to their position beyond the bungalow, by the road junction. This was only thirty yards from and below the Jap stronghold on the terrace; and any movement was punished immediately. The plight of the wounded was appalling, many of them having to lie out all day in the sun.

But one great thing had been achieved: the road was now open and the tanks could go through towards 5th Brigade.

The Dorsetshires weren't the only regiment in action that night, and it is necessary to go back a few hours. About 0100 hours, a heavy mortar barrage came down on Summerhouse Hill, the spring grenades began landing among the Durham Light Infantry slit trenches, and men from three Japanese battalions rushed into the attack. They were held, but kept coming on again and at 0500 hours gained some success. According to 'Tank' Waterhouse: 'The men of the leading ranks carried no weapons but bags full of grenades. Owing to sheer weight of numbers they broke through, and got on to the plateau on top of the hill. Here they went round shouting "Tojo" and blessing the Mikado....' Then they started to dig in. A period of confused fighting followed in which men seemed to be moving in all directions, and positions kept changing hands in bloody hand-to-hand fighting. For a while the gunners manning the 99th Field Regiment O.P. were completely cut off; and the Garrison Commander (Colonel Theobalds) emerged from his dug-out to find a section of Japs digging in only five yards away. These he shot dead immediately. The commanding officer ordered a counter-attack to go in at first light, from two sides, and a comprehensive fire plan was worked out. Some time after 1030 hours the 25-pounders opened up from the Jotsoma box, then the Durham's mortars joined in, firing 1,300 rounds. At the agreed moment Lieutenant Greenwell sounded a blast on his hunting horn and led the battle patrol into action. Simultaneously Captain Shuttle led a composite company from the other flank. A good many Japs had already been killed by the barrage and those who stayed to fight it out were killed, many with the bayonet. Unfortunately, to prevent fire coming from the flanks, Kuki Piquet had been blanketed and some Japs managed to disappear through the smoke. The situation was restored; but in repelling these attacks the D.L.I., had suffered further casualties and were now pretty exhausted. Seeing their condition, Brigadier Shapland reported to Grover that they must be relieved, and arrangements were made for the Royal Welch Fusiliers to take over the following day.

*

The flanking movements of 5th Brigade, and the increasing pressure from inside the Kohima perimeter, made an immediate impact on General Sato. From his tactical headquarters on point 5120, near the eastern fringe of Naga Village, he could watch the press of trucks, jeeps tanks, and armoured cars on the road, and from time to time the Hurribombers, which swooped down on the positions in front of him. Day by day the weight of artillery had been increasing and his intelligence reports kept announcing that more and more troops were pouring through Dimapur and coming to the front. Sato was now receiving no reinforcements, nor supplies of food and ammunition, and his stocks were beginning to run low. The plan to drive 5,000 oxen from the Chindwin had turned out a ludicrous failure and indeed only a fifth arrived. Sergeant-Major Imanishi, who set off with 270 head of cattle, reported to Divisional headquarters with only fourteen. 'The remainder,' he said, 'are dead, worn out on the journey, or fell down into the valley.' It was quite obvious, in fact, that if Sato sent off Miyazaki with three battalions to join in the attack on Imphal (as ordered by Mutaguchi) his chances of taking Kohima Ridge would be nil. So he ordered Miyazaki to stay where he was at Aradura, with the two battalions of 124th Regiment, and told Captain Watari of the 1st Battalion, 138th Regiment (badly mauled, it will be remembered, during its attack on the Durham Light Infantry) to support Colonel Fukunaga's 58th Regiment in its continued offensive against the centre. When Mutaguchi heard the news a flow of angry signals came from Maymyo. These repeated the order in no uncertain terms and reminded Sato of the penalties of disobedience. But Sato stuck to his guns; Mutaguchi could do as he liked, he said, but no troops would leave Kohima. Relationships between the two generals, already strained, deteriorated even further.

Miyazaki's position was difficult. He'd always believed that, if the main objective were Imphal, then it had been wrong in the first place to send a whole division to Kohima. From a tactical viewpoint, he realized even now, Mutaguchi was right. But Miyazaki was a man of character and no opportunist; his loyalty, he decided, was to Sato, his divisional commander, so he did as the latter told him and secured the left flank on Aradura. This decision was to have an important bearing on the final stage of the battle.

In passing one should note that Sato had reacted just as Slim had intended he should when he gave his order to Stopford that the maximum pressure should be exerted at Kohima. This fact seems to have escaped the attention of historians so far; but time may prove it to be one of the most important decisions this great commander ever made, an example of his rare military genius.

These were anxious days for Slim, nevertheless. The battles at Kohima and Imphal were balanced precariously in the scales; and the outcome of neither could be regarded as a foregone conclusion. Already his staff were telling him that operation 'Stamina', the airlift to Imphal, was failing to deliver the planned tonnage of stores, and he knew that Scoones was getting anxious. Worse still, the rains were under four weeks away, and what their effect would be both on the R.A.F. and on the infantry struggling in the mountains it was impossible to say. One thing was certain: there was a good deal of bloody fighting ahead, with no chances of spectacular results. And results were what Mountbatten and the Chiefs of Staff desired with a passionate longing. Only the dry, dedicated figure of Sir George Giffard was shielding Slim from a rain of brickbats, both military and political. In war courage is not only displayed in the front line.

Apart from tactical problems, Slim was also engaged in supply problems himself. At Kohima the 3.7 howitzers, those magnificent mountain guns with their high trajectory, were now silenced, the crews being put on ground defence work; and the 25-pounders were rationed too. Smoke shells, vital for blanketing enemy flanking positions during attacks by infantry, could only be obtained in negligible quantities. Angrily Slim railed at G.H.Q. India, and the departments whose job it was to produce and forward the ammunition; he received comforting replies that all was well, that vast quantities of ammunition had been sent to the front. 'We can prove to you,' they said, 'that there is no shortage of ammunition on your front.' But, except in a trickle, the munitions never came, and what happened to these vast supplies Slim never discovered. Rumour had it they were finding their way into the arsenals of the Congress Party for the eventual war between the Hindus and the Muslims. And rumours in India usually have some truth in them.

*

'Are the troops fresh?' Napoleon asked Marshal Ney at breakfast one morning. 'Yes, Sire,' replied the barrel-cooper's son. 'It's been raining all night.' This remark was forcibly recalled by the staff captain, 5th Brigade, as he put his head out on the morning of the 28th April to find the whole area awash and the rain still pouring down from black, swirling clouds. This was not the monsoon, the experts informed him. This was merely the 'chota barsat' or little rain. But as he and many others observed, whatever it was, water was still water—and mud was mud. The battle must inevitably enter a new phase.

Chapter Seven

Delay and Crisis

The 27th, the last dry day for some weeks, was eventful both on the left flank and in the centre. After a stiff artillery concentration, laid on by Harry Grenfell, the Camerons attacked the hill separating them from their objective at the road junction, and took it without opposition. The rest of the brigade moved forward to find itself among the bashas (bamboo huts) of the Reinforcement Camp. From their positions on a thickly wooded hill to the south the Japanese machine-gunned and sniped the brigade, and Victor Hawkins was lucky to escape when a burst tore up the ground a few inches from his feet. The Japs, cut off at Merema, also shelled the brigade with a 75-mm. gun, causing a dozen casualties among the Worcestershires. The brigade, therefore, removed itself to less exposed positions and began active patrolling, to ferret out the Japanese. Then, after a warning message from John Grover, a troop of Lee tanks arrived from the 149th Regiment R.A.C. with a troop of light tanks from the 45th Cavalry, and some sappers in armoured carriers. Hawkins immediately set the Lees the task of securing the water point on the Nerhema road, which they did.

But now the next hill to the south had to be dealt with. Patrols reported that it was held only by a ring of snipers and light machine-guns, but there were about 200 Japs in the valley to the north. When warning was given, the latter would immediately scramble up the hill to their positions. Bereft of artillery support because of the ammunition shortage, Hawkins decided to try and get a patrol on to the hill, followed by a company, then a battalion. The Lancashire Fusiliers were invited to take on the job, zero hour being fixed for early the following morning.

All day during the 27th, John Bowles and his men of the Dorsets somehow held on to their position at the road junction below the D.C.'s bungalow. They saw the tanks move by and go up towards 5th Brigade, and another troop swing round to the right, in front of them, on their way to help their own 'C Company in the Club area. This was the second attempt to get a tank up the drive towards the D.C.'s bungalow, but it was no more successful than the first. The C.R.E., with tremendous effort, had manœuvred a bulldozer round, and after this had improved the slope of the drive, a medium tank managed to follow it half-way to the top. Then, at the critical moment, some Japs who realized what was going on began sniping. The tank slewed round to return the fire and smashed into the bulldozer, reducing it to scrap-iron. This put paid to the efforts for a while, but then the C.R.E. had tackle brought up and for hour after hour the sappers struggled to winch the tank up the slope. But it was all in vain. With darkness coming on, the tank had to be released to go back to its laager, and the Dorsets had to battle on as best they could.

Their role, and especially that of John Bowles' company on the knoll at the road junction, was increasingly difficult. But Bowles and his men knew the vital function they were performing in this stage of the battle; knew that while they hung on the tanks could keep getting round to help smash the Japanese bunkers all along the back of the ridge. Fortunately, the divisional 25-pounders could help them, laying down a concentration within twenty yards when called upon. After dark on the 27th, as Colonel Fukunaga's men launched attack after attack, the guns were called upon with great urgency. The Japs came from positions across the road, to be shot down in droves. Hour after hour the shells rained down, breaking up the attacks before they could be properly launched. The Dorsets suffered heavy casualties; they were wet, tired, and rocked by the hurricane of sound that roared round them. But not a position gave way.

So to the 28th April, which, as already noted, dawned wet and muddy. It brought a surprise too. At 0830 hours a dozen Oscar fighters arrived to strafe the box at Zubza. By now the troops were so conditioned to the fact that every plane in the sky was friendly, that at first they did not give them more than a cursory glance. It so happened that at this moment the sun had broken through the cloud, and an officer spotting the planes observed 'how pretty they were as they rolled and turned against the sky, with the light flashing on their wings and fuselages'. But as they began manœuvring to come in to the attack, memories of France and the German dive-bombers swept to the surface. The cry went up: 'Look out—they're Japs! They're going to bomb us!' As most people knew, the Ack-Ack guns were being used in a ground role, the R.A.F. having undertaken to maintain complete superiority, so there was nothing for it but to bolt for cover. Men ran for the nala bed which skirted the box, dived under trucks, hurried mules in all directions. For a while a mixture of fighting and administrative units surged round in a confused mass; then the leading plane took a run and dropped a stick of four bombs near the gun-sites. There were four explosions. Then each plane came in turn, systematically straddling the crowded box. By some accounts this went on for ten minutes, by others seven, but then some Hurricanes came up and a dog-fight ensued, after which the Oscars roared away over Garrison Hill. Luckily there wasn't much damage, though the 100th A.A./Anti-Tank Regiment suffered some casualties, including two battery commanders. The hero of the occasion was undoubtedly a sapper subaltern called Brunel-Hawes. Taking shelter in a shallow drain, he had the presence of mind to count the bombs falling from the Oscars, and compare the total with the number of explosions. This showed a deficit of six, so running down to the road, where the dud bombs seemed to have fallen, he began searching for any detonators which might have become separated. And there they were—two of them slap on the tarmac. A third was snatched away just before a truck ran over it.

As might be expected, the arrival of their fighters was an immense fillip to the Japanese infantry, who were beginning to imagine that their Air Force had deserted them; but the enthusiasm soon turned to bitter disappointment, as Sergeant-Major Imanishi has recorded: 'As soon as the enemy aircraft came up, they ran away without fighting. This was a terrible discouragement to us.'

In itself the airstrike was small and rather ineffective, but as a warning it could hardly be more important. By now the single road had five brigades plus divisional and corps troops operating on it and the crush of traffic was reminiscent of the Brighton Road on a Bank Holiday. Trucks, jeeps, gunner quads, guns, tanks, armoured cars, mule columns and specialist wagons belonging to R.E.M.E. were surging along it from morning to night. Altogether, the road was a magnificent target for aircraft, and if the Japanese decided to send over planes in strength, the maintenance of the forward troops would become a virtual impossibility. There could be no movement at night either to help matters, as the Japs had still not retired completely from their flanking positions in the hills.

Curiously enough the Zubza airstrike coincided with a scare that the pressure against the road might increase. During the night a report reached Grover's headquarters of an enemy patrol near milestone 34 (that is two miles back from Zubza), and soon afterwards the translators sent a copy of one of Sato's orders to

Colonel Torikai, the 138th Regiment, telling him to make nuisance raids across the Zubza Valley, with a view to interrupting communications. In the light of this, it seemed that the airstrike was part of a coherent plan; so Grover contacted Stopford, and it was agreed that the 4th/1st Gurkhas of 33rd Brigade which had now come under command should move forward to milestone 32. Now it seems that there must have been a mistake in the translation and that the date of the order was the 7th April, not the 25th. It was on the 7th that Sato sent the troops across the valley, which held up the 5th Brigade at Bunker Hill, and fought the Royal Scots at Khabvuma. However, at the time, Grover was not to know this, and could do no other than conclude that his L. of C. was being threatened again.

On Garrison Hill the Dorsets began constructing head cover; and at his precarious position by the road junction, John Bowles and his men gratefully took the rations brought up by the scout cars and sent some of the wounded away. The company was weaker now, but still confident and in control of things.

Lieut.-Colonel Garwood, the C.R.E., had now received Grover's permission to try and bulldoze a track up the southern face of I.G.H. Spur. (His first plan, it will be remembered, had been turned down flat.) On the morning of the 28th, the Dorsets were delighted to see a giant bulldozer arrive, protected by a Lee tank fore and aft. These drove round the Jap positions, selected their spot, then began cutting into the steep slope. After some hours a rough track had been made to the top, and the bulldozer backed down so that the sappers could fix a chain. Then, with a roar and a great churning of mud, the bulldozer tried to pull the tank up the track. For a while he had some success; but then, for some reason, the bulldozer driver had to climb down and make an adjustment to his blade and the tank chose this moment to go into reverse. Like a crazy monster, it swept downhill, pulling the bulldozer with it; then the chain snapped and the bulldozer went crashing down on its own till it was completely wrecked. Another effort had come to nothing. Squatting in the foul stench of their bunkers around the tennis court, the Japanese were no doubt delighted.

On the left flank, with 5th Brigade, things didn't go too well either. The patrol of the Lancashire Fusiliers which was leading the operation soon ran into trouble on the jungle-covered slopes of Firs Hill, and commanding officer, Willie West, had to commit a company. Coming under light machine-gun fire, the company dealt with the enemy posts successfully and made good progress to within 150 yards of the top of the hill. West, therefore, decided to send a second company in support, and then to close the rest of the battalion forward. But, as things turned out, this decision was a bit too precipitous. Hawkins writes: 'The last 150 yards to the top were covered with very thick bamboo through which visibility was nil, and the original delay to the patrol caused by the snipers had given the Japs time to man their positions along the crest.' From his O.P., Hawkins could see what was happening, as there was a bald patch near the top of the hill across which the enemy could be seen streaming. West then called up Hawkins on the radio to say that if only he could have some artillery support, he thought he could still reach his objective. Hawkins, it will be recalled, had been warned that no guns would be available for this operation, but with the Lancashire Fusiliers pinned down, he asked Lieut.-Colonel Harry Grenfell to see what he could do. Grenfell immediately radioed the C.R.A., Brigadier Burke, who switched a couple of batteries to the task. But first they had to range, as the country was difficult; and to make sure that they didn't get hit while this was going on, the Fusiliers had to be pulled back from positions they'd already gained. However, after a while, the gunners came on to tell Grenfell that they'd finished ranging, and zero hour and a hurriedly contrived plan were agreed. The gunners were to soften up the top of the hill, and the 150 yards leading up to it, then the Fusiliers were to go in as fast as they could before the Japs had clambered back into their fire positions.

But it didn't work. To quote Hawkins again: 'The bamboo was so thick that the Fusiliers couldn't get in quick enough, and when they started forward met heavy opposition.' The Japs, it now appeared, had followed up the withdrawal of the Fusiliers, and sited a strong screen of snipers and machine-gun posts in the bamboo. These steadily shot off the officers, five being wounded and five killed. However, the men pressed on steadfastly, and in places advanced to within twenty-five yards of the top, where they met fire from the main bunkers. West called up Hawkins again, to tell him that he might still take the objective, but at the cost of many more casualties; and even then he wasn't sure he could hold it at night. After some discussion, Hawkins gave the order to withdraw. The total casualties were fifteen killed and forty-four wounded. Though the Japs undoubtedly lost some men also, their position was still intact.

The 28th, incidentally, was the Emperor's birthday. Prisoners captured a few days previously had said that it would be marked by a general offensive along the whole ridge, and all troops were warned. In fact, the attacks, though supported by artillery and mortar fire, were limited in scope and were directed against the sector held by the Royal Berkshires. In places they succeeded in penetrating the positions, and the Berkshires were forced to get out of their trenches to start fighting with the bayonet. During the confusion, a company commander rang up battalion headquarters to say that a party of Japanese had invaded his cookhouse, where they were 'throwing tins about and howling fiendishly'. Colonel Bickford replied shortly that he should 'get in and deal with them'; but the company commander reported that his whole headquarters had been wounded, except for himself and a signaller. Nothing much could be done till daylight; but then a party hunted down all the Japs who had penetrated the perimeter and shot them. At this juncture a solitary Japanese came out from his hidey-hole and stood in the open, screaming defiance and staggering drunkenly towards the troops now facing him. For a moment the Berkshires looked on silently at this strange spectacle, this pathetic ending to the Emperor's birthday. Then someone let off a burst, the screaming stopped, and the Jap sank to the ground.

Whether Mutaguchi attended any birthday celebrations at Maymyo isn't known; but he did send a signal to Sato, cancelling his order to send three battalions to Kanglatongbi. Sato was therefore spared any immediate threat of disciplinary action; but Mutaguchi made it quite clear that he hadn't forgiven him for his gross disobedience. However, forgiveness was not what Sato needed at this precise moment; he needed food, ammunition and medical supplies. And still they didn't come.

*

On the right flank, the 4th Brigade column were still struggling through the jungle on the foothills of Pulebadze. In three days of heartbreaking exertion and labour, they had covered territory which on the map amounted to about four miles. For the last twenty-four hours, the rain had been adding to their torments, soaking them to the skin, and rendering the tracks treacherous and slippery. Often they weren't negotiable at all by men carrying heavy loads, and the S.S. Company had to fix toggle ropes to the trees and haul them up. By the 29th the whole column was so exhausted that Brigadier Goschen decided to close it up and let the men rest for a day. The site chosen was a valley, lying a mile to the south of Pulebadze, which the Norfolks christened 'Death Valley' and the Jocks, with their wry sense of humour, 'Happy Valley'. It was a vile spot. Everybody was wet to the skin, and tried to sleep 'on ground that was a quagmire'. One of the Royal Scots recorded: 'There were among the giant trees, rank shrubs with glaucous leaves so thick on the ground that it was hard for a man to move about.' Captain Morrison, who was searching for a suitable site for his regimental aid post, 'dropped through a tangle of bushes into a riverbed below'. 'What a foul night...' wrote one of the Jocks. 'The coldest, dampest, unhappiest night of all—rations not plentiful, and next morning a little breakfast of bully, biscuits and cheese, all mixed up in a mess tin.' Parts of this foul valley were never touched by the sun, and there the vegetation was dank, fungus-encrusted, and stinking. Some of the fungi were luminous and glowed horribly at night, giving the whole jungle an air of phantasmagoria. The Norfolks, Captain Hornor records, were in a 'deep jungle-clad cleft, with an icy stream running down it, with such steep sides and so deep that... a perpetual damp mist overhung everything. Where it had been difficult to get a fire going before, here it was nigh impossible and the moss-covered trees and boulders combined with the gloom and cold rain might well have depressed the troops had they allowed it to do so.' Exhausted though they were, the troops wanted to get on.

John Grover wanted them to get on, too, so that the brigade could be co-ordinated into the major operation he was now planning. As the calendar reminded him, not to mention the Corps Commander, his division had now been in action for twenty days, and it was high time that an offensive was launched against Kohima Ridge. His plan, shortly, was as follows: 6th Brigade were to take F.S.D. Hill, then Jail Hill, aided by tanks which would round the corner by the Dorsets' position; 5th Brigade would capture Naga Village. And 4th Brigade would occupy Aradura Spur, block the road, then attack G.P.T. Ridge from the south-west, in co-operation with 161st Brigade, which was to advance from the west, after occupying Two Tree Hill and Congress Hill. Owing to the shortage of artillery ammunition, the gunners were to support 6th Brigade in the centre, and 5th Brigade were to be given 'Lifebuoys', the American flame-throwers which had just been received. D-Day was fixed for the 2nd May.

But hardly had the plan been made than it had to be modified, so far as 4th Brigade were concerned. Grover learned that the position regarding the transport aircraft (which would be needed to supply the Brigade later on) was shakier than ever, as Mountbatten was being pressed hard to send the planes he had borrowed from the Mediterranean back again. Some rugged horse-trading was going on between the British and the Americans, between the soldiers and the politicians, and what would happen was anyone's guess. But one thing was quite clear: all the aircraft which remained would be needed for the lift to Imphal. The only sensible solution, therefore, was to order 4th Brigade to head direct for G.P.T. Ridge, or as direct as Mount Pulebadze would allow. This decision was signalled to Brigadier Goschen on the morning of the 29th and immediately patrols went forward to reconnoitre routes and cut tracks.

While 4th Brigade were resting, and 5th Brigade were patrolling and wondering how on earth they'd capture Firs Hill, the Royal Welch Fusiliers of 6th Brigade made their way into the Kohima perimeter to relieve the Durham Light Infantry. Since the siege had been lifted, the area had been subject to a further eleven days of bombardment, desperate hand-to-hand fighting, and bloodshed, and like everyone seeing it for the first time the Welshmen weren't favourably impressed. The leading companies had to crawl, an officer recorded, 'through the shallow, muddy communication trenches to take over the forward dug-outs and foxholes...coming under occasional fire from snipers overlooking the area.... It was strewn with empty cartridge cases, ammunition boxes and abandoned equipment—the debris of earlier fights which there had been as yet no chance to clear up. The most lasting impression of all was caused by the stench of decaying bodies, half buried or lying in the open between the lines. In some of the slit trenches, rotting bodies of Japanese were used to form the protective parapet.... Space was so limited that dug-outs, latrines, cookhouses and graves were all close together. It was almost impossible to dig anywhere without uncovering either a grave or a latrine....' During the hours of daylight it was now possible to carry up supplies of ammunition, wire, water and food from the road, but the garrison still had to rely a good deal on air-drops. 'In the late afternoon some half a dozen Dakotas, flying in line ahead, would come up the valley, circle low round Garrison Hill, and release their many-coloured parachutes. A good few of the precious parachutes drifted away to the enemy's lines... some lodged in the trees.' Great care had to be taken to get the latter down, because of snipers. A favourite method was to keep shooting at the cords, or the branches of the trees, till they came down. Altogether the troops at this period were never short of food or ammunition. Some loads were dropped without parachutes, notably tins of chloride of lime, intended to deal with the plague of flies which were breeding on the dead bodies. If any of these free-drop loads hit anyone it was certain death, so there was a good deal of scampering about as they came down, 'to land in a cloud of choking white powder'. The silk parachutes themselves were very much coveted as they provided cover and warmth, in the absence of blankets. Some troops even lined the walls and floors of their dug-outs with them, making curtained doorways, so that they looked more like miniature harems than anything else. When the Royal Welch Fusiliers first joined the garrison, water was still rationed to a pint a day, very much as it had been during the siege, and washing and shaving were still forbidden. Thanks to the R.A.F., the ration was gradually increased to three pints; but even so it all went 'for brewing up'.

Lieut.-Colonel Garwood and his sappers, aided by a Major of the R.E.M.E., had yet another go at getting a tank up on to the tennis court, but again they failed. Just at the critical moment the cable broke, then an enemy 37-mm. anti-tank gun opened up and scored a couple of hits. John Grover decided that all attempts to get a medium tank up by this method should be abandoned for the moment. However, the following day, a light tank was got up successfully and fired a number of rounds into the main bunker on the tennis court, before being hit by a Jap anti-tank gun, which damaged the turret traversing gear. But it was quite obvious that the 37-mm. gun wasn't heavy enough to do any real damage to the bunker.

All day on the 30th the heavy showers continued and the evening closed in with low clouds and mist. The staff supplying 5th Brigade were getting increasingly worried, as the R.A.F. could not possibly drop all their demands, and the tracks up from the Zubza nala were getting worse all the time. The Pathans had stopped leading their mules up the khudside and were now *driving* them up like cattle. Often the mules would slither down again, crash against the trees, and splinter their bamboo 'carriers'. Sometimes the loads would come off altogether and go sliding down the valley. By some miracle, the bulk of the supplies kept getting through... though how long this would happen as the monsoon got really going was problematical.

While on the subject of supplies, it may be worth recording the vast bulk and variety of supplies that a brigade requires to keep it in action. Apart from the air-drops, 5th Brigade demanded on the night of the 30th April, and received next morning:

1,600	blankets
100	coils of barbed wire
1,000	gauzes
10	rolls of flannelette
30	suits of battledress
50	cardigans

10	bales of fodder
100	gallons of petrol
50	gallons of high octane
150	razors
160	Indian Type Compo rations
1,000	water-sterilizing outfits
4	drums of mosquito cream
4	drums dubbin
60	rounds 3-inch mortar H.E.
60	rounds 3-inch mortar smoke
20	mule loads of jam and tinned fruit
15	mule loads of vegetables
16	gallons of rum
100	pairs of boots
18	bags of mail

All this by mule-train, across a rain-soaked valley. This may help to explain why in Burma 'logistics' [as the Americans called them] always figured largely in any operational planning. It may also explain Slim's sharp comment to anyone who asked him why he didn't 'fling a couple of divisions' across the Chindwin, or elsewhere. Only amateurs fling divisions... not professional soldiers.'

During the whole of April the bickering by signal had continued between Sato and Mutaguchi. On the 8th, after the latter had signalled 'Congratulations on your splendid achievement in capturing Kohima,' Sato replied: 'It is not your congratulations we want but food and ammunition.' On the 20th he signalled: 'We captured Kohima within three weeks as promised. How about Imphal?' To this Mutaguchi answered: 'Probable date for capture of Imphal 29th April.' Sato waited till the 29th had gone by, then on the morning of the 30th signalled: '31st Division at the limit of its endurance. When are you going to destroy Imphal?' To this there was apparently no reply.

*

If April died in a pall of black cloud, May came in with a burst of bright sunshine and blue skies. The staff captain, 5th Brigade, noted: 'The shadows come racing across the mountains in a never-ending pageant of blues and mauves and deep purples... for wild, dark, lush beauty, there's nothing to touch Assam.' He was writing from the viewpoint of Zubza; but the men of 4th Brigade, now sweating it out on the flanks of Pulebadze, no doubt had different views. Through the heavy rains, the going had become so difficult that the 143rd S.S. Company was now having to hack out a route to the Assembly Area through primeval jungle. The slopes were so steep that steps had to be cut and hand rails fixed; and even then loads had to be passed up by a human chain. Progress was cut down to a mile a day. A party from the Royal Norfolk succeeded in getting right on top of Pulebadze, and noted that 'from here it was possible to see the reverse slopes of the positions which 6th Brigade was fighting hard to recapture, and which were unobserved from any other point. 99th Field Regiment thereupon shot their guns and the Japanese must have wondered how the previously unobserved shooting had suddenly become deadly accurate. The gunners enjoyed themselves.' The account continues:

> 'At over 7,000 feet the air was cold and clear and for once it wasn't raining, and below the whole battlefield was spread out: Naga Village, Gun Spur, Treasury, Hospital Hill, D.I.S. Ridge, Garrison Hill, Jail Hill, the road running through a cutting between them, and to the southward, Aradura.'

Down below, things weren't so calm or peaceful. It was now

realized that the Nagas couldn't accompany the column any further, even if they'd been willing, as on their way back to Khonoma the previous evening, a Japanese patrol had attacked them and killed two. Whether surprise had been lost, it was hard to say, but certainly the Nagas couldn't keep travelling to and from the column on their own. The best hope was that the column would make contact with the road, or someone coming up from the road, before its supplies ran out.

Meanwhile, Brigadier Goschen had selected a feature for the jumping-off place for the assault on G.P.T. Ridge. This was a high pimple, to be known as Oaks Hill, and all day on the 1st May the 143rd S.S. Company were reconnoitring a route to it. But progress was slow; one route proved so precipitous that they had to turn back to find another, and before mid-day it became evident to Goschen that all hopes of taking part in an operation the following day must be abandoned. He therefore signalled Grover that it would be the 3rd May before he'd be ready. Grover accepted his explanation and in turn got on to Stopford. But, though appreciating the difficulties 4th Brigade were under, Stopford wasn't too pleased at all, and rang up Grover at 10.30 p.m. to say he must get going on the 3rd. The battle could hang fire no longer. 'A thoroughly depressing day', Stopford noted in his diary.

It was a depressing day for Mountbatten, too. The threat to his transport aircraft had grown to such an extent that he was now keeping them from day to day. On this day he signalled the combined Chiefs of Staff that two courses were now open to him, neither of which would admit half-measures. He could hold on to the aircraft till the road was open and Imphal relieved; or he could send them away, as ordered. If the latter course were adopted, however—as he forcibly pointed out—the Chindits would have to be withdrawn, Stilwell would be forced to retreat, and Scoones' 4th Corps would have to fly out of Imphal, leaving their guns, equipment and stores behind them.

In turn, the Ledo Road would have to be abandoned. In other words, the whole front would collapse; the Japs would achieve their objectives; and the blow to Allied prestige in the Far East would be so heavy that it might never recover. No immediate reply was received to this signal and, with increasing anxiety, Mountbatten held on to the aircraft.

No major action was fought this day, though as always patrols were out, and some minor clashes occurred. The regiments were busy organizing themselves for the coming offensive, and new units were coming forward. Of these the 4th/1st Gurkhas took over Two Tree Hill, half a mile to the west of Jail Hill. They were a young unit, with young officers, commanded by Lieut.-Colonel Hedderwick. (Brigadier Warren told Grover that, in his view, their youth and inexperience were such that they should not be put into a battle.) Their Brigade was the 33rd, of General Messervy's 7th Division, the two other battalions in the brigade being the 1st Queens and the 4th/15th Punjab. Soon the whole brigade would be drawn into the battle.

Victor Hawkins was already directing his attention towards Naga Village and subalterns of the Worcestershires and the Camerons were slipping through the Jap defences with patrols, pinpointing strong points, and bringing back information on such details as to 'where they slept and their hours of inactivity'. Hawkins wrote: 'I cannot speak too highly of the work these boys did. They came back sometimes exhausted, but never failed to respond to my call for more.' But how he could move his brigade on to Naga Village while Firs Hill still held it was difficult to say. A second attempt by the Worcestershires and Camerons to infiltrate on to the latter had failed, though fortunately without great loss.

On the 2nd May the bad news continued. Three Naga porters, on the 4th Brigade supply route, were met by a Japanese patrol, which was evidently lying up in wait for them. Their loads were taken, then they were beaten up, and left tied to trees. The Japanese patrol (or what was thought to be the same one) was later ambushed by the Royal Scots, but it was now clear that the enemy had knowledge that a column of some size was operating in the Pulebadze area, and hopes of achieving surprise were dwindling rapidly.

Progress was still slow. And before noon Goschen was forced to signal Grover again and say that he couldn't be ready now till the 4th May. This was a heavy blow to the divisional commander, especially as he knew that Stopford and Slim would be arriving any moment to receive a report on his progress. Accounts of the meeting which ensued vary widely. According to Stopford, Slim 'was obviously upset' that the major attack on the ridge 'had not started long ago'. Slim, on the other hand says: 'I was determined not to push Stopford beyond the pace that he considered wise.... He was the last commander to drag his feet....' Grover records: 'Slim was very insistent on the need for speed, very largely for political reasons. He evidently thought we had been going rather slowly, but appeared surprised at the size of the country. He was also a little sceptical as to the strength in front of us— though later events proved that we were correct and he was wrong.' There is little point in trying to reconcile these accounts. The reality of the situation, the need for taking Kohima and reopening the road was known to all three generals; and the reasons for the delay, whether valid or otherwise, were at this juncture of secondary importance. In this context, it is quite clear that Slim and Stopford had no alternative but to press for immediate action; and that Grover had good cause to think them somewhat unreasonable. This kind of situation is common in war, and is repeated right down the chain of command.

Before leaving, Stopford told Grover that he 'must push 5th Brigade into Naga Village' the following night. Grover passed the order on to Victor Hawkins, asking him to work out a plan which would be discussed with a liaison officer (bearing

Grover's ideas) who would arrive next morning. Hawkins' reaction wasn't favourable. He says: 'I didn't like it a bit. Not only were the Japs still on Firs Hill, which covered our only route, but it meant *again* passing the whole brigade across the Jap front and then this time through their lines... and planting ourselves in the middle of them on the most important tactical feature of their position. I foresaw a nasty time ahead of us.' But, despite his personal forebodings, Hawkins went ahead with his usual energy; he again grilled Phillips of the Worcestershires, and Peter Cameron and Neil White of the Camerons when they brought back their patrols. He also considered a report from Captain Mackay of the Camerons who said 'he had found a way round the enemy flank'. Firs Hill was naturally causing him enormous worry; and he seriously considered fighting a third action to gain it, with the help of the tanks. But the tank commander's reply was: 'Unless we can get a bulldozer to help us, it isn't on, so far as we're concerned.' So that was that. Hawkins had to consider how he could get round the hill with the minimum risk, and came to the conclusion that a whole battalion would have to picket the lower slopes of the hill. This would leave two battalions for the main operation, with no troops left to guard the 'tail'. When Major Robertson, the liaison officer, arrived, it soon became obvious that Grover hadn't yet received all the information regarding the Jap dispositions and (in Hawkins' eyes) his plan was unworkable. Hawkins' own plan was much bolder and therefore much riskier. He'd decided to use the Camerons to occupy Naga Village and Point 5120, a high feature on the far edge of it; and, as silence was a prerequisite of the operation, he'd laid down that they should travel as light as possible, wearing gym shoes. The track to be used was the only one reported by patrols to be free from Japanese weapon pits. The timing was vitally important too. Patrols had reported that the Japs slept between three and five in the morning, so the whole operation would have to be completed in that time. Hawkins reckoned that if the Camerons left at 0200 hours they could cover the two miles and reach Point 5120 within an hour. Once they'd succeeded, they were to report by code, so that the Lancashire Fusiliers could follow on. The Worcestershires, picketing Firs Hill, would remain in position till receiving orders to close. The tanks would remain with them and act as an escort, before returning to Division.

When Robertson took details of this plan back to John Grover there was some consternation among his staff. The dangers of the operation leapt from the page. If the Camerons were heavily attacked on route, if they couldn't get into Naga Village, if the track proved to be held, if the enemy companies on Firs Hill decided to come down and hit the brigade while it was on the move... one could go on endlessly. But, as Grover had to ask himself: what was the alternative? The brigade was doing no good where it was, and he'd received urgent orders from Stopford to push it into Naga Village. Slim had also sent a message direct. Courageously, Grover agreed to Hawkins' plan, and gave permission for him to go ahead. Like Hawkins himself, he was very worried; but relations between these two men were excellent, and their trust in each other was complete. Also Hawkins was lucky....

All day during the 2nd May the Royal Norfolk, with a company of the Royal Scots under command, toiled onwards to Oaks Hill, the new assembly area. Captain Hornor says: 'The climb... was very trying, all ranks being much overloaded, and this in spite of a great amount of ammunition, battle batteries, and rations which could not be carried having been buried. As from the start of this move no more fires were allowed, the physical strain began to be apparent. It was a weary 2nd Norfolk which led on to Oaks Hill through the S.S. Company....' The jungle was so thick on this feature that nothing could be seen;

and Goschen decided that to reduce the risk of discovery to a minimum, only one reconnaissance party would be allowed. This didn't please Robert Scott at all, especially when he discovered that he would be allowed only two representatives on it. After a sharp exchange, Goschen increased the number from two to eight, and the commanders of the leading companies were included. The time fixed for the reconnaissance was 0700 hours on the following morning.

While the Royal Norfolk were slogging towards Oaks Hill, the Royal Scots were occupying a feature above it, known as Pavilion Hill. Here the Japs were more active, and put in an attack on the leading platoons at mid-day. Fortunately, they had come uphill in the open and the machine-gunners were able to deal with them. However, at dusk, before two companies had even had time to dig in, the cry 'Banzai! Banzai!' was heard in the thick jungle around the perimeter, then the Jap machine-gunners opened up, and the spring grenades started coming over to explode among the slit trenches. After this the infantry came in with their usual spirit, and though many were shot down, others pressed on, and a section of Major Menzies' company was overrun. As darkness fell, and the confusion grew, it seemed that the enemy might penetrate the position in some strength, but a section commander, Lance-Corporal McKay, rallied his Jocks, and they tore into the Japanese. For a while there were shouts and cries and the sight of desperate in-fighting, but McKay and his men gained the upper hand, and the situation was then restored by the platoon commander, Colin Black. Two more attacks came in at the same spot, the Japanese probably reasoning that if they could wear the platoon down, sooner or later it would have to give. But it didn't; and eventually, with their own losses mounting, they gave up. During the action, an enemy machine-gun section had tried to establish themselves on a high feature, overlooking the whole position, but McKay picked them off with his Sten gun. For this, and his other actions that night, he was awarded the Military Medal, while Colin Black won the Military Cross. In all the Royal Scots lost only six men, but when daylight came they found Jap bodies in the jungle all around them. Some had rolled down the hill till stopped by trees, and others were lodged precariously on narrow ledges. There was one amusing incident during the action, when the commanding officer sent Major Menzies a 'rocket' because his company were using too much ammunition. To this Menzies replied: 'It isn't my men that are blazing away—it's the Japs.' A dangerous moment occurred when the second-in-command, Major Hayward, joined in the job of priming Mills grenades. After watching his efforts, those around him made a hurried departure.

From the scale of this attack on the Royal Scots, and the fact that the Japanese had pushed troops so far up towards Mount Pulebadze, it was obvious that their strength on this flank had increased. On the evening of the 2nd, Grover discovered why. The 4th/1st Gurkhas, now occupying Two Tree Hill, found a telephone line running up to a Jap O.P. Intelligently, they cut it, then laid on an ambush, and when the Japs arrived to repair the break, killed them and stripped their pockets. The men were identified as belonging to the Colonel Miyamoto's 124th Regiment, part of the force which had been intended for Kanglatongbi. This was the first news Grover had received that they were on this flank, and it made him glad that he had changed the plan for 4th Brigade. If it had gone down Aradura Spur to cut the road, Miyamoto might well have been strong enough to cut it off; and without air supply, its position would have been serious.

On reaching his headquarters, Stopford received information from his Intelligence officers that 'a prisoner stated most definitely that the Japs had been gradually withdrawing during the last week and that he realized Kohima would fall'. Stopford seems to have accepted this report and asked Brigadier Wood to phone its contents to Grover, 'as an urge to keep thrusting forward'. But, as events were to show, the prisoner, like most Japanese, told his interrogators what he thought they'd like to hear.

*

The 3rd May was the final day of preparation before the offensive against Kohima; it was a day of great activity and great tension. The troops had no illusions as to what the battle would be like, even if they were successful; their commanders knew the price of failure. At 0700 hours, guarded by an escort of Major McGeorge's S.S. Company, Brigadier Goschen's reconnaissance party moved off, working its way on to the lower slopes of the Aradura Spur before turning north towards the objective. According to one account: '... the same view of jungle five yards away, to which everyone was well accustomed, was all that could be obtained; had the chance of discovery permitted climbing a tree an equally entrancing view of tree tops could have been obtained....' Altogether, the reconnaissance seemed pretty hopeless, but after some hours of crawling and scrambling, a spot with some sort of view was found. From here part of Jail Hill could be seen, and short of it, a corrugated roof, which was taken to be on the objective. After Goschen had obtained such information as he required, he took his party back again, leaving Robert Scott and Lieut.-Colonel James, of the 99th Field Regiment, to study the ground further. The bearing on the tin roof was 55 degrees, from which Scott calculated that the bearing of the axis of advance must be no degrees. As the objective was still invisible, this was only a rough calculation; and, in fact, for a major attack, the whole reconnaissance had been very inadequate. But surprise was paramount; and nothing more could be done.

At 1300 hours the remaining compo rations were shared out,

each man receiving tea, milk, and sugar for a day, five biscuits, a half-tin of bully, a small tin of pilchards, a spoonful of butter, a little tinned cheese, and some jam. The orders from brigade were that there were still to be no fires, which meant that the men wouldn't get a hot drink. As they would be fighting all the next day, this was more than Robert Scott could tolerate; and he ordered a pit to be dug near the regimental aid post, six feet deep and twelve feet square. This was then roofed over and an immense pile of shavings was made. Then at dusk, when any smoke escaping wouldn't show, a large fire was lit and the mess tins were boiled. Gleefully the men collected for their beloved char. But when Goschen turned up, to find that his orders had been flouted, he was naturally incensed, and asked Scott what on earth he thought he was up to. With his tongue in his cheek, Scott said the hot water was needed to treat jungle sores, and this produced such an explosion that it seemed likely for a moment that he would be placed under arrest. Fortunately, any such development was out of the question on the eve of a battle; and in the nick of time, Captain Mather produced a man who actually had been treated for sores. At this, Goschen cooled down again—and finally agreed to the char. In view of the events a few days later, this clash between Scott and Goschen has a peculiar irony.

The rule of silence caused some difficulties too; company commanders had to move from platoon to platoon, whispering the orders for the attack, and after them the platoon commanders and section leaders. Most of the night had gone by before the whispering was over.

A comprehensive fire plan lasting forty-five minutes had been laid on with Division. The two 5.5 guns which had been found in Dimapur by Pat Burke, and were manned by gunners from the division, were to shell G.P.T. Ridge 'cap on', with the object of making shell-holes which would provide cover during the period of consolidation. When the Norfolks had formed up 'at the edge of the jungle' Robert Scott was to inform Goschen, who in turn would inform Division and then immediately they would start the fire plan. The Royal Scots would block the track to the north, then on receipt of orders, move in bounds on the same axis as the Royal Norfolk. But with so many unknown factors, as Goschen remarked, the plan had to be fluid....

To return to the centre: John Bowles and his men were still holding out by the crossroads, beyond the D.C.'s bungalow, but only just. On the evening of the 2nd, the Japs had brought a 75-mm. gun down the road from Treasury Hill and shelled them at 300 yards' range. All communications went, and Jock McNaught, the commanding officer, had no means of knowing how badly they were being hit. The gunners got on to the area from where they imagined the fire was coming, but failed to stop it, and things began to look very serious. However, at eleven o'clock, Corporal Mansfield and two men managed to get to McNaught, through the enemy lines, with their damaged 18-set. They also brought a message from their company commander to say that things weren't very good, and he'd been losing a lot of men. McNaught sent back a message that he'd send Alan Watts and 'B' Company the following morning, and Mansfield set off with another radio set to replace the damaged one. Somehow he got through. On the morning of the 3rd, the divisional artillery put down a smoke screen, aided by the battalion mortars, and the relief took place. Geoffrey White writes: 'I confess to feeling a large lump in my throat as I watched the twenty-eight survivors of the hundred-odd of my old company clamber up the hillside to battalion headquarters. Blackened and red-eyed, John Bowles' men had, for five and a half days, hung on by the skin of their teeth against almost overwhelming opposition in the most exposed position... they had kept the road open and had killed a large number of Japanese.'

In daylight on the 3rd May, Sergeant Seale of the Dorsets carried out a brilliant patrol towards the tennis court. His object was to occupy the large bunker on the north-east corner, and by skilful use of ground he got to within five yards of it. This was the bunker which 'C' company had reduced in their first attack, and it seemed pretty certain that it hadn't been reoccupied. Seale and his men took a good look at it and moved round to find the entrance, but failed. Then he came under heavy fire from the water tower and had to withdraw; but not before he'd had a quick look round at the lay-out of the Jap defences. This information, added to what was already known, enabled McNaught to get a much clearer picture of the situation. It also increased his respect for his opponent, who it had to be conceded 'had a grand eye for ground'. As Geoffrey White put it:

> 'He concentrated his defence in the area of the tennis court. With a very strong post dug well in under the water tank at the south-west corner—that is below the old club-house—and strong bunkers along the south end—far end to us—and in the bank which separated the tennis court from the club square above it, he only had to wait for us to emerge on to the tennis court and let us have it.... One thing stood out a mile: it was absolutely essential either to get a medium tank on to the tennis court or manhandle a gun into such a position as to blow the devils out of their holes at very close range in support of an infantry attack.'

But how to get a tank on the tennis court? Garwood and his sappers had been trying for a long time now and were still no nearer success. Fortunately, they hadn't given up.

This battle of the Dorsetshire Regiment around Charles Pawsey's tennis court was a most extraordinary one; and without a detailed model of the ground, most difficult to understand. What one must keep in mind though is that the positions of the two armies were close, sometimes within fifteen yards, and interlocked. The Japanese positions, as usual, all supported each other; one could not get at one without being shot up from two or three others. The curious terraced conformation of the ground played an important part too; the Japs— always great diggers—had got so far in to the banks that nothing landing from the air could touch them. Artillery and mortars were quite useless. However, on the evening of the 3rd news arrived from Major Rhodes of the 149th R.A.C. that he wanted to have another crack at getting a tank up the drive to the bungalow, and Captain Jock Murrills (who had been with John Bowles at the road junction) agreed to guide him round. 'B' Company under Major Alan Watts were briefed for an attack, and suddenly the Dorsets were filled with new hope.

On the 5th Brigade front things went quietly during the 3rd, the troops resting in preparation for their coming exertions during the night; but the gym shoes were causing headaches among the 'Q' staff. Understandably, no mention had been made of the fact that they were an operational necessity, and so the order wasn't dealt with as a matter of top priority. However, at 1100 hours on the 3rd, the staff captain 5th Brigade received a call from 'ADOS', the senior ordnance officer in Dimapur, to say he'd collected 3,000 pairs together and sent them off. The staff captain reported this to Colonel Simpson, the A.Q. at Division, warning him at the same time that he'd no mules to send them up on. At this Simpson exploded, but then agreed to find the mules and send them to milestone 42, under Mervyn Preston, one of his staff. But by 1300 hours, the gym shoes still hadn't reached Zubza, and Simpson came on the line again angrily to demand what was happening. Frantically a search began up and down the road to locate the missing lorries, which now, so it appeared, had either vanished into thin air or gone over the khud. By this time the 'G' Staff had joined in the flap and were threatening to cancel the whole operation, if the shoes didn't arrive in the next half-hour. They were essential, they said; they were vital... the divisional commander was most concerned. Then, when the staff captain found himself mumbling the old nursery rhyme 'because of a horseshoe the battle was lost….', the convoy arrived, and was rushed forward to milestone 42. Here the precious packages of footwear were bundled into the bamboo carriers, and the carriers strapped on to the mules. The latter had been waiting some hours now and were stamping their feet and milling round in a crazy circus. The business of threading straps through holes and buckling them up was an utter nightmare, and for a while it looked as if the Pathans would take out their rifles and shoot some of the mules to stop the rot. But suddenly it was all done. And just as a message arrived from Division to say that, if something didn't happen soon, 'it was all off', the leading mule led downhill towards the nala. If the episode hadn't been so desperate, it would have been highly comical; it was certainly the kind of snag that military textbooks never allowed for.

But the gym shoes didn't provide the main crisis of this day. General Scoones at Imphal realized that the supply situation was becoming very serious, and even if the R.A.F. and the U.S. A.A.F. went flat out in the fairly good weather, which he hoped would prevail till the 21st May, his reserves would have fallen below the safety level. He therefore signalled Slim that his administrative situation now dictated the date by which the Imphal Road must be open. This critical date, he said, could be postponed somewhat if the ration scale were reduced, or if the airmen could fly by night as well as day. Failing that, some of the fighting troops would have to be flown out.

At the precise moment that Scoones despatched this signal, Slim was on a visit to Stilwell, so did not receive it till the following day. Before he had time to deal with it, however, a signal came from Air Chief Marshal Sir Richard Peirse, advising that the transport aircraft on loan from the Middle East must be withdrawn by the 8th, *in four days' time*. A blow of these dimensions, coming at a critical moment in the battle of

Kohima, and the siege of Imphal, might have shaken a lesser man. But Slim remained cool and outwardly unperturbed. With Air Marshal Baldwin's agreement he sent messages to Sir George Giffard and to Air Headquarters, S.E.A.C., forcibly pointing out the disastrous consequences of withdrawing these seventy-nine aircraft. Giffard, that much underrated soldier, immediately saw Mountbatten and supported Slim, saying that if the aircraft were taken he could not answer for the consequences. That afternoon, Mountbatten told Giffard that the aircraft were to be held, and that he personally took full responsibility. A few hours later, Mountbatten received a telegram from Winston Churchill, the Prime Minister, which read: 'Let nothing go from the battle that you need for victory. I will not accept denial of this from any quarter, and will back you to the full.'

By the time Slim heard this good news, the offensive on Kohima Ridge had been going for some hours.

Kohima Ridge, with I.G.H. spur in the foreground.

F.S.D. Hill on Kohima Ridge, scene of some of the fiercest fighting. The trees in the foreground are hung with the remains of parachutes from air supply drops.

The Deputy Commissioner's bungalow at Kohima, in a photograph taken before the War.

The ruined tennis court and terraces of the Deputy Commissioner's bungalow, July 1944.

The main street of Kohima, seen after the battle.

Lord Louis Mountbatten, Supreme Allied Commander South East Asia, at the memorial to the West Kent regiment on Garrison Hill.

Garrison Hill, key to the British defences at Kohima.

Angami Nagas in full dress.

The Naga village and Kohima Ridge, seen after the battle.

The battlefield of the Naga village at Kohima.

Naga women and children.

Dug-outs in the Naga village.

Naga girls.

A bulldozer at work on the Kohima–Imphal road.

Men of the Royal West Kents visit the grave of their former comrade Lance-Corporal John Harman, who was awarded the Victoria Cross posthumously for gallantry, 8 April 1944.

(*above*) Grover and Stopford.

(*left*) Major-General John Grover, commander of 2nd Division.

(*below*) Brigadier 'Daddy' Warren, commander of the 161st Indian Brigade.

(*below*) Lieutenant-General Montagu Stopford, commander of 33rd Indian Corps, Imphal.

Lieutenant-General Kotoku Sato, commander of the Japanese 31st Division.

Lieutenant-General Renya Mutaguchi, commander of the Japanese 15th Army.

Kohima in 1965.

Chapter Eight

Attrition on the 4th May

At dusk the men of the Worcestershires, the Cameron Highlanders and the Lancashire Fusiliers buried their boots and put on gym shoes which by then had been taken from the mules and sorted roughly into sizes. Then just before nine o'clock the Worcestershires moved off to start picketing the tracks running down from Firs Hill, so securing the left flank of the other two battalions when they advanced. Unfortunately the moon was near the full and movement could only take place when the clouds obscured it. The Worcestershires were therefore delayed and, later on, the Camerons. The latter took four and a half hours to form up in the assembly area, although the distance from the furthest company was only one and a half miles. However, at midnight, the 'all clear' was given, and a message sent to Victor Hawkins. Soon the Camerons were collecting on the edge of the perimeter near the road, and Hawkins had a word with Peter Saunders, whom he reported 'to be in good heart but not minimizing the task in front of him'. Saunders was a delightful character, with a wonderful sense of humour and a natural Highland courtesy. After some rather austere periods with previous commanders, the battalion had been very much relieved when he took them over, and though even now they hadn't quite got accustomed to some of his unorthodox habits, they trusted

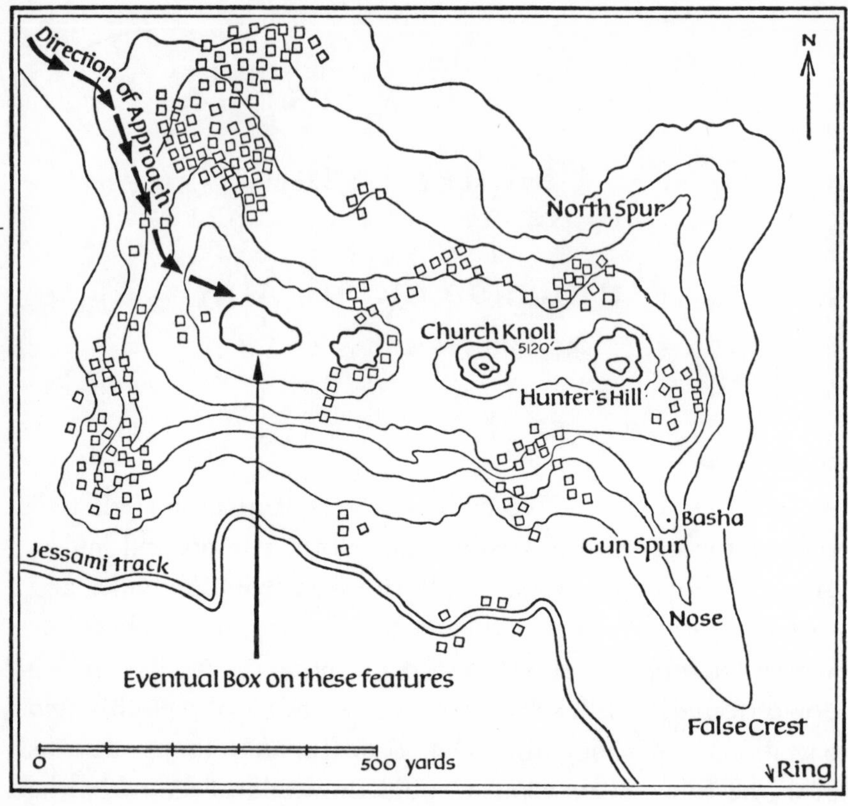

him completely. Saunders had another attribute (shared with Victor Hawkins) which, it was hoped, would stand him in good stead this night: he was considered lucky.

Just before midnight everyone was ready. Hawkins wished Saunders the best of luck, and Saunders passed an order to Captain Neil White, commanding the guerrilla platoon, who led off along the track. According to Colin Hunter, who commanded 'D' Company: 'There was a ghostly moon, and patches of mist. Our nerves were taut and we kept expecting trouble. Sometimes we heard noises and thought the Japs were around, but it was our own chaps further forward. The track zigzagged up and down and there were frequent halts as the column bunched then strung out again. The journey wasn't very long, really… but that night and in those circumstances it seemed almost endless.' Fortunately, the information brought back by the patrols had been accurate and the Japs were sleeping. White's men surprised three of them, and killed them without trouble. But it was hoped that no more would show up... the last thing anyone wanted was the noise of shooting.

As already explained, the Naga Village sprawled over the high ground to the north of Kohima. There were four features strung out in a line from west to east, the third one being known as Church Knoll or Point 5120, and the last, Hunter's Hill. These two hills, which had been terraced by the Nagas were connected by a saddle, and to the north and south of them were two features known as North Spur (thickly covered with jungle) and Gun Spur. The Camerons' plan was for the leading two companies to occupy Naga Village up to Church Knoll, then 'D' Company to pass through and occupy Hunter's Hill, while 'C' Company acted as a link on the saddle. All this had to be accomplished by first light. The officers had studied air photographs of all the features and hoped to locate them without difficulty; but, as they knew only too well, ground looks very different from eye-level, and especially at night.

The advance went on steadily, if slowly. Firs Hill was passed, then hill after hill on which the Japs were sleeping. Later the leading company became conscious that there were bashas up on the left, presumably the north-western fringe of the village. The next feature was the road, a danger point if the Japs had it covered, but White's men went across without a sound, and the companies followed, to begin scrambling up the hill. Even now there was not a sound from the Japs; no reaction whatever. The leading companies began deploying, and, as their officers located Church Knoll, began siting platoon and section positions, and occupying them. Then 'D' Company under Colin Hunter came forward, streaming down into the saddle, then up again on to Hunter's Hill. Here some Japs were found sleeping in the bashas, and the Jocks killed them with the bayonet. So far, the whole operation had gone with wonderful precision, and exactly as planned—except for one thing. Before Colin Hunter and his company could dig themselves in on Hunter's Hill, it was light.

Having left detailed instructions with his second-in-command, 'Bimbo' Howard, Victor Hawkins lay sleeping for the first two hours of the operation, but at 0400 hours he woke up, to ask if there was any signal from the Camerons. Nothing had been heard at all. The only good news was of a negative kind: that no shooting had been heard, so, Hawkins records, '... slightly encouraged, I hoped against hope.' His real worry now was that once the Lancashire Fusiliers moved out with Brigade Tactical headquarters, 'they would be horribly placed if the Jap reacted violently, as by all the rules of war, he should do'. The Fusiliers would be moving or fighting with the enemy above them on the high ground, and coming down on top of them. 'Moreover, the ground was so steep and in places so thick that to fight a controlled battle, and, if necessary, a withdrawal, would have been almost impossible.'

The great enemy now—apart from the Japanese—was daylight, and it was approaching fast. If news didn't come soon, Hawkins' position would be a little short of desperate, his brigade split in two, and neither half secure. The wait was the most agonizing of his whole career. Then at 0500 hours, just as the light was coming on, word came from the Camerons. This gave the news that they had reached Naga Village without opposition and were now occupying the eastern knolls. Hawkins decided to push on with the Lancashire Fusiliers at once. He says:

> 'It was an uncomfortable feeling moving along the road and track, right across the Jap front, knowing that he was above us and should be able to see everything.... However, things went well until we crossed the road to ascend the hill. As I reached this point there was some shooting from the side of

the hill, and an alarm that the Jap was coming in. Luckily this was exaggerated. There was a small party of them but the Lancashire Fusiliers pushed them back and we went through. We had achieved what looked impossible, and completely surprised the Jap by a manœuvre which, on the face of it, was contrary to every principle of war.'

Immediately the Lancashire Fusiliers got firm on the ground, holding the northern, western, and southern sides of the perimeter, and by 0700 hours Hawkins made contact with the Camerons in front. But now things were happening. The Jap had come out of his sleep and was beginning to fight.

Taking a quick look round, one of the first things that Hawkins realized was that the ground looked very much bigger in reality than it had done on the map; and the task of holding the whole hill was too much for a brigade. Also, the jungle and the bashas on the spurs to the north and south provided the enemy with ideal cover from which to infiltrate or snipe. He also noticed that the saddle between Church Knoll and Hunter's Hill could be swept by fire from both spurs. As to the village itself, Hawkins noted that it was in a foul state. 'Thousands of flies, and filth of every description, including the innards of pigs and cows to which the Japs had helped themselves, made the surroundings disgusting.' However, at this precise moment, hygiene had to come second to the tactical situation, for, as Hawkins could hear only too clearly, the Jap pressure on the Camerons was increasing steadily.

Colin Hunter and his company had not long started digging in when the sniping started, from North Spur. His own men were being hit, and those of Allan Roy's 'C' Company in the saddle. Then the Jap mortars opened up, and the position deteriorated even further. C.S.M. Tommy Cook was killed at this time, a great blow to the Camerons. Apart from being one of the 'characters' of the Regiment, he was a magnificent fighter who had distinguished himself in the first action on Bunker Hill. The 5th Brigade mortars now came into action, to try and keep the fire down, but without great success. About noon, Hunter made his way back over the saddle to find Peter Saunders, and give him the situation. After some discussion Saunders ordered that the company should hold on till just before dark, then withdraw to Church Knoll.

The withdrawal from Hunter's Hill, as subsequent events were to prove, was one of the great tragedies of the battle of Kohima, but Hawkins had no alternative but to sanction it. Apart from his recent observation as to the size of the ground, there was the further consideration that the Worcestershires were still back beyond Firs Hill. This meant that he couldn't push any more troops forward, to help the Camerons, as to have done so would have offered the Japs a chance to split the brigade in two. 'It was better, I thought [so he recorded], to make certain of holding the very important position we had won, than to grasp at more and risk losing it all.' Even *his* luck had limits.

How important the Naga Village was became immediately apparent, as Hawkins moved around, keeping an eye on the siting of the perimeter. 'The observation from the top of the hill was magnificent. We not only overlooked the complete Kohima battlefield but right into the back of the Jap positions. Immediately below us and running away to the south was Treasury Ridge... and beyond this Garrison Hill. The road to Imphal which we were trying to open... passed behind Jail Hill, then turned south-east.* It was in the area of Garrison Hill to G.P.T. Ridge that the heaviest fighting was taking place, and we had a grandstand view of it.'

* From their first day at Kohima the Japanese had appreciated the importance of this position and had occupied it. However, according to Colonel Yamaki, the shelling and air bombing was so devastating that they couldn't hold it. As he says, 'the game was to the long cannon'.

At the centre of that fighting was the Royal Norfolk. Leaving their position on Oaks Hill at first light, they scrambled down the steep slope, to be met by heavy small arms fire, and a message came back from the leading company commander that he was going ahead to reconnoitre. At this Robert Scott announced that he would wait ten minutes, and lay down to sleep. Before this period was up, however, word came that there was a strong bunker 100 yards ahead, which had already inflicted five casualties on the leading section. Scott therefore ordered that a company should contain the bunker, while Major Hatch with 'D' Company took the lead and found a way round to a flank. So the column pushed on again, till another bunker was located. This couldn't be outflanked, so an attack was put in which cleared it, though not without casualties. The column advanced again down the spur, but unfortunately there was a track along the spine of this on which the Japs had sited a number of positions. From these they began sniping as the column passed along below them in the jungle, causing a good many casualties, and unfortunately these fell in the undergrowth, where the stretcher-bearers had a difficult time finding them. Lieut.-Colonel James of the 99th Field Regiment was sniped, and while being carried back on a stretcher was sniped again and killed. This sort of thing happened time after time, and the calls for stretcher-bearers became so frequent that they had to dress the casualties and leave them where they were, to be picked up later. Whatever happened, the column dared not slow down. Captain Hornor writes: 'The feeling of complete helplessness of the winding column in single file is something not experienced... in open warfare.' The commanders, in fact, found it so difficult to get information that they moved further and further forward. Robert Scott ended up among the leading sections.

Fire discipline and the conservation of ammunition had been stressed during the whole campaign, and especially on this march. 'The men were very reluctant to shoot at noise only; they waited, as taught, for a target. The target never appeared, and casualties were mounting with no apparent dividend.' The result of this was that when Scott shouted for fire to be opened, a soldier replied: 'But, sir, we can't see the target!' This reply provoked 'a long string of imprecations' from Scott, who promptly moved over towards the source of the fire and began hurling grenades. This action seems to have had the desired effect, so from now on every burst from the Japanese was answered with a shower of grenades from the Norfolks, and the situation improved considerably. Later on, parties of Japs appeared in the open, to be dealt with by rifle or Sten fire. Company Sergeant-Major Derry was observed to shoot down three of them, from a standing position, before they could reply. In places the undergrowth was so thick that the only method of progression was by crawling; but still the advance retained its momentum, driven on by the enormous figure of Robert Scott, bearded and satanical, swearing horribly, and carrying a sack of grenades, which he had great delight in hurling at any suspected enemy post. His great heroic spirit so infected the column that, when a bunker was charged, the men broke out into shouts and cheers, and these went echoing down the ranks in a great crescendo. The speed of Major Hatch's column, in the lead, became so great that gaps began to appear and Scott ordered a halt to reorganize and make a fresh plan, and, incidentally, to make a temporary repair to his pipe which had been damaged during a long crawl.

After a brief conference at 1435 hours, the battalion reconnaissance party went forward with most of two companies, covered by a creeping barrage put down by the 99th Field Regiment. The jungle began to thin out, though visibility was seldom more than twenty yards. The brief halt had luckily not impaired the momentum, and the troops rushed post after post as it came into view. A good many Japs ran away, to be shot down by rifle fire, but those who stayed to fight were bayoneted. Robert

Scott was now brandishing his revolver, shooting down Japs in between bursts of invective against any soldier who looked like slowing the pace. Later, after killing an enemy officer, he picked up his sword which he now brandished, threatening to cut down any Jap who got in his way. As it approached the objective, the column was now almost going at the double, and Scott realized that if the battalion kept on at this pace they could gain the objective without waiting for the artillery barrage. (It will be recalled that the orders for the operation had laid down that Scott should halt on the edge of the jungle and call for fire.) He believed that although the intensive shelling might demoralize the enemy, it could not compensate for the loss of impetus. He therefore ordered Major Henry Conder, his second-in-command, to bring up the remainder of the battalion and requested that a company of Royal Scots should secure his left flank. Unfortunately it couldn't be spared, and the snipers were allowed to operate unchecked. But now the objective was straight before the Royal Norfolks and they swept on, using Brens, rifles and bayonets only. Nothing could stop them now, and in minutes they were on G.P.T. Ridge, killing any Japanese who came to fight in the open, firing and grenading the bunkers, then hurriedly fanning out to consolidate. Shouting for his signaller and the radio, Scott called up Division, as Goschen was now out of touch:

'I am on G.P.T. and am consolidating. Casualties pretty heavy but we've killed a hell of a lot of Japs.'

'But you can't be on G.P.T. You haven't had the fire plan yet.'

'I am I tell you. You'd better send someone up to see.'

Unfortunately, in the excitement, two platoons had overrun their objective, and came under heavy fire from a bunker position, about forty yards to their left front, later known as 'Norfolk bunker'. For the next hour, attempts were made to get those caught in the open back over the crest, which was a very desperate business. No smoke grenades were available, and the positions were too close for the artillery to put down smoke. Fortunately some of the Manchesters were available with their medium machine-guns and they put down such a volume of fire that rescue operations were able to go ahead. It may be added that Robert Scott and Henry Conder aided the fire from the Manchesters with Brens which they had positioned on a flank. From time to time, argument broke out between these two distinguished officers as to which one was doing the prettier shooting. During this period, Captain Mather and his ambulance men did great work, moving to and fro across the ridge, and bringing in stretcher cases under fire. Many of the wounded, unfortunately, were lying in such exposed positions that they couldn't be moved. As Hornor remarks: 'Lying in hastily dug holes and Jap slit trenches, sheltered from the rain by what little could be scrounged, their cheerfulness and fortitude was amazing and not a complaint was heard even from those very seriously hit.' Major Twidle lay out in the open for twenty-four hours, periodically visited by Captain Mather. In all, three officers had been killed and six wounded; among the other ranks there were nineteen killed and ninety wounded. This loss was heavy, but the gain of G.P.T. was a considerable one.

Before dark, two companies of the Royal Scots formed a box 200 yards above the Royal Norfolk, and Goschen made his tactical headquarters with them. All night the process of consolidation went on.

*

While 5th Brigade and 4th Brigade were attacking on the flanks, 6th Brigade attacked in the centre, their objectives being the line of hillocks, Kuki Piquet, D.I.S., F.S.D., and Jail Hill. The morning at Kohima had dawned dry but misty, and at 0740 hours, when the Vengeance bombers came over for their first strike, some low cloud blew up Zubza Valley, and slowly rolled over

Garrison Hill. However, twenty minutes later, a message reached John Grover, in his tactical headquarters overlooking the battlefield, that the strike had been successful, the sky to the east being clear. During this time, the tanks supporting the Durham Light Infantry for their attack on F.S.D. Ridge were rumbling round the corner beyond the D.C.'s bungalow, to come down the back of the objective. Meanwhile the leading infantry companies were moving across country to link up with them, which they succeeded in doing. The attack went in, but immediately the troops came under fire from enemy positions on the flanks, the cloud having lifted at just the wrong moment. There was a halt while the artillery dealt with the enemy positions causing the trouble, then the attack continued, the troops scrambling as best they could up the steep slopes towards the crest of the ridge. The light tanks, having failed to get up one track succeeded with another and began firing straight into the bunkers. The whole place was honeycombed with them, many concealed in the undergrowth, and the operation was a foul one. Every bunker had to be dealt with individually, and every Jap killed individually. While this was going on, the remainder of the battalion under Lieut.-Colonel Brown were moving along the road in carriers. But rounding the corner by the D.C.'s bungalow, they came under heavy fire from the D.I.S., and Brown ordered his men to scramble out of the carriers and get into cover. They did this with great speed, and then the carriers slewed round and got away. Brown then radioed Brigadier Shapland to tell him what had happened, to be ordered to withdraw through the Dorsets on to Garrison Hill. Brown barely had time to put these orders into effect, than a Jap 75-mm. gun opened up and he was killed immediately. The battalion was now without a commanding officer, and remained so till late that evening.

By the time of Brown's death, the two companies on F.S.D. and D.I.S. were already in trouble. One company had made its way along the ridge towards Kuki Piquet, imagining it to be in the hands of the Royal Welch Fusiliers, but it was still held by the Japs, who brought down automatic fire with murderous effect. Man after man cried out as he was hit, and rolled down the slope till he was stopped by a tree. Eventually the remnants of these companies and a company of the Royal Welch Fusiliers went to ground on the F.S.D., where their plight was desperate.

At mid-day, seeing the tanks on F.S.D. Ridge, Shapland decided to put in an attack on Kuki Piquet with the Royal Welch Fusiliers. Support was given by the brigade mortars, who put down a concentration of devastating accuracy, then two companies advanced to the attack. Immediately they came under heavy fire and several officers were hit; every Jap position was supported by several others, and they were all untouched by the mortar fire. If the companies had advanced further they would have been wiped out and the only course was to withdraw. Even so, the losses were heavy, and the wounded lying out in the open could not be brought in. One platoon, however, did secure a lodgement on the end of F.S.D. and, after dark, two other platoons went forward to reinforce it. Here, though harassed by snipers, they managed to scrape shallow holes with their entrenching tools, and kept hanging on. Fortunately, the tanks were able to help them.

While this desperate fighting was going on along the whole ridge, the Dorsets were carrying their epic 'battle of the tennis court' to a new phase. About mid-day, Major Ezra Rhodes brought his tank along the road, rounded the I.G.H. Spur, and the sharp corner by the road junction, where a company of Dorsets was still holding on, and, guided by Jock Murrills, made for the drive up to the bungalow. Though attempt after attempt had failed, Rhodes was now confident that he would succeed, as Murrills knew every inch of the ground. Slowly the nose of the tank slewed round, and pointed up the drive. A change of gears and it lurched forward and slowly, haltingly, began finding its way up the slope, changing course awkwardly in the confined space, but somehow keeping to the drive. It was halfway up, three-quarters, farther than any tank had been before. Then it reached the top. Breathlessly in their trenches, a company of Dorsets waited. Then, as the tank advanced towards the bungalow, blasting the bunkers as it went, they leapt into the open and charged forward. At first the Japs were confused, and lost heavily as the shells tore into their bunkers. But then the posts sunk into the bank came alive, and the infantry suffered casualties and had to withdraw. Then the tank, which was having great difficulty in manœuvring itself with the hatches down in such awkward territory, had to retire also. Though robbed of success, this was by far the most promising 'set' in the tennis court battle so far; even before the smoke had drifted away, the Dorsets were busy planning another for the next morning.

Even by 1500 hours Grover was getting anxious about the men on F.S.D. and D.I.S., and told Shapland to start laying on defensive fire tasks, and to send wire forward. At 1630 hours, he also gave orders that a troop of tanks should stay forward, helping the men of the Royal Welch Fusiliers to hold Kuki Piquet for the night; news that they'd come off it didn't reach him till two hours later, when Shapland came on the line. The withdrawal was a great disappointment to Grover, as he had seen more Japs streaming down the back of Kuki Piquet, to be caught by the D.L.I., and imagined that things had gone well. However, he told Shapland that Kuki Piquet must be won back. And he repeated his order that wire and grenades must be got forward to the men on F.S.D. immediately after dark. Acknowledging these orders, Shapland reported that the Dorsets in the D.C.'s bungalow area were now rather weak, and asked permission to withdraw them. This request Grover refused, pointing out that relief at this stage would prejudice the whole operation.

Though with the oncoming of night the battle died down in some sectors, in others it kept flaring up. Robert Scott decided that he could not get his wounded in until the large bunker ahead of his position was reduced, so put in an attack with his carrier platoon. This dealt with part of the position, but then came under heavy fire from bunkers lower down the slope, which hadn't previously been located. The platoon commander was killed and several men, so the attack had to be called off. And the wounded from the carrier platoon lay in the open with the men who had fallen earlier.

The men of the Royal Welch Fusiliers, clinging to their position just below the crest of F.S.D., came under command of a quiet, unassuming subaltern called Ogburn. Before dark a tank had worked its way up to the position, but on the orders of Brigadier Shapland it had been withdrawn. The brigade mortars were then put on instant call, and when the Japs started attacking Ogburn rang up Colonel Braithwaite, asking for D.F. fire, which came down in a matter of seconds. It was so close, though, that Braithwaite thought that some of the shells must have landed in Ogburn's position so rang him up, asking:

'Are you all right, Ogburn?'

'Yes, fine. Thank you, sir.'

'That D.F. fire was pretty close, wasn't it?'

'Yes, sir. Bloody close—but bloody comforting.'

So Ogburn held on. During the night there was a curious incident when a Major from another unit made his way up to the position and ordered him to withdraw. Being somewhat doubtful, Ogburn rang Braithwaite, who in turn rang up Shapland. The brigadier's reply was very short and to the point: 'Get that Major on the line and tell him to place himself under command of Lieutenant Ogburn. Tell him also that if he moves an inch I will court-martial him. The position must be held.' And so it was.

Just before dusk the Camerons had begun withdrawing from Hunter's Hill. When Colin Hunter returned to his company, after giving Peter Saunders his report, it was to find that the position had deteriorated even further. One of his officers, Bill McKillop, had been hit in the throat, and many more men had been killed or wounded. Waiting till the covering fire came down, the Camerons began filtering down the hill and across the saddle. Here the fire was quite heavy, and more men were hit, before the company was in the relative safety of the position dug by men of 'B' Company. This was on the oval, terraced feature called Church Knoll. Here things were not a great deal better, as the Japs kept sniping and mortaring. To begin with, the night was clear and bright, but later on it clouded over, and then after midnight there was a violent thunderstorm and the rain poured down. Crouching in their shallow trenches, the troops were hungry, thirsty, and wet—and still the mortar shells kept exploding among them. When the deluge finished, the mist rolled down the bill, and the Japs chose this moment to come into the attack. They were in great strength, and despite the gallant efforts of the mixed force of Camerons and Fusiliers, part of the position was overrun. In the darkness and mist, as so often in this battle, the fighting became close and confused; and among the shouting, the firing, and the cries of the wounded, it was difficult to make out what was going on. Colin Hunter and his company headquarters eventually found themselves with no one in front of them, and it was quite obvious that the Japanese had got on to the position in strength. In the darkness and confusion it was found impossible to organize a counter-attack, and by daylight it was seen that the enemy were in occupation of the Knoll. In this action thirty-eight men of the Camerons were killed or wounded, and the Lancashire Fusiliers suffered heavily also.

The Japanese mortar section had not confined their efforts to Hunter's Hill; the main position on Naga Village was bombed also, and brigade headquarters received special attention. Lieut.-Colonel Harry Grenfell, of the 10th Field Regiment, was badly wounded by one of the mortar bombs. In his command post, Victor Hawkins was becoming increasingly concerned about the fighting on the eastern sector. The attack was a heavy one, as he could tell, and all he could do was hope that somehow it would be held. Then he heard feet running past his dug-out, and put his head up to discover that the Jocks were going by. At this point, he did not know that Saunders had sanctioned the withdrawal, so formed up his brigade-major and staff to man the broken stretch of perimeter. Later he heard from Peter Saunders that the Jocks had lost their way in the darkness, but were being shepherded together and reorganized. (Actually, parties of Jocks and Fusiliers were streaming back into the perimeter all the next day.) The remaining hours of darkness seemed very long; but the Japs were content with gaining Church Knoll and did not attempt to penetrate any further. When the sun came up over Pulebadze the two battalions were still firm on the ground; and Hawkins gave orders for the Worcestershires to come forward.

Summing up the day's battle, the hardest and bloodiest his division had yet experienced, Grover wrote: '5th Brigade's night march in between located enemy positions was an epic performance. When the news reached me, I could hardly believe it.... 4th Brigade's march over the Naga hills and through untracked dense jungle is also an epic... its attack this afternoon was magnificent—Willie Goschen can't say enough for the determination of the Norfolks and for Robert Scott's personal leadership.... 6th Brigade seem a bit under the weather—their plans for F.S.D. and Kuki Piquet went badly wrong, owing to enemy machine-gun sniping....' Jail Hill, one of the main Japanese positions, hadn't yet been reached, and the fighting in the centre would obviously be harder yet.

Altogether though, despite some reverses, the courage and the dash of the division had been tremendous. Grover could feel proud of his men.

*

The problem which faced the Royal Norfolk on the morning of the 5th May was the large bunker which had defied capture by the Carrier Platoon the previous night. It lay across the track down to the road and, until it could be reduced, the only route for bringing in supplies and evacuating the wounded was the one used by the battalion in the assault. This was long, exposed, and open to ambush by enemy patrols. The bunker could not, however, be attacked with any real hope of success before its contours had been plotted in more detail and Captain Randle therefore decided to carry out a patrol, which he did with great courage, and plotted the routes for each of the three platoons. The attack was then timed for dawn on the 6th. On the whole it was a quiet day for the Royal Norfolk, after their exertions on the previous day. However, the sniping went on, and soon after a subaltern had been killed, Henry Conder, the second-in-command, was hit in the arm and leg. Refusing to be evacuated, he lay for some hours in a slit trench pretending to read Robert Scott's pocket Shakespeare. To all enquiries, he replied that he wasn't badly hit at all, and was just having a rest. However, as his wounds stiffened and the pretence was getting harder to maintain, Captain Mather gave him a shot of morphia and he was carried away on a stretcher.

For the last twenty-four hours, Brigadier Warren and 161st Brigade had been pressing forward on Congress Hill to make contact with 4th Brigade, but by noon had failed. The supply position was getting increasingly urgent; even the signs for the R.A.F. could not be put out because of snipers. Some time during the 5th, C.Q.M.S. Huckvale reached the unit, having trekked round from Khonoma. He had great news of the supplies waiting on the road—if only the battalion could reach them. Sadly the Norfolks told him about the bunker.

In the afternoon of the 5th, the Worcestershires successfully rejoined 5th Brigade in Naga Village, and began digging in on the eastern sector of the perimeter, facing Church Knoll. This regiment had a great knack of making itself comfortable, and soon (according to Major Elliott) 'we built strong bunkers with thick head-covers, which proved most effective, as some bunkers had direct hits from 75s, but the occupants were uninjured. Each bunker held three or four men with sleeping quarters below ground. The cooking was done by platoons, and some of the cookhouses were below ground.' Despite these tendencies towards domesticity, the men of the Worcestershires were left in no doubt as to their duty, and each section had a copy of Victor Hawkins's Special Order of the Day:

> 'On no account will anyone retire from their positions if the area gets overrun by the Japanese. If they infiltrate into the position, they will be left and dealt with by the bayonet at the first opportunity. This hill must be held at all costs.'

During the day Hawkins, with the help of Major Ken Daniells of the sappers, began reconnoitring a new route across the Zubza valley for evacuating the wounded and bringing in supplies. The R.A.F. were already coming over, and most of their drops landed inside the perimeter, but nevertheless a mule track was badly needed. Hawkins also had a shave, having found a moment to glance in the mirror to see 'an old greybeard' staring at him. Now he understood why the Worcestershires had been grinning at him as they marched in.

Though things were quieter with the flanking brigades, in the centre 6th Brigade fought on to try and achieve what it had failed to do on the 4th April. The Royal Berkshire and the Durham Light Infantry on Garrison Hill and F.S.D. were now so depleted that they had to be merged into a composite battalion, and the 4th/7th Rajputs from 161st Brigade had to be sent forward to reinforce them. During the morning the tanks of 149th Regiment R.A.C. succeeded in rounding the D.C.'s bungalow corner again, and running down the back of the position to get into the F.S.D. Expecting this move, the Japs had erected an elaborate road block, and covered it with mines, and some time elapsed before this was cleared. However, the tanks got into the F.S.D. again and carried out great execution, blowing four machine-guns out of the Water Tank bunker, and destroying some other positions. One Jap who ran out towards the tanks to hurl grenades at them received a shell to himself.

It had been hoped that the tanks had also dealt successfully with the remaining bunkers on Kuki Piquet, so the Royal Welch Fusiliers were launched into the attack again, under cover of mortar smoke. One company worked round the far side of the hill to mop up the snipers, while the other went for Kuki Piquet itself. Here the Jap lay doggo until the attackers had gone past, then began shooting them in the back from some concealed bunkers. It was now evident that the enemy had dug himself in to the lower convex slopes of Garrison Hill, below our forward posts, so that nothing could touch him. As Grover recorded somewhat wryly that night: 'They certainly are experts at siting defensive positions.' The Royal Welch Fusiliers lost fifty men, and achieved almost nothing. The battalion casualties including killed, wounded, and missing were already 189, and that figure included eighteen officers. And the Japs were still as strongly entrenched as ever. The battle in the centre was developing into a long nightmare of attrition and death.

The only bright spot in the centre, in fact, was the next set in the tennis court battle, played by the Dorsets. Coming round again in their tank, and mounting the drive to the D.C.'s bungalow, Rhodes and Murrills found that the Japs had profitably spent the previous night in digging a ditch across it. Fortunately, however, it wasn't quite long enough, and, after some masterly manœuvring, the tank managed to avoid the ditch and drive up towards the tennis court. Again, the men of 'B' Company, now under Dick Purser, leapt from the trenches and surged forward to reach the enemy bunkers. Some of them succeeded in getting inside the bungalow, and hunted the Japs from room to room, killing ten of them. But after this things began going wrong; the Lee tank couldn't find a way up the bank on to the tennis court, nor could it depress its guns sufficiently to deal with a machine-gun post which held up further advance by the infantry. So again, a retreat had to be ordered. This raid, however, like the others before it, increased the Dorsets' knowledge of the Jap position considerably, and they were still confident that, given time, the battle would be won. But close positional warfare, whether in the Ypres salient or the Kohima perimeter, is a costly business, and the daily wastage through casualties, even though the regiment was not engaged in any major action, was considerable. A reorganization had to be carried out to allow the unit to remain in action.

Just before ten o'clock, Brigadier Wood arrived at John Grover's headquarters to discuss the situation, before reporting back to the Corps Commander. One of the first things that Grover had to tell him was that he was fast running out of troops, and unless reinforcements could be found it would be impossible to carry on. They then went on to discuss the further operations against the F.S.D., Kuki Piquet and Jail Hill, Grover mentioning that he could not attack the latter till the 9th May, as Stopford had asked him to sort out his battalions into their correct brigades, and this would take a couple of days. The Lancashire Fusiliers, which belonged to 4th Brigade, were now with 5th Brigade; the Dorsetshires, which belonged to the 5th Brigade, were now with the 6th; and 4th Brigade now had only two battalions. During the rapid and complex moves at the beginning of the battle, it had been inevitable that the units should become mixed up; but no one was happy about it. The brigadiers had trained their formations to work as a team, and each brigade had its own character. Hawkins, in particular, was badly missing the Dorsets, and wanted to get them back.

About noon, Brigadier Wood phoned Stopford to give him a resume of the discussions. Stopford accepted Grover's plan in principle, but absolutely refused to wait another four days for the attack on Jail Hill. On being informed of the reasons for the delay, Stopford announced that Brigadier Loftus Tottenham would be coming forward at once with the remainder of the 33rd Indian Brigade, the 1st Queens and the 4th/15th Punjab. (The other battalion, the 4th/1st Gurkhas, was already on Congress Hill, under command of Brigadier Warren.) These units would provide troops for an attack by the 7th. Despite Grover's very good reasons for the proposed delay in attacking Jail Hill, and the fact that he did not know till this moment that 33rd Brigade would be coming to his aid, Stopford seems to have considered that his plan showed a want of resolution. He therefore announced that he would be going forward to 2nd Division headquarters that afternoon to see Grover in person. Relationships between Mutaguchi and Satohad already deteriorated; from now on professional relationships between Stopford and Grover were to deteriorate also.

Chapter Nine

The Black 7th

As Stopford drove forward on the afternoon of the 5th May, a squadron of Oscars roared down the valley to machine-gun the road. Fortunately an air-raid warning had just been received by the administrative boxes, and the sirens sounded. The troops enjoyed themselves thoroughly putting up a barrage of small-arms fire, and the tracer seemed so thick at times that it was a miracle that the enemy planes weren't hit. However, as the anti-aircraft fire thickened, they lost formation, then wheeled and flew back towards the east. A few casualties were caused, and some vehicles slightly damaged, but nothing very serious. Probably the raid was a morale-booster for the Japanese infantry, or at least a reminder that their air force still existed.

Once closeted with Grover, Stopford at once began impressing his viewpoint: that the Japs should be given no rest whatsoever. 4th Brigade, he considered, should start 'infiltrating down G.P.T. Ridge before daylight tomorrow and establish a strong standing patrol on Congress Hill'. The attack on Jail Hill was brought forward to the 7th, and it was to be followed two days later by an operation against Treasury Ridge, also to be carried out by 33rd Brigade. Before he left, Stopford gave Grover some important news, which he had just received by telephone from Slim the previous evening: that Major-General Frank Messervy would be arriving with 7th Indian Division headquarters. He would take over 33rd Brigade (which belonged to his division), 23rd L.R.P. Brigade, which was still operating on the left flank of the 2nd Division, and would also be allotted 268th Indian Brigade, and the Lushai Brigade. The battle could then be fought on a two-division front, as it should have been from the beginning, had the size of the Japanese threat not been so underestimated. Grover received the news with great satisfaction; not only because the arrival of Frank Messervy would take a great load off his shoulders; but also because with two divisions to administer, the Corps staff would be more fully employed. As things had been so far, with the anomalous situation of a Corps commanding *one* division and attached troops, Grover felt he had the staff on his neck.

As Stopford left, Loftus Tottenham arrived. According to an officer who knew him well: 'He was a fine-looking man with a strong and forceful personality. He had a delightful sense of humour and a fund of risqué stories. The moment you met him you realized that he was a commander. He was in no way brilliant, but he was brave and dashing.' Others have described Loftus Tottenham as 'a bulldog of a man… tenacious, stubborn'. Later in the battle, these qualities were to be put to a severe test; certainly it was fortunate that such an experienced brigade should be available at this phase of the battle. Raw troops were utterly useless at Kohima. After Tottenham came Warren, who informed Grover that as soon as Bunker Hill had been captured—the feature, it will be remembered, now facing the Royal Norfolk—there would be no difficulty in occupying Congress Hill and so securing the start line for 33rd Brigade. Plans were discussed and reconnaissances arranged. Meanwhile, the situation hinged on Robert Scott and the Royal Norfolk.

During the evening the 1st/1st Punjabs and the 4th/1st Gurkhas pushed forward to make contact with 4th Brigade; rations were taken forward and casualties were brought back. At first the men of the Punjabs objected to being detailed as 'coolies for British troops', but when they saw the number of Jap corpses lying about, their attitude changed. They carried the wounded down almost impossible muddy slopes, along tracks cut through virgin jungle. The British troops were filled with admiration for them, and for the way they kept their feet and their balance in the most appalling circumstances, never letting go of the stretchers or overturning them. As Grover noted: 'No British troops could have done that job.' This was the first contact in action between the men of the 2nd Division and top-flight Indian troops, and there can be no doubt that it did something towards creating a bond of comradeship.

Having seen the ground, Loftus Tottenham had no illusions as to the task facing his brigade. As he says: 'We were faced with clearing five or six strongly defended positions.... This filled me with some dismay as, though I knew I could rely 100 per cent on the spirit of the troops, I did not relish the prospect of returning to my Division in a highly mauled condition.' The brigade had just borne the brunt of the Ngakyedauk Pass battle in the Arakan, and had been promised 'a good rest in reserve in the Assam Valley' before being committed to battle again. Medically, the troops had been classified as 'suffering from malnutrition as the result of the Arakan privations', and opinion was, that September was the earliest date they could be used again. However, here they were and facing the battle for Jail Hill. Apart from the difficulties of the objective itself, which was now honeycombed with bunkers and devoid of cover, Loftus Tottenham saw that there was a great danger from his right flank where the Jap positions on the reverse slopes of G.P.T. Ridge could shoot up his troops as they went in. He therefore urged John Grover that the flank should be cleared.

The initiative, therefore, lay with 4th Brigade, and, in particular, with Robert Scott and the Royal Norfolk.

All night it rained hard, and water came coursing off the hills. Some of the troops who had taken the precaution of digging channels round their dug-outs found that these were now the size of small rivers. The whole scene was sodden, desolate, and depressing in the extreme. However, the platoons of the Royal Norfolk, which had been detailed for the attack on Bunker Hill, went in as planned, helped by covering fire by the Brens and machine-guns on their northern flank. The general plan was that once the nearest bunker had been captured, the two leading platoons should exploit this success down the flanks. But what hadn't been realized was that a whole series of linked positions ran down the spine of the ridge towards the road. The left-hand platoon captured the first bunker as planned, but the right-hand one came into heavy machine-gun fire and was pinned down. Captain Randle, the company commander, spotted the position which was causing the trouble, and decided to go for it himself with rifle and bayonet. All that was visible was the narrow slit to the bunker, and Randle ran straight for it. Inevitably he was hit time and again as the Japs opened up on him at point-blank range, but somehow he went on, till he reached the edge of the bunker. Here, in a last act of self-sacrifice, he fell with his body across the slit, temporarily depriving the enemy of their field of fire. This enabled the rest of the platoon to come forward, and soon the bunker had been wiped out. But as it came to be realized, the enemy position extended right down the ridge and in such strength that three platoons could not tackle it, and the action was called off. It had been short, but costly. However, as usual, the dash and bravery shown by all ranks of the Royal Norfolk had been quite remarkable; Randle was awarded the V.C., and two other decorations were won.

The problem was, though, that the remaining bunkers still covered Jail Hill; and it was obvious that before Loftus Tottenham's men went into action, another attempt must be made to deal with them.

Apart from this action on Bunker Hill, the 6th May was for the most part spent in reconnaissance, administration, bringing forward supplies and ammunition, and an effort to relieve some troops and disentangle others. The Durham Light Infantry were relieved by the Royal Berkshires, and went back to Dimapur for a rest. 'A' Company of the Dorsets went down too; and the 4th Rajputs moved into Kohima to strengthen the garrison. The day was also notable for the fact that a staff officer from 33rd Corps, Brigadier Wood, went on to Garrison Hill for the first time to see conditions there. He reported them to be 'indescribably beastly, with masses of Jap dead and innumerable trenches and dug-outs which make it impossible to know the exact spots occupied by Japs until they should be induced to fire.' He also observed that these conditions 'would make mopping-up extremely slow'. Grover, who visited the place again, after an interval of some days, noted, however, that 'a good deal of clearing up has been done....' He took the opportunity to speak to the troops who looked to him very cheery, though 'they were badly in need of a wash and clean-up. They all have beards.' Though it was now three weeks since the siege had been lifted, there was such an acute water shortage that washing and shaving were still impossible.

Personal hygiene, in fact, was a great problem all through the battle. In many areas it was even impossible to take off one's socks and shoes; Colonel Bickford of the Royal Berkshires noted that when his unit was relieved from Garrison Hill he 'had not loosened his shoe laces for twenty days'. In these circumstances, it was impossible to change pants or vests, usually considered a daily necessity in the tropics, and battle-dresses got caked with mud, sweat, filth, and blood. They also got torn through the constant movement through jungle, but had to be worn till replacements could be brought up, and an opportunity could be found to change. As a result everyone stank. Gradually, one got used to one's own smell, except occasionally on bending down, but the smell of other people was almost insufferable. It was quite common for officers to meet and talk, both start sniffing suspiciously, then realize that one was as bad as the other. Often it was impossible to deliver toilet paper to the forward troops, which meant that they had to make the best arrangements they could, and as there was no water to wash their hands with after defecating, a steady deterioration in hygienic standards was inevitable. This is not to say that everyone concerned did not make the greatest possible effort to help the troops in this respect; they undoubtedly did. But the circumstances of this battle made all such arrangements very difficult. As the weeks went by and as the flies kept multiplying, dysentery swept through the whole division. Hundreds of men went sick; even more remained on duty, though feeling wretched. From the early days of the battle, a bath unit had set itself up at Zubza, and this proved a boon to the troops whenever they could get back. To increase the bathing accommodation, forty-gallon oil drums were slit in half and served very well. To see fifty or sixty men all lying back in them, luxuriating in the hot water, and singing their lungs out, was a wonderful sight.

Also at Zubza was a canteen, where the troops could purchase toilet requisites, chocolate, cigarettes, and a limited amount of beer. Some of these stores were sent forward to the men in action, the purchase being initially paid for out of brigade and regimental funds. Even 5th Brigade, supplied by the mule column and the Naga porters, were kept provisioned with canteen materials. Also every tin of rations dropped by the R.A.F. contained cigarettes which were very welcome. Unfortunately, after the drops had been going on for about three weeks, a genius in G.H.Q. India worked out a bill for the total amount of cigarettes dropped, and sent it to 5th Brigade headquarters. Here the staff captain asked Victor Hawkins what he should do about it, to be told: 'You can tell G.H.Q. that until the Japs have paid for the proportion they've got, we shan't consider paying for ours.' This reply was sent on and provoked a rather stern document from a gentleman in Delhi. This in turn was sent to John Grover and nothing more was heard; but it was understood that the government had agreed to pay for the cigarettes, both those smoked by our troops and by the enemy.

While dealing with behind-the-lines matters, and especially with correspondence, it may be worthwhile mentioning the flood of paper which hit the division from behind, once news had percolated through to the various Commands that it was in action. At one sticky moment in the battle, the staff captain 5th Brigade noted that the following mail reached him by mule column:

1. The Pay Office wanted to know the authority by which the brigade paid wet sweepers Rs25 per month at Galunche in 1943.
2. No. 83 Sub-area wanted to know what the brigade did with three tables on loan at Mahableshwar in October 1942.
3. Legal Aid wanted Private Smith speaking to as he wasn't writing to his wife. [Smith had been dead three weeks.]
4. Divorce papers in respect of Private Brown came back as one deletion hadn't been initialled.
5. The Railway Accounts Branch wrote to say that when Sergeant Jones travelled from Poona to Ooticomund in March 1943 the warrant wasn't marked 'by the quickest route'. They were therefore charging by the longest route and would like Rs57 As8.
6. Forces Radio wanted two men from Coventry to broadcast home.
7. Two cooks were wanted for a cooking course.

There were also, in this batch, three courts-martial at various stages of development, nine pamphlets, a brochure on how to make apple dumplings, and the War Establishments for most unlikely units. As the battle dragged on, no opportunity offered itself to staff officers and adjutants for dealing with such paper matters, their volume increased to appalling dimensions. The issue tin boxes were crammed to suffocation, and sandbags were then stuffed full. A favourite dodge was to leave these in the open, hoping that they'd be destroyed by enemy action; but the curious thing was that however thick the mortar shells came down, and whatever else was hit, the paper remained inviolate. And when the boxes or sacks were put on mules, they were the ones which never went over the khud. (Conversely, mules carrying rum or anything important were always the most accident-prone.)

Apart from such unwelcome paper as that listed above, the battle, of course, generated its own. Apart from situation reports, and intelligence summaries, there were casualty returns, all the documentation involved in promotions, citations for awards, and letters to relatives of the fallen. More than one commanding officer, after a hard day's fighting, would swear horribly as his adjutant brought a stack of paper work into his dug-out. If a brigade or a unit was out of touch for even a few days, the mail multiplied fantastically. It was not uncommon for 5th Brigade to receive fifteen to twenty mule loads of it, and 4th Brigade, after their chukka round Pulebadze, had some tons. At all times tremendous efforts were made to get mail to the forward troops.

Many officers had standing orders for newspapers and magazines which arrived with amazing regularity. Devotees to *The Times* crossword carried on as usual, though a few days in arrears; what infuriated them more than anything, though, was when the issues crossed, and they received the solution to a puzzle before the puzzle itself. Sometimes, if a clue seemed more than usually tantalizing, these devotees would risk life and limb to consult a brother officer in a neighbouring slit trench. A newspaper which came daily and free was *Seac,* the 14th Army paper edited by Frank Owen, with its ebullient leader headed 'Good morning'. It is fashionable to make fun of these wartime service papers now, and certainly, if glanced at today, their tone does strike one as somewhat brash, and artificially hearty. But *Seac* was doing a specialized job, and on the whole it did it very well.

These comforts were very welcome and much-prized; but they were few, and, now the rain had set in, life was very uncomfortable indeed. About this time an officer wrote:

> 'Apart from flooding roads and rendering jeep tracks unjeepable, it has a bad effect on the morale of the troops. The infantry, as usual, get the worst of it. Living in water-logged slit trenches, their boots sodden, their food, when they get it, cold and mushy, life rapidly becomes intolerable. In the forward areas, groundsheets and gas capes are the men's only protection and they are useless against the torrential rains. The men are therefore compelled to sleep in wet blankets on the slushy ground. It's amazing how they keep going.'

The cooks, as in most armies, were a tower of strength, and whenever the tactical situation permitted would go forward to their companies and prepare a hot meal. Warm food inside one's belly in these circumstances is one of the most marvellous feelings a man can have. The rations themselves remained remarkably varied, even when delivered by air-drop. On the 14th May, for example, the semi-beleaguered 5th Brigade had the following for lunch: sardines, beetroot, peas, tinned pears, biscuits, butter, jam, and tea. In the evening there was a stew with meat and potatoes. This couldn't be called luxurious, but, compared to the food British troops have endured in previous wars, it was plentiful and varied.

The plight of the wounded has been touched on before, especially with reference to 4th Brigade. Though there was a good deal of rain before they finished their 'hook' and attacked G.P.T. Ridge, conditions then were nothing like as bad as they became later on, when the rain poured down steadily, day after day. By then 4th Brigade and 6th Brigade fortunately had a firm link to the road, but 5th Brigade, up in Naga Village, still had to rely on the Nagas and the precipitous trail across the Zubza valley. Of the situation in mid-May, the staff captain wrote:

> '... having been patched up at the A.D.S., the wounded must endure the nightmare three-hour journey down the precipitous slope into the nala, and across it, and up on to the road. This, on a swaying stretcher carried by four faithful Nagas, often as not under mortar fire. Then a forty-three-mile trip by ambulance down the tortuous road into the torrid heat of Dimapur. Then later on a two-day journey by train to Shillong or Chittagong. Then God knows what. Am continually amazed at the patience of the troops; they he still beneath the blankets, white with pain, but uncomplaining. It's a miracle that so many survive.'

The trail across the Zubza valley, it should be noted, was not only used to bring wounded down, but to take supplies up. Usually trouble was taken to see that the two columns didn't meet, but on at least one occasion they did. The track at this point was narrow, and flanked on one side by a cliff face and the other by the khud. Understandably the doctor leading the wounded column wanted the mules to go back but that was impossible, the track being too narrow for them to turn. The only solution, therefore, was to ask the Pathans to edge their mules against the cliff face, and hope they'd stay docile, without lashing out with their hind legs; then to see if the Nagas could squeeze past them. As there were about seventy mules, this meant that each wounded man had seventy chances of being kicked to his death, which rather lengthened the odds against the whole party surviving. However, the Pathans spoke gently to their charges in a language they understood, and slowly the column quietened down. Then, at a signal from the column commander, the grinning Nagas eased forward with the first stretcher, gripped the cliff edge with their toes, and shuffled happily along it. Then the next party came... and the next. Within half an hour all the wounded were past the mule column and on their way towards the nala.

At Kohima this kind of crisis and improvisation occurred almost daily in the business of evacuating wounded; and every time, the Nagas did what was demanded of them. How many lives were owed to the courage and skill of these remarkable hillmen will never be known; but the figure must certainly run into thousands.

A vivid and accurate description of the life of an ordinary Jock in the 5th Brigade box, up at Naga Village, was written, while still in action, by Major W. B. Graham, of the Camerons.

> 'He is awakened by a shake, while it is still dark. He is fully clothed, and probably has been for weeks. He does not sit up because the roof of the fox-hole is only two feet from the floor. Instead, he slides forward to his stand-to post, where the floor has been deepened. The other two or three occupants of the fox-hole are doing the same thing, pushing aside the slightly sodden blankets they have been sharing. One is already awake, as he was the last on 'stag' or sentry. If possible, there should never be fewer than four in a fox-hole, or stag comes round too often. Even with four it comes round twice in a night, as it is forbidden to do more than one hour consecutively.
>
> Equipment on, rifle or automatic in the hand, grenades ready, all are now staring out into the blackness.... In fifteen minutes it will be first light... and fifteen minutes after that it will be stand-down, that is, unless the mist fails to clear.

But all being well, they can mount a single sentry at, say quarter past five, and the day has started.

No one, however, gets out of his fox-hole, though it may be cramped and hurriedly dug. Fox-holes are all inter-supporting and integral parts of a defensive position, but in a way they are independent units. There should be no movement between them by night, and as little as possible by day. One man may have to crawl outside to perch over the hole dug to meet the needs of nature. Another will be preparing the morning 'brew' with the aid of a Tommy-cooker, a tin with petrol or meth, as fuel. It is the only method of cooking allowed when in contact with the enemy.

The arrival of the ration columns, whether by coolie, mule, motor transport, or plane, is the main event of the day, not only because the actual rations are so important, but because along with them comes the mail, the rum issue, and *Seac,* the Army newspaper. Mail is received like manna, for it is the only link with another world.... In the early morning, however, the arrival of the rations is in the vague future. The first business of the day is to get organized. Then, if there is nothing doing, rest. Always rest—at any moment it may cease to be possible....'

But to return to the main stream of events.

All day on the 6th there were meetings and discussions about the coming attack. Loftus Tottenham was more concerned than ever about his right flank, and about three o'clock went forward with Lieut.-Colonel Grimshaw (who had now taken over the 1st/1st Punjab), Lieut.-Colonel Goode, of 149th R.A.C., and John Grover, to look at the ground. It was now agreed that G.P.T. Ridge must be cleared to join with Congress Hill before the main operations for the capture of Pimple Hill and Jail Hill could be launched. After the reconnaissance was over, John Grover worked out the following plan: the Punjabs were to clear the bashas in front of their position and move forward to contact the Royal Scots on Congress Hill; a company of the Gurkhas would then pass through the Punjabs and, in co-operation with the Royal Scots, would clear G.P.T. Ridge; after that had been done the Punjabs would occupy Congress Hill; and then the Queens would capture Pimple Hill and Jail Hill. The operation was somewhat complicated, and dependent on close co-operation and accurate timing; but it was the best that could be arranged in the time.

It poured with rain all night, and the troops, bivouacked on the sodden slopes, got little sleep. The Queens especially, who had just moved forward, had a miserable time of it; and movement was more difficult than ever.

However, soon after dawn, the Gurkhas and the company of Royal Scots detailed to clear the remaining bunkers on G.P.T. Ridge began preparations for the attack. A bazooka barrage went down on the Gurkhas' objective, from forty yards range, but had little apparent effect. P.I.A.T.s (a form of spring mortar) were tried, grenades and concentrated machine-gun fire, after which the 2-inch mortars put down a smoke screen and, under cover of this, Captain R. F. Gibson-Smith, his company officer, 2nd-Lieutenant Rae, a havildar and eight sepoys charged the first bunker. Gibson-Smith was killed and Rae wounded almost immediately, and three of the Gurkhas were knocked out also. Lieut.-Colonel Hedderwick then seems to have decided that a pincer movement would have to be launched, covered by the bazookas; and as the company had no British officers left, said he would lead the attack himself. But no sooner had he moved forward from one of the Norfolk trenches, which he was using as a command post, than his brilliant green shirt attracted a sniper's attention, and he was shot through the chest. At this, Brigadier Goschen's orderly (a Grenadier guardsman) jumped out of his trench, rushed forward to seize Hedderwick, and pull him into cover. Before he succeeded in doing so, however, the sniper got him too. Then Goschen ran forward, seized hold of his dying orderly and under heavy fire began dragging him back to the trench. But the inevitable happened and Goschen was shot. Robert Scott, who had been standing in the same trench, rushed to him and succeeded in carrying him back, but in a few minutes he died in Scott's arms, without regaining consciousness.

Altogether, the Gurkhas' attack on the bunker, gallant as it was, had led to disaster. As the men were now leaderless, an officer of 4th Brigade ordered them back.

The occupation of Congress Hill had gone according to plan and by 1100 hours, the news of the Gurkhas' failure had not reached Loftus Tottenham or Grover. According to one account, the former said at this time that 'he considered the 4th/1st Gurkhas were adequately dominating G.P.T. Ridge', and agreed that the Queens should commence their advance at 1130 hours, an hour later than originally planned. So at noon the divisional artillery opened up, and for twenty-five minutes the shells roared overhead to explode on Pimple Hill, then Jail Hill. The concentration was so heavy that the whole area shook. Great columns of earth shot into the air and the trees splintered and fell. As the concentration came to an end, the Queens moved forward, 'C. Company under Major Rothery in the lead. By noon they were firm on Pimple Hill and 'B' and 'D' Companies began to advance through them for the attack on Jail Hill. The plan was to push one platoon up the right-hand side of the hill, and two platoons up the left, but these hadn't climbed far before fire was poured at them from both flanks. The Japs still had some bunkers on the rear slopes of the D.I.S., which brought machine-gun fire to bear, and there was a minor spur running down to the south-east of G.P.T. Ridge where they were dug in too. Neither area was accessible to artillery or mortars. Inevitably the men of the Queens began falling, their bodies rolling down the bare hillside, or being caught by the tree stumps, but the rest went on with amazing courage. They sought out the bunkers and began dealing with them methodically, though the apertures were hard to find, and the extent of the defences beneath the ground they couldn't guess. Though hit in the arm, Sergeant Burt led his men against one bunker. They captured it; and he immediately led them on to the next, but here he was hit by a grenade which the Japs had rolled down the hill. This time the wound was in the neck, but, lying on the ground, bleeding and in great pain, he shouted: 'I'm paralysed down one side, but I can still throw grenades: let me have some.' He then told his men to move round a flank, while he wriggled himself forward towards the bunker, so attracting the enemy's attention by hurling grenade after grenade at them. The platoon surged forward and captured the bunker, but by the time they got back to Sergeant Burt he was dead.

Despite local successes, however, the situation was deteriorating rapidly, and it was becoming clear that if 'D' Company and 'A' Company which were now supporting them stayed on the hill much longer they would be wiped out. The Japs had brought a 75-mm. gun into action, and were shelling both Jail Hill and Pimple Hill. At 1400 hours, Major Shaw rang up his battalion commander, Lieut.-Colonel Duncombe, and said: 'My right platoon's held up almost at the bottom of the hill and is taking casualties. The other two platoons have reached the top but are having a terrible time, under heavy cross-fire. Only fourteen men are unwounded.' A further report showed that 'A' Company's position was just as bad; they were only a quarter of the way up the hill, but even so suffered from the devastating fire from both flanks. Duncombe reported the situation to Loftus Tottenham, who got on to the gunners and they did their best. But with the Japs dug into the reverse slopes there was nothing for it but to bring the Queens back. At 1500 hours Loftus Tottenham gave the necessary order, and the gunners succeeded in smoking out the whole area on the flanks. Slowly, and carrying their wounded, the Queens withdrew from Jail Hill and then from Pimple Hill; the failure was bitter, and costly.

At four o'clock Loftus Tottenham and Duncombe came to report to Grover, and the action was discussed. It was clear that earlier assessments of the position on G.P.T. Ridge had been both optimistic and inaccurate. Keeping the Japs there occupied was not enough; they would have to be wiped out. And something would have to be done, too, about the D.I.S. Loftus Tottenham was of the opinion that the bunker where Hedderwick and Goschen had been killed 'could not be taken by mere assault... somehow it would have to be blasted out of existence.' Grover sent a message to Robert Scott asking his advice on this point, to discover that he agreed absolutely. The bunker was covered, he said, 'by sniper posts both behind and dug right in under Bunker Hill'. In view of this Grover arranged to send Lifebuoy flamethrowers to 4th Brigade, to see if they would help.

But there were some things worrying Scott, who was now temporarily commanding the brigade, even more than bunkers; and they were food and water. The latter was practically finished, and the troops' rations would run out at breakfast the following morning. The trouble was that the Japs had built bunkers and sniper posts along the jungle track which had been cut to 4th Brigade, and the mule columns couldn't get through. Grover therefore contacted Loftus Tottenham who undertook to supply a company of Gurkhas as porters and some Punjabis as escort. These were to be pushed through that evening by another route.

Arrangements were put in hand at once and the supplies brought forward to a loading point. The Gurkhas took two 2-gallon tins each, or the equivalent in rations, and headed towards G.P.T. Ridge. Meanwhile, a liaison officer from Robert Scott reached Grover with a message, emphasizing the serious situation facing 4th Brigade. The men were very fit and cheery, this said, but definitely weakening. They hadn't had a hot meal for ten days. Fortunately, a later message arrived to say that the supply column had got through with 100 gallons of water in tins, and rations.

Temporarily the position was saved; but if the brigade was going to find strength to clear Bunker Hill, and the remaining enemy positions down to the road, some more comprehensive arrangement obviously had to be made, and in the evening Grover called a conference to thrash things out. At this it was agreed that the sappers should cut a new mule route, under the protection of 33rd Brigade, that supplies and wire should be pushed through to the Royal Norfolk area, and casualties should be evacuated by the following evening.

Lastly, Grover saw Colonel Duncombe and asked him to pass his warmest thanks to all ranks of the Queens for their gallantry on Jail Hill.

*

The 7th May and the three days that followed were probably the bitterest time in the whole battle of Kohima. After thirty-four days and nights of close and bloody fighting, after hunger, thirst, discomfort, after appalling casualties, the enemy still held the main bastions of their position. No bombs, shells, mortars, flame-throwers, or grenades could seem to shift them. The 3.7 howitzers, which could have reached many of their positions, were silent through lack of ammunition; and no amount of railing, correspondence, argument, or anything else, could produce any. The Japs had lost thousands upon thousands of men, and reports kept saying they were weak and diseased, and running short of ammunition. But all the British, Gurkha, and Indian troops knew was that as soon as they got near a bunker, the fire poured out of it just as mercilessly as ever. The British battalions were now reduced to three or four hundred men; some had less.

Few could muster four nominal rifle companies. All were desperately short of officers; and platoon commanders were almost non-existent. It would be untrue to say that the division faltered; but in these days, officers and men would sometimes look at the great ring of mountains encircling them, and wonder how on earth it could be taken, how flesh and blood could possibly stand much more... and how things would end. Everyone now had some friends buried on the black ridge of Kohima or in the hills flanking it; a good many people had lost all their friends there. Also, for every man killed, three or four had disappeared into distant hospitals and would not be seen again for months, if ever. Altogether there was a growing feeling of desolation.

The curious thing was, though, that despite its horrors, despite its unquenchable thirst for sacrifice, Kohima Ridge still seemed to hold a fascination. Troops coming back from the dirty, flea-bitten rest camps in Dimapur would smile, even laugh, as they trudged up Garrison Hill again and saw the familiar sights. Life as it existed before the battle now seemed very, very far away; and in some perverted manner the Ridge had become the nearest thing to home.

*

If these were black days for the Allies, they were black, too, for General Sato, as it was quite evident that the supply system had completely broken down. In private discussions with Mutaguchi before the offensive began, he had been assured that the longest period he would have to maintain his Division in its independent role was fifty days from the 15th March, that is, till the 3rd May. In a further meeting on the 15th January with Lieut.-General Kunomura, Chief Staff Officer of 15th Army, and Major Usui, the staff officer dealing with ammunition supply, the following programme had been agreed: 15th Army would undertake to supply eight tons of ammunition per day from the beginning of the operation; it would also forward 250 tons of food and stores within the first twenty-five days, that is, between the 15th March and the 8th April. Sato told Kunomura that the rations his column was carrying with them, both on the men and the pack animals, would be exhausted by the 5th April at the latest, so supplies from 15th Army would be vital after that date. Later Sato received written confirmation of these arrangements and a confirmation that after fifty days—by which time, of course, according to Mutaguchi's schedule, Imphal would have fallen—normal supply would commence along the Imphal road. On the 4th May, having received no assurances from Mutaguchi, Sato signalled General Kawabe direct, pointing out that 15th Army had failed in its responsibilities towards his Division and no supplies had arrived. (According to statements by Sato's staff, the only supplies which ever did arrive were 500 artillery shells, brought in jeeps by Major K. Takata, Commander of the Field Transport Brigade, on the 21st May. Sato, it seems, questioned Takata closely about 15th Army's intentions and asked him whether he would be given any transport. Takata replied that all the available transport had gone to 33rd Division. This statement, according to one officer, hardened Sato's determination to act as he thought fit, even against orders.) General Kawabe, not surprisingly, did not reply to Sato's signal but sent it on to Mutaguchi, who in turn told Sato in plain language that he must not signal Kawabe direct. He added that Sato would find food at Ukhrul, which the latter took to mean that supplies had been pushed forward to this point. What Mutaguchi meant, however, was that Sato would find food in the villages around that area, if he sent back foraging parties. When Sato realized this he became incensed and immediately drafted signals to Count Terauchi, Commander-in-Chief South East Asia, and even to Imperial Headquarters in Tokyo. At all costs he intended that the Army should realize the grave situation in which he had been placed.

By now Sato must have realized that his chances of taking Kohima had virtually disappeared and all he could do was hang on to his positions as long as possible. With his numerous casualties, no troops were available for Manipur and the last platoons on the high ground above Jotsoma were being withdrawn to help defend the Aradura Spur. No reinforcements had come through, and he knew that none ever would do. His battalions along the Jessami track were reporting that the 23rd L.R.P. Brigade was approaching it in six columns and nothing could prevent their cutting it. The southern track from Tuphema, on the Imphal road, was still open, but in time there was the possibility that that would be cut too.

To make matters worse, there was the complete failure of Mutaguchi and his 15th Army to capture the Imphal Plain. All the fears of Lieut.-General Yanagida and some other commanders were now being realized, and at least the suspicion must have entered Sato's mind at this time that the whole offensive was doomed. Latest intelligence reports reaching Sato indicated that not only had the advance of the 15th and 33rd Divisions come to a standstill, they were even being pressed back. To try to get things moving again, Mutaguchi had ordered Tanaka, Yanagida's successor, to break through into the plain, via Bishenpur. For this task, the 33rd Division had been reinforced by two infantry battalions, tanks, and infantry; and the target date was fixed for about the 20th May. Mutaguchi still exuded confidence; but it cannot be said that his plan for a new offensive enthused either Sato or anyone else. At this time Lieut.-General Hata, Assistant Chief of Staff at Imperial General Headquarters, who was visiting Burma, received pessimistic views, especially from officers in the administrative services, and later on his return to Tokyo he reported to Tojo that 'the Imphal operations stand little chance of success'. But Tojo had just received that morning a more favourable report from Kawabe and didn't hear Hata out.

But to return to Kohima: though Sato unquestionably maintained command of his men, a good deal of grumbling had started among the troops, who considered that his headquarters (at Chakhabama) were too far back, and that he personally did not spend as much time as he should have done in the front line. On one occasion a soldier of the 58th Regiment, who was sent back with a message, remarked on arrival: 'From this distance the battle seems like a dream.... You would not know it was going on.' The extent of the feeling is hard to assess, but certainly the troops compared Sato unfavourably with Miyazaki, who made his headquarters with regiments or even battalions, and was never far from the sound of the guns. Through this close contact Miyazaki came to know large numbers of officers and N.C.O.s by name and his personality and professional ability made an enormous impression throughout the Division. The 58th almost worshipped him.

However, whatever the dissensions or grumblings in the ranks, discipline still remained unimpaired and every position was held to the last man. It was something of a wonder to British officers to learn how few men there were in some positions. The secret was that the Japanese did not fight to their front if they could fight to a flank. This meant that they had to rely on neighbouring bunkers for the protection, that is 'to cover them', while they covered their neighbours. This system involved a good deal of training and discipline, and a consistently high standard in the siting of posts; but it did make the maximum use of fire power. British and Indian troops were psychologically incapable of such tactics, each man preferring to fight to his front and remaining responsible for his own protection. Also, of course, though recognizing the need for head cover, the British hated being entombed in bunkers and liked the free use of their weapons, denied by Japanese-type bunkers. But these bunkers did allow the Japanese to bring down mortar fire on their own positions, when under attack, and time and time again drove the

British and Indians from them before they could dig in. And in Burma the Jap mortarmen were the counterparts of the German machine-gunners in the First World War.

*

On the evening of the 8th May, Brigadier Stevens came back to 33rd Corps headquarters to report that Grover did not think he could mount a major attack against Jail Hill till the 11th. Stopford immediately got on the phone to tell Grover that this wasn't good enough; he must get on. Grover's view was that there was no sense in sending more men to be killed on the position; the remaining bunkers on G.P.T. Ridge simply had to be dealt with first, and, as Robert Scott had affirmed, they could not be taken 'by mere assault'. Grover's plan was for the Gordons of the 100th Anti-tank Regiment to take a 6-pounder to pieces, get it up on to the position, and blast the bunkers out of position one by one. But before this could be done a new track would have to be constructed and a special pit dug by the sappers. This job would take twenty-four hours, that is up to the night of the 9th, and it was hoped that the bunkers would be ours by the 10th. It was also necessary to lay on an operation against the D.I.S. and F.S.D., to be co-ordinated with the Jail Hill and Pimple Hill attack. The 11th, therefore, was the soonest the battle could be laid on. Still unhappy with the delay, Stopford said he would send Brigadier Wood the following morning with his ideas for a surprise attack within twenty-four hours.

Stopford's increasing demands for speed were understandable enough. He was expecting a visit from Slim the following day and knew that the reopening of the road was in the forefront of his mind. In fact, Slim announced that the difficulties of supplying Imphal were so great that by the end of May 4th Corps would have no reserves left. And just at that time, when more aircraft would be needed, the seventy-nine transports were due to leave for the Mediterranean front. Mountbatten might succeed in holding on to them, of course, as he had done before; nevertheless, every day that the road was cut meant a greater strain on air resources, and a greater strain on the high command. While Stopford and Slim were discussing the situation, Brigadier Wood reported back from John Grover. On examination, the latter's plan seems to have proved more reasonable; in any event, it was accepted, Stopford noting that 'it seemed to have a very good chance of success'.

The generals then turned to the role of Frank Messervy's 7th Division, which was now to start operations on the left flank, and Stopford explained that his plan was a concentric advance on Mao Songsang, the great ridge about twenty miles to the south. Messervy was to start from Naga Village and move via Chakhabama and the Kezoma–Kekrima tracks, having taken command of 161st Brigade, 33rd Brigade, and 25th Mountain Regiment. As Slim departed, Messervy arrived, and plans were discussed in more detail. But though Messervy's advance would help a great deal with the problem of reopening the road, it couldn't start until the battle of Kohima was over. And this prolonged engagement hadn't even reached the last phase.

Chapter Ten

A Hole in the Centre

At 2200 hours on the 10th, the Queens left their bivouac area to begin the approach march towards their forrning-up line, the first phase of their new attack on Jail Hill. The men were tired, even before they started, as their nights had been disturbed by Jap patrols worrying the troops in the hills above them. The weather had been good for the last twenty-four hours, but now it was turning to rain again, and the men slithered on the slippery ground, and cursed as the water trickled down their necks. The route, says Major Lowry, 'lay through thick undergrowth, up and down hundreds of feet of steep hillside', and though the distance was only a few miles, the journey took till just after 3 a.m. on the 11th. Here they waited, with the Punjabis, who were to attack the D.I.S., on their left. The latter were in great heart, recorded Major Arthur Marment, and 'anxious to avenge the death of the large number of the Queens lost a few days previously'. Their adjutant, Major R. A. J. Fowler, had translated a short passage from Shakespeare's *King John* into Urdu—'Come the three corners of the world in arms and we shall shock them. Naught shall make us rue'— which became: 'Dunia ka char kunion se larne dena, aur ham log unke kafi mardenge. Kuch bhi nahin hamko assosi denge.' This, says Marment, 'had a most tremendous effect on the troops'.

In the darkness and silence, the Queens and the Punjabis waited. Then (to quote Lowry again): 'At 0440 hours it was whistle, shriek, and screech, and everything came down with a rending crash and clatter—machine-guns, anti-tank guns, artillery and mortars—a most impressive noise. The slopes to the left, above and to our right were silhouetted by the explosions in the darkness. We had one or two shots from something, which landed in the Company, one falling behind us and one in the area, but no one was hurt....' At 0500 hours, as the barrage ceased the leading companies crossed the road and, firing from the hip as they went, the men began tackling the bunkers at the foot of the hill. The left-hand company continued to make good progress, the men crawling slowly towards the crest, but the other company found the going difficult and was pinned down. Within half an hour daylight came and things got worse. It was soon evident that the enemy positions on the reverse slopes of G.P.T. Ridge, and on F.S.D., were still held and pouring out machine-gun fire. The operation looked a repetition of the abortive affair of the 7th.

What had happened was that despite the help of the 6-inch anti-tank gun the Norfolks had still failed to eliminate the bunkers on the tip of G.P.T. Spur. On the F.S.D. the Royal Berkshires were still fighting, but though they had captured some bunkers, with the help of pole charges, the job was slow; and the Jap positions at the top of the hill and on the reverse slope were still holding out.

On the D.I.S., the Punjabis (supported by a company of Gurkhas) were having an equally difficult time. To the stirring music of their dhols and saranais (drums and pipes) playing 'The Wounded Heart', they had dashed into action, carrying their religious books with them. In the first wave went the Jats and Sikhs, their war-cries shrilling above the noise of battle, as they surged across the road ringing the D.I.S. to secure a tenuous finger-hold. Then, led by Colonel Conroy, 'Raj' Fowler, and Whitmarsh Knight, the Khataks and Punjabi Mussulmen went through them, and got up on to the hillside. Marment, who, seeing that the companies were losing men, went forward to help, says: 'It was extremely difficult... we were being hit from F.S.D. and Jail Hill and had taken 130 casualties. It was impossible to move because snipers seemed to be everywhere, and we could not make much impression on the main bunker.... We were digging with our hands, grabbing every tin to fill, and getting as tight to the ground as we possibly could.'

But to return to Jail Hill. Lowry's company on the left had succeeded in reaching the crest by 0600 hours, having shot about a dozen Japs as they ran away, but now, as Lowry records, 'movement forward was a very hard and costly business.' He goes on: 'As far as I could see there were three bunkers barring our way, and there were others firing up the hill about 100 yards distant. Under cover of grenades I took about six men forward so that we were only about eight or ten yards away from two of their bunkers....' The men began worming their way forward and got on to and inside one of the bunkers, but many of them became casualties from machine-guns on the flanks. However, by 0830 hours, Lowry's company had established themselves on the high ground and were looking down at the Japs; the other company on their right had made some progress, but did not have such good ground to move across. They were troubled, too, by a machine-gun which was firing straight down the road. Energetically trying to redeploy his forces, Lowry went back to his company headquarters and radioed for smoke to be put down on the flanks. He could not make this request via the gunner O.P., as the set had been knocked out, and the operator and the O.P. officer's runner killed. Once the smoke was coming down, Lowry began organizing an attack on the bunkers sited on the rear slope of the hill. He says: '... I started the ball rolling by whistling over some grenades, and then we all ran forward. But the terrain was not easy; horizontal tree stumps and the odd trench to negotiate. As we were going down the slope we caught the blast of about three light machine-guns and rifle fire and, of course, grenades, as we tried to negotiate the obstacles. This, I am afraid, resulted in many more men dropping; we were pinned at about ten to fifteen yards away, and there appeared to be only six or seven of us there. I halted the assault... and we took up positions in the broken ground and just took on the Japs by firing at any that showed themselves.' After this there was a sniping duel, and then the grenades started going over. 'It was the nearest approach to a snowball fight that could be imagined. The air became thick with grenades, both theirs and ours, and we were all scurrying about, trying to avoid them as they burst. This duel appeared to go on non-stop for an unreckonable time.'

At 1030 hours the four company commanders managed to get together for a conference. They decided that as the two leading companies were so weak—they could barely muster two strong platoons between them—they should consolidate the ground they had gained, while a third company attempted to work round to the left, and the fourth to dislodge the Japs from the ridge running down to the road.

All this time the stretcher-bearers were moving to and fro to get back the casualties. Some of them who crossed and recrossed the lines of fire, hour after hour without being hit, seemed to bear charmed lives.

From about 1015 hours, as Lowry recalls, 'and at odd intervals during the day, there were low sweeping clouds and mist which, of course, brought some rain. This was one of the few occasions when we welcomed this thick mist and rain, as it meant that we could move around a little without being sniped from behind us. When the sun came out for periods we had a few more casualties.... For the rest of the day we dug like beavers—everything we could find, plates, mugs, bayonets, and entrenching tools—not so much digging as it is normally done, but by making a hole and burrowing and tunnelling ourselves forward below ground level. By the evening we were completely dug in and all section posts linked up.'

At 1800 hours a company of the 4th/1st Gurkhas moved across the road to support the Queens, immediately coming under fire and losing six men. On linking up, they observed that 'the Queens had gained one-third of the north-west portion of the hill, but the rest was very strongly held by the enemy... the positions we were on were very strongly enfiladed by enemy M.G. fire. There was no cover whatsoever, and any movement was met by a hail of bullets.' Gradually the two battalions linked up and a little more ground was gained.

To help the troops dig in, Loftus Tottenham had asked John Grover that the battlefield should be smoked out till dark, and the artillery began putting down their shells. However, after an hour, reports came through from the Punjabis that their troops were being hit by the canisters, and Colonel Conroy had been hit in both arms. The smoke barrage therefore had to be called off. Fortunately, however, the heavy rain clouds came down on the ridge, giving the forward troops some relief from snipers, and the stretcher-bearers a chance to remove casualties.

At 1600 hours, a company of the 4th/15th Punjab, aided by a 6-pounder, put in an attack on a bunker at the rear of the F.S.D., which was causing trouble to the Queens. But the whole area was swept by cross-fire from light machine-guns, and it became obvious that tanks would have to be brought in to deal with the situation. The 4th/15th Punjab were therefore ordered to clear the road block between Jail Hill and D.I.S. and sappers were laid on to deal with the mines.

Only one battalion had any real luck that day: the 1st/1st Punjab, who found Pimple Hill unoccupied and dug in without interference.

All the night of the 11th it rained, and the Queens and the Gurkhas on Jail Hill, the 4th/15th Punjab on the D.I.S., and the Royal Berkshires on the south end of F.S.D. had a miserable time of it. The Gurkhas managed to get forward food, rum and ammunition, but not all the troops were so lucky. The Queens had no sleep at all, as they were so close to the Japs that grenades were coming over all night, and the L.M.G. fire was almost continuous.

Of his experiences on Jail Hill that night Lowry has written: 'We had a 50 per cent stand-to all night, but we were virtually all awake. It poured with rain throughout, and it was one of the noisiest nights imaginable. Jap machine-guns and our light machine-guns were punctuated by grenade and mortar fire. Three of the enemy bunkers were only ten or fifteen yards away, and the grenading was a little unpleasant.

It was a bleary dawn on the 12th, cold and with the rain still sheeting down. The clouds hung low over the mountains and the whole of Assam seemed foul and dank. At six o'clock John Grover was already in conference with Loftus Tottenham, and it was agreed that his troops 'should get solid where they were, then feel forward....' They also discussed the situation in the F.S.D. area, which it was hoped would improve when the tanks got through. Later a report came through that the Japs had made a road block past the D.C.'s bungalow bend, but this turned out to be merely a stack of 37-mm. shells, which seemed to indicate that they were running short of anti-tank mines. The tank commander decided to run over them, which he did without any ill-effects, and soon the leading tanks had linked up with the Queens on Jail Hill. Their object was to shoot up the bunkers on the reverse slopes, which they proceeded to do at very close range. Lowry, whose men were on this flank, recalls: 'It was an amazing sensation as the tanks shelled these bunkers. We had to lie flat on our stomachs to avoid debris and even the shells... as the positions they pounded were literally only fifteen yards away, but we had no casualties at the end of it.' Two bunkers were dealt with very successfully, and the Japs streaming away from them were caught by the Manchesters' machine-guns. A bunker by the road was shot to bits, and the corpses were seen 'to be blown clean up into the air'. This improvement of the situation enabled Lieutenant Hamilton to lead his platoon against the Jail buildings which had defied capture on the previous day, and take them. Two companies of Gurkhas, supported by tanks, attacked bunker positions on the western and south-western slopes of the bill, pressing on with great determination. Two bunkers were reached and captured, but the third, which held out, was surrounded, the Gurkhas digging in within ten yards. All through the day sniping continued and there were casualties among both battalions, but it grew less, and towards evening men were allowed to slip down the hill to fill their water-bottles. From his command post, Grover had been watching the attack by the Gurkhas and noted the behaviour of one of the Japs. 'He ran out of the bunker and, after pausing to take cover a couple of times, eventually dropped into a firing position behind a tree—a very cool customer.' Others strolled out of their bunkers unarmed and walked off, 'three miraculously getting away with it'. At three o'clock, twenty Japs were seen running down the far side of the hill. But whether they walked or ran, it was good to see them go; this was a new development in the battle.

At 1500 hours the Grants began shooting up Jap positions on D.I.S. and F.S.D., and the 4th/15th Punjab and the Royal Berkshires went into the attack. The Punjabis on the D.I.S. met considerable opposition, and were unlucky when their tank jammed its gun. However, they kept plugging away and eventually cleared the whole feature, except for one small bunker which was left for the following day when another tank could be brought forward. Meanwhile, the Royal Berkshires continued their attack on the F.S.D., and soon after four o'clock when a second tank came up to join the first (to quote Grover) 'there was the sound of bunkers cracking hard—a good sound'. Their fire was directed by Sergeant Garrett of the Royal Berkshires, until his company commander took over with his radio set. No Japs ran from the F.S.D. during the day; in fact, they fought on with great bravery, despite their heavy losses and the hopelessness of the situation, once the tanks were confronting their positions. None surrendered, though corpses littered the area, and about forty men were buried in their bunkers. One of these was a battalion headquarters, 'as big as a cathedral and full of galleries'. It was also full of papers and equipment; and before the action was over the Royal Berkshires had captured a 75-mm. gun, two regimental guns, eighteen machine-guns, and a good deal of ammunition.

'A depressing day for the Japs...' Loftus Tottenham remarked, as he left Grover's headquarters that evening. It was also a depressing day for 5th Brigade, as their commander, Victor Hawkins, was wounded, while going forward on reconnaissance. He was the third casualty among the brigadiers of 2nd Division, Theobalds, who had taken over from Goschen, having been hit the previous day. Two commanding officers (Hedderwick and Brown) had already been killed, apart from a high proportion of company and platoon commanders. The Japanese snipers certainly stuck to their job. By a coincidence, Robert Scott was standing next to Theobalds when he was hit, just as he had been with Goschen, and so twice took over the brigade. Scott had been hit several times himself, and for days a large bloody bandage adorned his head. On seeing this, soon after the battle of G.P.T. Ridge, John Grover said to him: 'Perhaps you'll now apologize for your truculence when I asked you to take steel helmets on the march round Pulebadze.' Unfortunately, Scott's reply isn't recorded.

'Just rain... rain and misery,' wrote an officer on the night of the 12th, which was just as wet as the two nights before it. But still the troops stuck it out on Jail Hill, on the D.I.S., and F.S.D. Ridge; Loftus Tottenham had called for one final effort, and they weren't going to let him down. Their tenacity was rewarded. At dawn, patrols from the Queens and the Gurkhas probed forward to find the enemy bunkers empty. The main bunker on the top of the hill was large enough to hold fifty men, and had steel loopholes, taken from the Assam Rifles barracks, which could be closed against grenades. It was so deeply dug into the hill and covered over that no shelling or bombing could touch it. The whole hill was honeycombed with tunnels and interlinking bunkers. As the Queens mopped up they caught sight of fifty Japanese streaming back from the Treasury position, to the north, and put in some very effective shooting. But everyone was anxious to leave Jail Hill, which an officer described as 'an unattractive place, battered, barren, scattered with debris and thick with the most disgusting flies'.

The Japs were not only leaving Jail Hill and the Treasury. Before daylight the men of the Royal Berkshires on F.S.D. Ridge woke up to find that they were running away down the rear slopes, and left their positions to chase after them. The enthusiasm was so great, in fact, that they had to be called back and warned not to overdo things. The Royal Welch Fusiliers probed forward to find Kuki Piquet unoccupied; they also found a grim reminder of the bestiality of war against the Japanese. Tied to a tree was the skeleton of a soldier whose shoulder flash disclosed that his regiment had been the Royal West Kents. In his battle-dress were a dozen or more slits, the poor fellow having been used for bayonet practice. At the same time as the Queens and the Fusiliers were probing forward, the 4th/15th Punjab sent a patrol on to the top of D.I.S., and this was found unoccupied too. As Marment recorded: 'The Japs were either dead, buried, or had packed up... it had been a wonderful show. All was quiet and someone thrust a bacon sandwich into my hand. I have eaten a lot of bacon since then, but no bacon sandwich has ever tasted quite so good again.'

One of the Japanese strong-points that the Punjabis had to

face on the D.I.S. was the bakery, and as the rain poured down on them during this foul night of the 12th it occurred to Marment that the story of the three little pigs might amuse his men. So, translating this into Urdu, he told it to them, and when he came to the refrain which runs: 'We'll huff and we'll puff and we'll blow your house down!' ('Ham apne hunkar se apke ghar kaundar denge!') the men roared with laughter. The morale of this battalion, after its losses during the action and the foul circumstances of the last forty-eight hours, was amazing.

The situation, therefore, on the morning of the 13th was that the whole central sector of Kohima had fallen, with two exceptions: the D.C.'s bungalow and the tennis court. Here the fighting was as stubborn as ever.

In dealing with the main offensive, it has been necessary to neglect the Dorsets for a while, but it shouldn't be imagined that the battle of the tennis court had died down. Day by day they'd been probing, patrolling, and fighting; and getting ready for 'the final set'. On the 11th, after some concentrated fire from a 6-pounder which had been dragged up on to the hill with immense effort, an attack had gone in against that old sore, the bunker in the north-eastern corner. It had failed, but not till several Jap positions had been identified for the first time. Then, on the 12th, the sappers decided to bulldoze a track straight up Hospital Hill Spur and into the perimeter from the rear, so that a medium tank could be pulled up on to the hill. This was a difficult task, as the ground was sodden and the gradient steep; but the sappers went on doggedly and by afternoon the job was done. Then the Lee tank arrived and, watched breathlessly by the troops, gradually manœuvred itself forward, chucking up mud with its tracks, slithering, and occasionally halting but never giving up. Before night the miracle had been achieved and the Lee was found a position by the cookhouse. News spread round the slit trenches like wildfire and suddenly everyone was very excited. '... nearly every man who could get away from his post came to look at this monster,' wrote Geoffrey White, 'the dragon, which was to help us annihilate the stubborn defenders of the bungalow on the morrow.' White and his commanding officer, Jock McNaught, were so elated, in fact, that they 'recklessly squandered half a mug of water each on a shave!'

The plan for the morrow's attack was as follows: with the help of the Lee, a platoon would get a hold of the north-eastern corner of the tennis court, and then would move along under its covering fire, clearing the positions dug into the bank below the club. A second platoon would move round the right, clearing the water tank, and the tin shed area; while a third would advance over the captured tennis court area and advance towards the bungalow terrace. This third platoon would link up with the platoon still holding the spur above the road junction. To reduce risks to a minimum, the Mountain Gunners were invited to manhandle a 3.7 howitzer up the bank to a site to the south of the position, which would give them a good shoot at the tin huts and the water tank. They could also take on other targets as required.

But first the Lee had to descend the club bank and get itself on to the tennis court, and a good many anxious eyes were on its commander, Sergeant Waterhouse of the 149th R.A.C., as he drove forward to attempt this task. The track had been widened and reinforced the previous evening, but the job was still difficult and after so many days of this battle no one was going 'to count their chickens'. However, having contemplated the bank for a moment, the tank slid down and suddenly its nose was on the base-line. Geoffrey White continues:

> 'We had done it at last! Anxiously we watched for any Jap reaction as the tank slowly swung round and started to serve. There was no nonsense about foot faults: Sergeant Waterhouse just let the Nip have it with his 75-mm., firing straight into their bunkers at a range of the length of a standard tennis

> court. On the first round... the infantry moved forward and the 3.7 howitzer opened up and let the enemy have fifty rounds fire at point-blank range, up their sterns. With great skill, Sergeant Given manœuvred his platoon round to the north-east corner, where he deployed and started setting about any opposition he could find. On the right, Sergeant Cook waited until the gun-fire had switched and then got in among the shell-happy Nips.'

As the 3.7 finished firing, about fifty Japs were seen leaving their positions, to run away past the Commandant's bungalow and into the nalas below. Immediately everyone who could bring a gun to bear opened up and the remnants of this party were pursued by bullets till they reached the slopes of Treasury Hill, eight hundred yards away. Meanwhile, Sergeant Given moved round the tennis court, directing the Lee's fire to any position which still showed, signs of life. Soon it became obvious though that the garrison had all been killed or had fled, so the Lee turned and moved forward to the edge of the terrace overlooking the bungalow itself, and under the cover of its gun the infantry went through. The bungalow itself was cleared with one casualty, the only one sustained that day, and then Major Chettle took over the mopping-up operations. This entailed searching out the bunkers, getting up to the slits under covering fire, lighting the fuse of a pole-charge, then pushing it through the hole. The charges were originally twenty seconds, which gave the Japs time to pull off the fuses, so, realizing this, Chettle cut the fuses down to four seconds and hoped that he and his men could get back before the bunker went up. With one exception they did. When he temporarily ran out of bunkers, Chettle searched out any likely hole which might be harbouring Japs and stuffed a 25 lb. tin of ammonal down it. This process went on right into the night, but when it was over the entire area had been cleared; sixty Jap dead were counted and many more must have been buried or blown to bits when their bunkers went up. Richard Sharp, the B.B.C. War Correspondent who had attached himself to the Dorsets, recorded an account of the day's action which was broadcast a few days later; it was one of the few graphic descriptions of the fighting in Assam that the people at home were ever granted:

> 'It's difficult to make sure of facts in this catch-as-catch-can type of warfare, but I know we've taken the tennis court, because I've been on it this afternoon. The men who took it... have been plugging away at that tennis court for sixteen days, and when I got there at noon they were on it at last. In these sixteen days they'd become personal enemies of the Jap there, who used to taunt them at dusk, calling across the tennis court: "Have you stood-to yet?" Today they're on top and they walked on their toes, laughing among the bulges in the earth of dug-out roofs.... There was a company commander—a robust man with square, black jaw covered with stubble. The skin between his battle-dress trousers and his tunic was bloody, and he swayed as he stood with his legs straddled. But his brain was working at full speed, and he laughed and shouted at his men as they went eagerly from fox-hole to fox-hole with hand-grenades and pole charges—that's twenty-five pounds of explosive at the end of a six-foot bamboo....
>
> Now all that's left is the litter of war—piles of biscuits, dead Japs black with flies, heaps of Jap ammunition, broken rifles, silver from the District Commissioner's bungalow. And among it, most incongruous of all, there's a man cleaning a pair of boots, another boiling tea, and an official photographer [Antony Beauchamp] who used to photograph Mayfair lovelies, saying: "Move a little to the left, please."

And there's another chap reading an "Edgar Wallace thriller" in a Sunday newspaper. Yes, today's been a great day for this battalion. Here's hoping they hold the tennis court through the night.'

They did, with no trouble. And the following day they were ordered back to Dimapur for a rest, with the other troops in the perimeter. For the first time in six weeks there was no fighting on Kohima Ridge.

*

Even before the attacks on the 11th developed, Sato realized that affairs were approaching a crisis and in an Order of the Day exhorted his men to keep fighting.

'The enemy are superior in weapons and firepower. Each and every man must look after his rifle as a mother her child. An uncared-for arm is a criminal offence, and any found with an unserviceable rifle, or no rifle at all, will at once be shot by his officer. You will fight to the death. When you are killed you will fight on with your spirit.'

But by the 13th, Sato realized that exhortations were in vain, that defeat was staring him in the face, and that his troops were being slaughtered to no purpose. He therefore signalled Mutaguchi and asked for permission to withdraw, the literal translation of the message running:

'Because of the heavy rain and starvation there is no time. Decided this Division, accompanying the sick and wounded, should move to a point where it could receive supplies.'

Permission was peremptorily refused, Mutaguchi signalling:

> 'It is very difficult to understand that your Division should evacuate under the pretext of difficult supply, forgetting its brilliant services. Maintain the present condition for ten days. Within ten days I shall take Imphal and reward you for your services. A resolute will makes the Gods give way.'

Sato signalled again, pointing out the plight of his troops, the hopelessness of his whole position, but Mutaguchi still would not budge. His new thrust with Tanaka and the 33rd Division would settle everything, he maintained; soon the Indian defences at Bishenpur would crack, and his victorious armies would then be pouring on to the Plain. Then Sato could be relieved.

But Sato had no faith in this latest thrust; he did not believe that Tanaka would be any more successful than Yanagida whom he had replaced. Yanagida, of course, was the second general to be relieved during the campaign, Yamauchi having been replaced by Shibata as commander of the 15th Division. Sato had been in close touch with these generals and when the news of their dismissal reached him he burst out angrily before his staff: 'This is shameful. If Mutaguchi considers himself a knight [i.e. has any chivalry] he should apologize for his own failure to the dead soldiers and the Japanese people. He should not try and put the blame on his subordinates.' According to some Japanese accounts, Mutaguchi disliked Yamauchi and Yanagida because he considered them 'pro-American', or at least thought they were too conscious of the American military potential. When they both displayed their lack of faith in 'the march on Delhi', it was inevitable that they would be replaced at the first opportunity. (Both Yamauchi, who had served as Assistant Military Attaché in Washington, and Yanagida were fine linguists. The latter spoke German and Russian as well as

English.) According to Takeo Komatsu (*The Imphal Tragedy*) the dismissal of his fellow divisional commanders released Sato (in his view) 'from the discipline of Mutaguchi's command'. This seems doubtful; but there can be little doubt that Sato now considered him untrustworthy in every respect, and realized that his dreams had far outrun his supply system. Nevertheless, Mutaguchi was still the lawful Army Commander, and a lifetime of professional soldiering demanded that his orders should be obeyed, however misguided, however futile, and no matter what the cost. So Sato fought on.

Though his left flank had been turned, and his centre pushed back, it should not be imagined that, from a defensive viewpoint, his position was now a weak one. Far from it: his flanks rested on two almost impregnable positions, Point 5120 at the north and the Aradura Spur at the south. Between these, running in a shallow semi-circle, was a whole series of good defensive positions: Gun Spur, Dyer Hill, Big Tree Hill, and others. And behind them there was Pfuchama, a great natural fortress, poised above the Imphal road. So long as Sato's men obeyed his order to fight to the death, these positions could hold up the British advance for weeks.

From the British viewpoint, the main hope was that the enemy would now have less and less time to prepare his positions, to dig those great cathedral-like bunkers. It was hoped too that, with his vast losses, morale would crack completely; but this was to prove only largely wishful hoping. As Slim has put it: 'The second phase of the battle was to be as hard fought as the first. The capacity of the ordinary Japanese soldier to take punishment and his fanatical will to resist were unimpaired.... I know of no army that could have equalled them.'

*

On the 14th there were two positions holding out, forward of what was now the main Japanese position: the remaining bunkers on G.P.T. Ridge, and Treasury Hill, between the D.C.'s bungalow and Naga Village. The Royal Norfolk and the Royal Scots began dealing with the G.P.T. Ridge bunkers, and this time the tanks were able to get up and join them. While one troop blasted the Japs from below, another moved round the back of their position, followed by the infantry. The Japs then opened up from Aradura with a 75-mm. and put over fifteen shells, which fell among the tanks, but did not damage them. This gun, which the troops had seen brought up on the back of an elephant, had been causing a good deal of annoyance. It was sited in a long pit, the back half of which had shell-proof cover; and the Japs' practice was to run it out, fire a few rounds, and then run it back again, before the 25-pounders could open up. Eventually the 75-mm. sustained a direct hit and was heard of no more. The mopping up went on during the 14th and 15th, and by the end of the time the ridge which had cost so many lives, and so much hardship and suffering, was in 4th Brigade's hands.

There was one extraordinary incident in this action. Searching one of the bunkers, some men of the Royal Norfolk found five of their regimental cap badges. They were taken to Robert Scott who immediately recognized them as the peace-time issue badges. They'd obviously been taken from men of the Royal Norfolk captured at Singapore. This discovery, providing as it did a link with their fellow soldiers in another battalion of the regiment, had a tremendous effect on the men. Stories of the Japanese treatment of prisoners had already reached them; and they were more eager than ever to take their revenge.

On the night of the 14th, two companies of the 4th/1st Gurkhas infiltrated on to the Treasury. Patrols from other units had reported it to be still held in strength, but no one could remember having been shot at from the position, and the Gurkhas (now commanded by Lieut.-Colonel Derek Horsford) decided to send their own patrols up there. Two came back to report the place deserted, but the third reported a few Japs there. Horsford therefore decided to send a company on to the position, which arrived safely and without meeting much opposition. The only Jap to come out and fight, in fact, was a sergeant of the 124th Regiment, who greeted the Gurkhas with grenades before being severely wounded. By next morning the whole battalion was on the Treasury, and though the Japs started mortaring there were very few casualties. Horsford wrote: 'The men were first-class; as soon as the shelling stopped, they got straight out of their semi-dug trenches and continued work on the defences.' When they weren't digging the Gurkhas were patrolling or laying ambushes, and captured several prisoners. As they were obviously going to spend some time in the position, while the front was reorganized, the battalion made itself comfortable, in the best tradition of the Indian Army. An officer of the unit wrote: 'Our Mess on Treasury caused great interest to all visitors, as it was almost completely underground. When Chris Nixon's piano had been installed, even the rain—which had a bad habit of pouring in through the earth roof—could not take away the look of luxury and splendour which the piano gave the Mess. A private of the Queens called Freshwater delivered water to us and took shelter in the Mess when shelling started one morning. His remark in Cockney, when he heard an officer start playing, confirmed our own feeling of uplift: "Cor blimey, I'm in 'eaven!" Unfortunately, the mortar officer's persistent efforts to harass the Japs provoked retaliation, and a bomb landed on the Mess roof, damaging the piano, whose dulcet tones no longer graced those barbaric hills.

On the 16th General Stopford went forward to have a look at Kohima. 'It was exactly like the Somme in 1916,' he wrote; One could tell how desperate the fighting had been. I am sure that our recent operations have been the biggest offensive show that the Japs have yet had to face… feel very exhilarated by the magnificent show which all battalions have put up.' But he did not let this exhilaration blind him to reality, and added: 'There will be much hard fighting ahead….'

Chapter Eleven

The Turning Point

On the 15th May, a brigadier with the formidable name of Michael Alston-Roberts-West walked up on to Naga Village to take command of 5th Brigade. He was a tall man with large features and a powerful intellect; and though not everyone liked him they came to admire him as a soldier. He was nine years younger than Hawkins, being just under forty, and the physical strain of action seemed to mean little to him. Somehow, from the beginning, he managed to give the impression that this brigade and this campaign was a minor incident in what was to become a major career; and his interest in people and things would be purely professional. He was an avid reader of newspapers, and once the *Observer* had arrived would take it to his bunk and be absorbed in it for some hours. On these occasions his staff dared not approach him, except on the most urgent business. He would sometimes become absorbed in the newspapers even after a battle had commenced, though always managing to switch his mind back at an instant's notice. Despite facets of personality and quirks of idiosyncrasy, there could be no doubt that West was a most professional soldier, and perhaps one of the finest tactical brains to be engaged at Kohima.

The problem facing him was the capture of Church Knoll and Hunter's Hill, the features from which the Camerons had been driven on that first night. For the last week, the Japanese had been solidly consolidating on them, digging into their terraced sides and constructing bunkers. Victor Hawkins had watched this process closely and day after day had sent out patrols. He also asked Richard Dupont, a subaltern in the Dorsets who was a professional artist, to draw him a detailed panorama and he sent this with his appreciation to Grover. In this he said: 'I am convinced that it will take a full-scale attack, with at least another brigade and possibly two, to capture these positions, and they will want all the artillery support they can get and even tanks....' However, as no further troops were available at this time, it was decided that the Camerons should try and infiltrate on to the positions by night.

To begin with things went well. Two platoons under Neil White and Peter Cameron got a footing on Church Knoll, but then they struck a bunker in which there were five Japs, of whom two were awake and opened fire with a machine-gun. All five Japs were killed, but surprise was lost and the whole position came alive. More machine-guns opened up, a shower of grenades came down from the terraces, one of which set fire to a Naga hut. The flames from this lit up the whole front and tracer bullets streamed from the Jap bunkers. There was nothing for it but to retreat, which the Camerons did, luckily with few casualties.

This failure had an immediate effect; any notions that the battle was nearly over, or that the fighting would be easier from now on, were dissipated. On the morning of the 16th, Grover sent for West, and the situation was discussed on a more realistic basis. The need was for tanks and 6-pounders; and Colonel Garwood, the sapper, was asked to start constructing a track. This he did at once, and two days later the tanks were winched up on to the 5th Brigade perimeter. Observing them, the Jap mortarmen put down some shells, but before long the tanks were in a more sheltered position and preparations for the attack went on again. It was to be carried out by the Worcestershires, on the 19th; one company to capture the forward slope of Church Knoll and another to move round the right of the objective, with its flank guarded by the Carrier platoon. When Church Knoll was in our hands, the other two companies were to pass through and attack Hunter's Hill. As a preparatory softening up, on the 18th, there was a strike by Hurribombers, which the men on the forward positions found the most frightening thing they'd experienced so far. As Major Elliott wrote: 'The target was only a hundred and seventy yards away, so the pilots were releasing their bombs right over our heads, which gave us the impression that they would drop into our trenches, instead of swishing low overhead on to the enemy bunkers.' However, the R.A.F. did its stuff most efficiently, and whatever damage was inflicted on the enemy the Worcestershires remained unscathed. On the following day there was to have been a second air-strike, but the clouds hung low and it had to be called off. The artillery opened fire at 0830 hours, and for some minutes plastered the two hills with shells. At the same time, the tanks opened fire on the bunkers observed on the forward slopes of Church Knoll. Pat Burke, the C.R.A., was with West in his command post, so fire could be directed at will. As the Worcestershires moved into the attack some enemy 75-mm. guns came into action, and though counter-battery shooting soon started they were never entirely silenced the whole day. The leading company of the Worcestershires managed to get within a few feet of the summit of Church Knoll, but here ran into heavy fire. As Elliott writes:

> 'The position was terraced, and on each terrace there were two or more Japanese bunker positions, with machine-guns covering the top of the terrace, so that whenever an attempt was made to climb up the five feet in order to rush these bunkers, the men were subjected to a withering fire at very

short range. While attacking one bunker, we invariably came under fire from one or two more.'

However, a number of bunkers were destroyed by direct fire from the tanks and the anti-tank guns. It was hoped that the Lifebuoy flamethrowers would destroy others, but their use was limited owing to the short range. However, the men using them showed great gallantry, especially Lieutenant Woodward. He succeeded in knocking out one bunker, and scrambling over the edge of the terrace, ran forward to occupy it. Before he could do so, he was fired at from another bunker, so turned and went for this with a grenade. He was shot dead, but the impetus of his charge carried his body forward so that it fell by the entrance to the bunker. Still the battle went on, hour after hour... when the flamethrowers wouldn't work pole-charges were tried, and the tanks and the anti-tank guns brought down fire whenever called on. Unfortunately, they could only reach the bunkers on the forward slopes, and as the Worcestershires moved round to the flank they ran into more trouble. Watching the battle from Kuki Piquet, Grover could see the Japs nipping out of bunkers, then running back and disappearing into fresh holes! One Jap ran from his bunker and stood hurling grenades, before being killed.

By three o'clock, by which time the day had turned to mist and rain, it was obvious to West that Church Knoll couldn't be taken before dark, let alone Hunter's Hill. Reports from the Worcestershire company commanders had reached him of 'five mutually supporting bunkers on the reverse slope' against which they were failing to make progress! At 1530 hours he therefore rang up Grover to discuss the situation. It seemed doubtful whether the troops could maintain their position on the forward slope during the night, so there was no alternative but to withdraw. Grover agreed, but ordered that work should be commenced on a track to get the tanks round to the far side of

Church Knoll. At about four o'clock, the artillery put down covering fire, and the Worcestershires came back to Naga Village, having lost forty in killed and wounded. Despite the weight of fire from aircraft, guns and tanks, the Japanese position was still intact.

On the 20th there were further disappointments. Early in the morning, West arrived to tell John Grover that all attempts to find a way forward for the tanks, or to find a possible route for a track, had failed. What he needed was medium artillery, which wasn't available; so Grover gave orders that the brigade 'should continue aggressive patrolling and offensive action against any bunkers they can get at, but not to stage any further operation'.

Having been foiled on the left flank, Grover turned his attention to the right, where 4th Brigade were still probing. All patrol reports were indicating that the Japanese position here was a very strong one; and that the enemy was watching every single track. How the division could burst through, it was by no means clear; as Grover noted at this time, two problems were always with him—shortage of troops and the job of finding adequate fire support.

The only encouragement he received at this time was from a rather intelligent prisoner who surrendered voluntarily, unwounded. 'I have reached the limit of endurance,' he said. His regiment, he added, was the 58th, and his company was down to forty men. All the officers had been killed or wounded and the company was being commanded by an N.C.O. For some time he'd had only rice and salt to eat, and the shelling was terrible... it had caused a lot of casualties. All this was good to hear—but no one expected a flood of deserters to follow.

Like Grover, Stopford had his problems at this time. On the 19th he received a letter from Giffard saying that the 2nd Division might have to be disbanded, to provide drafts for other British units in the 14th Army, owing to the shortage of manpower. Whether Stopford saw this as a first step towards the disbandment of 33rd Corps, it's not clear, but he certainly viewed the idea with horror, and immediately began working out a plan for obtaining reinforcements. This was sent off to Giffard on the 21st.

On the 23rd, Stopford called Grover and Messervy to a conference to discuss plans for their respective divisions. It had been agreed that the 2nd Division should operate on the right half of the front, 7th Division taking the left, so the two main obstacles now facing them were the Aradura Spur, and Church Knoll with Hunter's Hill, respectively. Grover proposed to attack Aradura with 4th Brigade and 6th Brigade, one making a frontal assault on the positions running up from the road and the other scaling the high ground towards the village. While this was going on, Messervy was to clear the two features confronting his position in Naga Village and be prepared to advance south on the 1st June.

The first operation to get under way was Messervy's. The guns of the 5th/22nd Medium Battery, which had just joined the Corps, were pounding Church Knoll, Hunter's Hill and North Spur, even while the generals were in conference. Nine hundred shells hit these positions in all, with devastating effect. According to A.J. Barker: 'As the heavy shells crashed down on the bunkers, baulks of timber and other debris were flung into the air. Not only did it appear that the defences had disintegrated and collapsed, but also that no one could possibly survive beneath the wreckage.' On the 24th and 25th the Hurribombers strafed the area, after a further artillery barrage, and with support from the tanks, the 4th/i5th Punjab (or the '28th' as they liked to call themselves, using their old title) went into the attack. As already indicated, this was a fine regiment with a proud record and traditions; even its junior N.C.O.s had seven or eight years' service behind them, and the V.C.O.s* and havildars a good deal more. Arthur Marment says: 'The plan was for the Khatak Company under myself to attack Church Knoll, whilst Stanley Berens went for Hunter's Hill. We went through the Queens and crossed the start-line to the second, and immediately encountered very stiff Jap 75-mm. fire. We ran like hares under our own 25-pounder barrage to the nala. I don't think I have ever got in quite so close under a barrage. The shells were all dropping about ten yards ahead, and of course one eventually dropped short, wounding several men.... Unfortunately my right-hand platoon could not cross the start-line on time owing to the very heavy 77-mm. fire, but with the others I reached the nala and our first attack progressed. It was only unsuccessful when we started to be heavily sniped from our right. However, when the rest of the company came up, and there had been another tank bombardment, we had another go. Once we reached the top, only to be beaten off by heavy fire.' Eventually, Marment's company was ordered to retire, having received twenty-three casualties. Berens, on Hunter's Hill, had had his radio knocked out and so the commanding officer could not contact him. Major 'Raj' Fowler therefore volunteered to go forward under heavy fire and to contact Berens, and helped to extricate his men from a very difficult situation.

It was a bitter day for the Punjabis; they had failed against these objectives just as surely as the Camerons and the Worcestershires. The Japanese positions seemed utterly impregnable.

The failure was particularly disturbing for Messervy and Stopford. The earlier attacks by 5th Brigade, on the 15th and

* V.C.O. is short for Viceroy's Commissioned Officer (Subadar and Jemadar). These men were roughly the Indian Army's equivalent to the British Warrant Officers, though their prestige and power were undoubtedly greater. Havildar is the equivalent rank of sergeant, and Naik of corporal.

19th, had not been supported by medium artillery, and it had been hoped that once these 5.5 guns were available, they would be able to hammer the Japs so hard that the positions must fall. But now, despite their help, and the skill and courage of the Punjabis, the situation appeared no better than before. The Japanese line still held and neither Grover nor Messervy could advance a yard further.

How was it that if the Japanese were so far gone with starvation and disease, as the Intelligence people believed, they were able to continue fighting with such determination week after week? Some clues are given by the statements of soldiers after they reached Japan. One of them said: 'The shelling grew to 3,000 or even 4,000 a day. I was always afraid when I was caught away from my bunker, but once I was inside it there was a wonderful feeling of relief.' When one considers how many shells some bunkers took without their inhabitants being wounded, the soldier's statement becomes immediately understandable. Undoubtedly, too, the bunker was very much suited to the Japanese mentality. This fact is borne out by the statement of another soldier: 'While we were actually fighting at Kohima we did not fear the enemy... but once we retreated and we were in the open, a deep fear for the enemy came upon us.' But there are other clues; as an N.C.O. put it: 'In the final stages of the battle many soldiers stayed in their bunkers because they were so far gone with starvation, malaria and beriberi that they did not have the power to move. Their clothes were soaked with rain and sweat, and filthy dirty... and they could never get out of the bunkers to dry them. All they could do, in fact, was rest against the fire-slit and pull the trigger whenever attacked.' Another factor to be taken into consideration is that not all the units had suffered equally. The 124th Regiment, for example, had some of its companies fairly fresh even at the end of May. Finally, there is the fact that from the early days of May the troops believed that they would be relieved by another Division.

Now we know, of course, that there was no Division which could possibly have come to their aid, but the troops did not know this, and this false hope undoubtedly buoyed them up day after day, as their own hunger and the military situation grew worse. It is difficult to believe that General Sato or his staff would have started such a false rumour, and where it emanated from it is now impossible to say; the important thing is, however, that the troops believed it.

Having noted the experiences of the Royal Norfolk and the Royal Scots in the thick jungle around Mount Pulebadze, it is interesting to read the anecdotes of Japanese soldiers in the same area. One of them remembered: 'Surprised by the noise of the bomb, a group of monkeys moved over our heads from branch to branch, some carrying their babies in their arms. One of these babies fell, but managed to clutch a branch before it hit the ground. The mother climbed down, rescued it, and hurried off with the others.' Like the men of the 4th Brigade the Japanese saw the luminous vegetation in the jungle and, as this anecdote shows, managed to use it to good effect: 'I tried to follow the soldier who was walking two or three steps ahead of me. It was difficult until he put what I thought was a luminous insect on his pack. It wasn't an insect though, so I discovered, but some leaves rotted to phosphorus. This made following him very easy.'

Reading these stories, the Japanese soldier seems very far from the superman who was feared throughout the East in 1942 and 1943; in fact, he seems just as human as any other soldier. But, nevertheless, his tenacity and courage were of an order seldom equalled. In fact, if Sato's men had not possessed qualities of this order it is difficult to see how they would have remained in being as a fighting force. This narrative by a subaltern of the 58th Regiment probably sums up the desperate circumstances of the 31st Division at this time, better than almost any other: 'Even the invalids and the wounded were driven to the front to help supply manpower. Even those with broken legs in splints were herded into battle, the malaria cases too. I have seen these going forward with yellow faces, the fever still in their bodies. I saw one man, whose shoulder had been fractured by a bullet, stagger forward to the front. Some of the wounded who were over forty fondly hoped that they would be sent home but even they were sent forward.'

*

While Messervy was attacking on the left, Grover was preparing his operation against Aradura, on the right. The front attacks against the Spur (which ran down parallel with G.P.T. Ridge) were allotted to the Royal Norfolk and the Royal Scots of 4th Brigade, while 6th Brigade, under Brigadier Shapland, would try and deal with the positions high up on the shoulder, in the area of Aradura Village. Grover had agreed to this operation by 6th Brigade, after being informed that 4th Brigade could not burst through towards the road unless their right flank was covered. During the 25th and the 26th, the Royal Berkshires, the Royal Welch Fusiliers, the Durham Light Infantry (now reduced to a headquarters and two rifle companies) and the 1st Burma Regiment, assembled on G.P.T. Ridge. The general plan Shapland had worked out was 'to move on a one-man frontage by battalion groups, stepping up from firm "bases"...' Guides would be provided by 143rd S.S. Company which had already reconnoitred part of the route.

A word of explanation is necessary here regarding the term 'stepping up'. It is a gunner term and means that unit A goes forward to position X, then as unit B arrives there to relieve it, unit A moves on to the next position. Brigadier Shapland was a gunner and to him, therefore, the manœuvre was quite a natural one. To infantry commanders, though, it was anathema, as it inevitably resulted in a period of some minutes during which both units were milling around in the same position, *and neither was firm.* When Colonel Braithwaite (Royal Welch Fusiliers) and Colonel Bickford (Royal Berkshires) heard the orders for the operation they were both horrified. Braithwaite protested strongly, and said that 'stepping up' was a manœuvre unknown to infantry. Why, he asked, couldn't his battalion leapfrog through Bickford's? Shapland explained that this was not in his plan, and insisted that the orders should be carried out as laid down. Braithwaite was so alarmed that 'he considered disobeying orders and asking to see the divisional commander'. Bickford was equally concerned and has recorded: 'I was convinced that the project would be disastrous and said so.' His objections to the operations were manifold. To begin with, there was no definite start-line to the attack, and the doctrine that 'the start-line should be parallel to the objective' could not be observed. Also, he 'hated stringing his battalion out in single file' along a jungle track. And finally, he 'could not see the point of capturing these positions which were high up in thick jungle and could not maintain observation of the road'.

To counter these objections, Shapland pointed out that 143rd S.S. Company had already been up on the Spur and reported it clear. But Bickford already knew that they'd had difficulty cutting a route through thick jungle—and they'd found some enemy positions. Apart from his other technical objections, these facts 'made him very sceptical'.

Shapland, it should be explained, had been C.R.A. to the 2nd Division, and was a well-liked and highly respected figure in it. But there is no use denying that his 'gunner methods' and way of doing things sometimes worried his battalion commanders. Gunners tend to be more intellectual, more precise and mathematical than infantrymen, while the latter tend to be more instinctive, more reliant on personal experience. 6th Brigade had had a very hard time during this battle (as in the Arakan campaign the previous year) and its casualties were very heavy. In recent actions it hadn't had the best of luck, and had been ordered to attack enemy positions which had proved to be very strongly held.

Altogether, the Aradura operation—at least 6th Brigade's part of it— started off in an atmosphere of depression; and then the weather became so bad that it was postponed till the 27th. For two days the troops crouched in their sodden trenches while the rain poured down and the mud grew thicker. The officers used the time to study the air photograph which had been taken by the R.A.F., and to watch for movement on the four features to be occupied, named in the operation orders as Matthew, Mark, Luke, and John. The Royal Berkshires, so it was now planned, were to capture the crest of the Spur, and John, then the Royal Welch Fusiliers, were to pass through them and capture the remaining apostles. The height of their objective was about 4,000 feet, but to reach them the troops would have to keep climbing, descending and then climbing again. In all they would probably be going up 3,000 feet.

If Bickford had been suspicious of this operation initially, now he viewed it with horror. The plan, he writes, was 'simplicity in itself, but lacking most of the information vital to a commander who had to carry it out.... Information about the enemy gave no details of estimated strength and armament, [his] defences or even where he was dug in.' The blurred aerial photograph he considered almost useless— 'the scale could not be estimated as no one knew the altitude at which it had been taken'. And ground observation did not help a great deal: 'For days we kept constant watch on the objective, through glasses from a vantage point on the left flank. No sign of movement or defences could be seen.' Also—'the perspective from the left flank from which the watch was kept bore no relation to that on the right flank from which the approach march had to be made. Each view presented quite a different picture, one across the hilltops, and the other into impenetrable jungle. As the crow

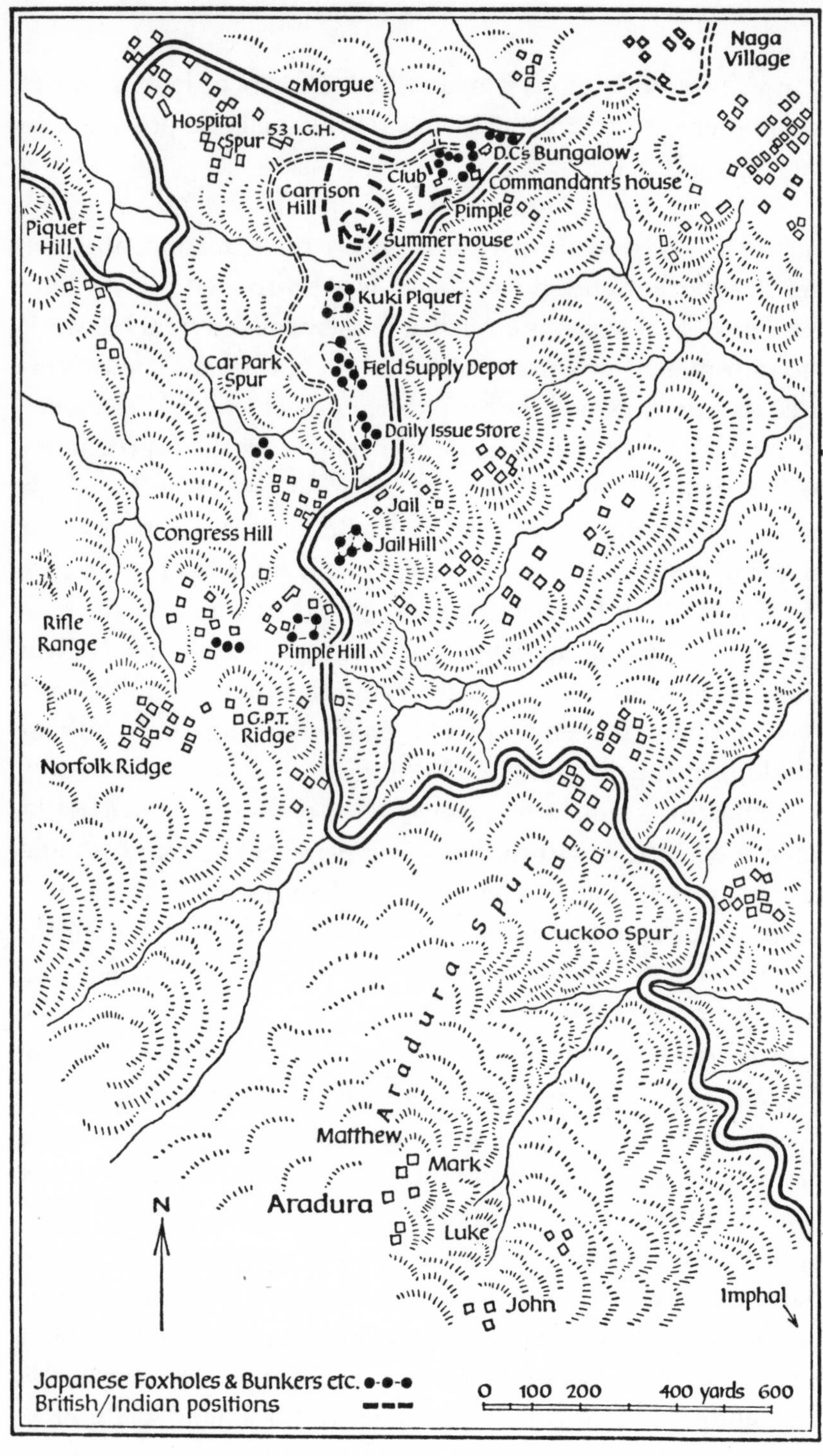

Naga Village
Morgue
Hospital Spur
53 I.G.H.
D.C's Bungalow
Club
Commandant's house
Garrison Hill
Pimple
Piquet Hill
Summer house
Kuki Piquet
Car Park Spur
Field Supply Depot
Daily Issue Store
Jail
Congress Hill
Jail Hill
Rifle Range
Pimple Hill
G.P.T. Ridge
Norfolk Ridge
Aradura Spur
Cuckoo Spur
Matthew
Mark
Aradura
Luke
N
John
Imphal
Japanese Foxholes & Bunkers etc.
British/Indian positions
0 100 200 400 yards 600

flew the distance could be roughly estimated, but as the climber ascended and descended it could not. [In this terrain] it could take four hours to move one man and his mortar a quarter of a mile, with or without the aid of a mule.'

On the morning of the 27th the rain was still bucketing down, but no further delay could be tolerated, so at 6.30 a.m. the Royal Berkshires passed through the Burma Regiment and entered the jungle. Ahead of the battalion was Major McGeorge, with his S.S. Company, and the Royal Welch Fusiliers were still on G.P.T. Ridge. The only communication between Bickford and Shapland at this time was by telephone; a signaller following immediately behind Bickford, unrolling a coil of wire as he went. The going was extremely bad, and according to one account:

> 'The ground began to rise steeply, through a dripping mass of vegetation, which limited visibility to twenty yards or less. Tall trees soared skywards, forming a vast umbrella that provided no protection from the rain. Lesser timber, decked with orchids, blocked their way. Glossy-leafed shrubs deluged them with water, thorn bushes caught in their clothing and equipment, and creepers ensnared their feet. The soft ground and undergrowth quickly became deep in mud, which on the steep slopes caused men to slide back on those behind. These conditions, coupled with an uncertainty of the enemy, made the pace intolerably slow.'

In Bickford's view, even this description does not give an adequate picture of the conditions his men were facing in this operation. He has written: 'First, the denseness of jungle. Bamboo... is so dense, and thorny, that even elephants cannot barge their way through. To clear a path... is a long, tedious business. Jungle not only provides a physical barrier but also restricts visibility to about ten to twenty yards; and therefore to move a body of men through it, deployed laterally, is almost impossible, as no one can see how fast or how far his neighbour has progressed. Single file is therefore the only answer, but how vulnerable it makes one to any marksman lying still and motionless by the side of the track! The noise of the advancing column cutting down the undergrowth gives ample warning to anyone waiting silently in ambush positions.' He also points out that expressions like 'heavy rainfall' give no real idea of the Assamese monsoon. 'It will fill a mess tin in half an hour', while the heaviest European rain takes several times longer.

As to the tactics employed, he continues: 'The peculiar conditions made it impossible to make normal tactical moves, as one would do in other parts of the world. No one in his sense would move a brigade up to the attack in single file, but... there was no other means of approach. To keep direction one would normally have prominent landmarks on ground and map as guides. Here there were none. Alternatively, in other terrain, one can march by compass, but in these conditions you couldn't take a bearing more than twenty yards ahead— and you'd be confronted with some impenetrable bamboo and have to make a detour.' Apart from impeding progress and making it hard to keep direction, these mountain-jungles provided other difficulties. As Bickford adds: 'No other climate in the world was so devastating to communications, particularly to infantry wireless sets. This meant that a commander could rarely communicate with his subordinates. If he wished to start the head of the column or stop it, a message had to be passed from hand to mouth.'

The track dipped into a ravine, then rose out again, almost vertical, and the men were only able to climb at all by joining their toggle ropes together and hauling themselves up. As with 4th Brigade, on the Pulebadze hook, machine-guns, mortars, and ammunition were being carried, and hauling them up the steep slopes was difficult in the extreme. Among the wet vegetation leeches abounded, and these wormed their way under the men's clothing to begin sucking at their blood. The damage they inflicted wasn't great, and the men knew how to burn them off with cigarettes, but they were another discomfort to add to the rain and the ground.

After a few hours, it was obvious that the men were getting very tired; but Bickford had no alternative but to keep going, even though the pace got slower and slower. Towards mid-day, the men began to think that they must soon arrive somewhere but the jungle still surrounded them and the path still led upwards. Then Major McGeorge came back to see Bickford to report that his company had lost the way. The maps were hopelessly wrong, he added, and how far the column was from the objective he couldn't say. Bickford decided that the column had better keep going for a while, but at about 1230 hours McGeorge came back again to say there was no sign of the crest, and he'd really no idea where they were. Faced with this dilemma, Bickford asked his gunner, Stewart Liberty, to call up his battery and tell it to put down some high explosive and smoke-shells on to the objective. Liberty did so; and a few minutes later the shells whined overhead and went travelling up the mountain. Explosions were heard in the distance but nothing could be seen; it was obvious that wherever the column was, it was a long, long way from the crest, let alone the four apostles. The hour for the attack had long gone by, so Bickford ordered the regiment to form a box for the night, then sent patrols probing forward to see what they could discover. In fact, they discovered nothing but more jungle; and at 1630 hours, McGeorge came back to report that he could find no way to the crest at all. Bickford reported the situation to Shapland whose tactical headquarters was with the Burma Rifles headquarters, and it was agreed that McGeorge should have another go at first light the following morning. At the same time the Royal Welch Fusiliers would come forward to 'step up' into Bickford's position, so that he could move up to the crest. So the troops dug themselves in to spend the night, 'drenched... exhausted... wedged against the trees to prevent slipping down the khud-side in their sleep, but unfortunately no one slept'.

While the Royal Berkshires had been looking for their objective, the Royal Norfolk and the Royal Scots had found theirs and were moving up to attack it. The Royal Norfolk at this time was reduced to less than four hundred officers and men, and the majority of those still serving were suffering severely from dysentery. 'Exposure, wet, fatigue,' wrote an officer,' had all told their tale....' However, the spirit of the unit was still remarkably good (as it was in the Royal Scots), many men refusing to be evacuated although they could have, legitimately. The Norfolks' first objective was 'Charles Hill', on the right of 4th Brigade's objective, the Royal Scots being allocated Basha Spur, on the left. The two leading companies of Norfolks were to move forward before dark and patrol towards the objective, and if it were found to be undefended, or weakly held, to occupy it. If, however, it was found to be strongly held, then an artillery concentration was to be called for and a full-scale attack put in. The Norfolks didn't like this plan (any more than the units of 6th Brigade liked theirs) but loyally put it into execution. At 0315 hours two companies moved forward in torrential rain, but before they were near the objective a report came back from a reconnaissance patrol that the position was strongly held. Robert Scott, who was well forward as usual with his tactical headquarters, therefore waited till the rest of the brigade could move into position and the barrage could come down. But the rain became so heavy that any operation was virtually washed out, and in the early afternoon the two companies were recalled. After a conference, it was decided by Shapland that the attack should go ahead the next day, and so the two companies dutifully went forward again. (The fact that they did so in such good order says a good deal for their stamina and discipline.) The going was rough and hard but fortunately the rain had stopped, and then the sun came up to greet a clear blue sky. At 0730 hours the leading company found the jungle thinning as they came towards their objective, and then the Japanese opened up on them from two bunker positions. These were situated just below the crest of a steep escarpment and had a commanding field of fire. A second company moved up to the left of the first, also came under fire, suffering several casualties, and the company commander, Major Murray-Brown, was only able to extricate his men through a most gallant and skilful operation. It was clear that no advance was possible against such a strongly held position, and an effort was made by men of a third company to work round to the right flank, but they hit trouble too. Despite repeated urgings from brigade headquarters to go on, Robert Scott realized that any further attempt would only lead to unnecessary casualties, so got his battalion firm on the ground where it was.

Meanwhile the Royal Scots had attacked the lower (eastern) end of the Spur, supported by tanks moving along the road. The country here was a bit more open but just as difficult. Towards the right, the last ten yards before the objective were so steep and slippery that ascent was virtually impossible. The men became spreadeagled in the mud, and the whole place was a death-trap. Only one soldier was able to reach the top and, try as they might, none of the others could join him. The troops on the left fared much better, and two companies succeeded in getting on to the objective. But the Japanese 'lay in swarms in the thick jungle on higher ground' and the Jocks were getting cut up so badly that it was doubtful if they could hold the position. Shortly after noon, Colonel Saunders, who was temporarily commanding the brigade, told Robert Scott of the Royal Scots' limited success, and ordered him to withdraw his battalion, move across to make contact with them, then attack Charles Hill again from the left. The disengagement was carried out under fire, but in perfect order, and the battalion then began to move round. At 1600 hours, after the two battalions had made contact, Scott called for artillery and a concentration was put down for ten minutes. Two weak companies of the Royal Norfolk went into the attack, but before they could reach the crest were brought to a halt by heavy machine-gun fire and grenades. Somehow, with Robert Scott shouting and cursing at them, these exhausted men found the strength and courage to attack up the last few yards of the slope. They reached the crest, to be pushed down again with more casualties. But the survivors went up again, and again, and again. Shouting at the top of his voice, Scott was pulling out grenades and hurling them over the crest to reach the enemy positions on the reverse slope. He was a demon of fire and fury; a fantastic, gigantic warrior, who did enough to earn one V.C. after another. But even he was not indestructible in a fire as hot as this. Suddenly he was hit and fell back down the slope. Major Murray-Brown, who took over command, realized the hopelessness of trying to capture the position and, having told Scott of his decision, ordered the withdrawal. Word was communicated to the Royal Scots, who withdrew also. Protesting and swearing volubly, Robert Scott was taken back by the doctors—one of whom he threatened to court-martial 'for evacuating me against orders'. Long after he had reached the A.D.S. and had seen John Grover he was still protesting; but the doctors had their way and he was put into an ambulance for Dimapur. This incredible soldier had seen his last day's fighting.

On the 6th Brigade front things had been happening too, and no less dramatically. At 0700 hours, when the telephone line had been mended, Shapland spoke to Bickford who reported that he'd had 'a quiet night'. Shapland therefore gave orders for him to move on towards the objective, and Bickford got his battalion ready to move at 0830 hours. He knew that there were Japs about, as word had come through that the S.S. Company had suffered some casualties while digging in the previous night, but how many he had no idea. Shapland was in the rear box, formed by the Burma Regiment, and at 0905 hours Braithwaite reported to him, as his battalion moved up to take over the position being vacated by the Royal Berkshires—or in Shapland's phrase, began 'stepping up'. The Royal Welch were pitifully weak at this time, consisting of three rifle companies of thirty men each, and a battalion headquarters. Their mortar platoon was put under command of Bickford for this operation, so virtually they were the strength of a single rifle company. The Durham Light Infantry were ordered to take over the route back from the Burma Regiment box and the Burma Regiment took the route running forward.

About 1000 hours Braithwaite and his men reached Bickford's position, and then the latter began moving up the hill again. Shapland came up with the tail of the column, and records that: 'At 1030 hours I moved my Tac. H.Q. forward to R.W.F. where I found the battalion deployed around the "table" top feature and the tail of the Royal Berks moving off.' An area of jungle some thirty yards across had been partially cleared and the Fusiliers began occupying the shallow slit trenches dug by the Royal Berkshires, and getting out their own entrenching tools to improve them. Before they had time to throw up the first shovelful of earth, however, they came under heavy fire. Braithwaite says: 'I moved over to speak to the Brigade Commander. It was then we were subjected to intense sniping, M.G. and mortar fire, together with exploding hand grenades. The Japs appeared to be occupying the whole of the face of the jungle in an arc on the battalion front, with the battalion in its weak state... unable to see any real target at which to fire. The front of the box suffered 90 per cent casualties, and the many wounded got back as best they could.' Major Owen walked forward to try and take command of the front of the box but was mortally wounded before he could reach it. Later, Braithwaite ordered 'A' company to try and work round to its right, only to find that it had blasted off all its ammunition into the jungle. Discovering this he countermanded the order.

Shapland writes: '... it appeared that a counter-attack was being built up. I saw a party of Japs moving down from the high ground above us, about half a mile away... into the valley between our small feature and, I think, the Pulebadze feature, but I can't be sure.' Shapland rang up John Grover to tell him what had happened, and the phone was hit as he was speaking. Shapland continues: 'Then the "nonsense" occurred—the forward company on my left "gave"—I think due to exposure to L.M.G. fire which was heavy and came through us. Braithwaite, I could see on my left, with his small Tac. H.Q. tried to rally them but without success. Just previously Owen was hit in front of me and then I got it.... When I came to I joined Braithwaite and ordered him to gather up the remnants and form a rearguard, but I fear the "rot" had set in and my next clear recollections are being helped by my "gun-man" in the 1st Burma Regiment perimeter.'

Braithwaite's recollection is understandably somewhat different. In his view the battalion had been led into a trap and the only sensible thing to do was to withdraw as quickly as possible. When Shapland, having been shot through the neck, came over to him, Braithwaite says he asked for permission to withdraw, and adds: 'At first he would not give me permission to order a withdrawal, though shortly afterwards I was granted that permission.... I knew that if we did not withdraw from the position the battalion would have suffered obliterating casualties to no purpose.' Braithwaite denies that his forward companies withdrew without orders; in his view 90 per cent of them were wounded and tried to get into cover so that someone could tend them. Shapland still holds to his opinion and wrote recently: 'I fear the forward elements broke and as far as I remember this started the rot.'

The situation was confused and desperate; and quite probably the various accounts will never be reconciled. Certainly there is ample evidence that the men of the Royal Welch came streaming down the hillside in disorder and badly shaken, though most of them were wounded. To this Braithwaite replies: 'We were led into a trap—but not on ground of our own choosing.' He points out that both Bickford and himself were against the operation and predicted disaster; and adds that he felt strongly, not for himself, 'but on account of the continued and unnecessary slaughter of these wonderful men of all ranks who had always fought so bravely'.

How did it happen that the Japanese were able to fall on the Royal Welch with such devastating fury? Shapland denies that it was an ambush, and thinks that 'it was a hook put in by the Japs when they discovered the Royal Berks on the "Table" either the night 27th-28th or in the early morning of the 28th... at the worst it was a local tactical success.' John Grover said at the time that 'it was a skilfully planned counter-attack.' Whatever it was, it certainly doomed the Aradura expedition.

The Royal Berkshires had only moved up a short distance when they heard the firing behind them. This journey, up and down precipitous slopes and through thick jungle, had taken, however, some hours. Colonel Bickford decided to dig in, a difficult task in these circumstances as the battalion was only equipped with entrenching tools and no picks and shovels were available. Also on slopes such as these and in heavy rain it was useless merely to dig slit trenches on their own as they would immediately fill with water; drainage trenches had to be dug also. Then head cover had to be provided against the inevitable mortar barrage. Soon after eleven o'clock, Shapland came on the phone to say 'he was in our old H.Q. and the Japs were firing at anyone who put his head out.' According to Bickford, he didn't seem very concerned, and said 'the R.W.F. have sent a patrol to deal with the enemy'. The firing could be heard going on and increasing in volume. Then at noon Major McGeorge came back to report that his company had found enemy positions along what they thought was the crest, though they couldn't be sure about it. He added that 'the going was impossible for heavily laden troops'. By the time the conversation between McGeorge and Bickford was over, the firing down below them was considerable and Shapland came on the phone again and told Bickford 'to use his discretion as to whether to move forward or withdraw'. Bickford wisely decided to stay where he was for the night. It rained heavily again, so his men spent their third consecutive night soaked to the skin; fortunately, however, rations came up next morning; and they were followed the next day by orders to withdraw.

So 6th Brigade abandoned its operations on Aradura. From them, Bickford has written 'several lessons can be drawn, and some of these, mercifully, were applied... in the jungles of Malaya. A commander at any level must accept more readily the advice of his subordinates— the men on the ground. He must say what is wanted and allow them to carry out his orders... in their own way. To move one man or a thousand through dense jungle in single file is a dangerous and intolerably slow operation. They must move in their own time and not be chased forward from the rear without regard to conditions prevailing. One cannot plan an attack unless one knows what one is attacking and the troops in turn must know and see what they are up against. This cannot be done without intelligence reports and personal reconnaissance. No one can act on the evidence of a blurred and deceptive air photograph.... More attention should be paid to... infiltration, as practised by the Japs....'

However, the situation at Kohima on the 29th May was that despite the most heroic exertions by their weakened units the operations of 4th and 6th Brigades against the left flank of the enemy had proved a disastrous failure.

Things had gone no better on the other flank. Undeterred by the failure against Church Knoll on the 25th, Frank Messervy laid on a strike by Hurribombers, which again blasted away at this long disputed feature. The 4th/15th Punjab went in for their third attack, taking flame-throwers and pole charges; but for the third time they were shot off the hill, and mortared and shelled. But with fanatical courage and a tremendous devotion to duty, they had another go. On this desperate action, Arthur Marment writes: 'The attack went in; the Sikhs on to Church Knoll and the Punjabi Mussulmen on to Hunter's Hill. The Sikhs got to the top but were again driven off by heavy mortar fire and a tremendous amount of defiladed fire. Then "C" Company had a go and, led by Colonel Thomas [the commanding officer during Conroy's absence] himself, got to the top, but it was just impossible to stay. The Jap held every bit of cover... Stanley Berens was mortally wounded... George Shepherd was wounded twice, and Colonel Thomas was marvellous in the way he brought in a very badly wounded Captain Forest who was to die soon afterwards. Captain Jeffrey was wounded too.'

Marment, during this action, was in the brigade command post, with Brigadier Loftus Tottenham and some of his staff, and at one point happened to ask his orderly to send up sandwiches for everyone. Half an hour later the orderly appeared, 'hopping and skipping in and out of the shell-holes with the sandwiches'. When he uncovered them, not only were the crusts seen to have been cut off but the plate was a china one with the regimental crest on it. Loftus Tottenham was somewhat amazed.

The attack failed.

Church Knoll and Hunter's Hill now seemed to be indestructible by any known means; the troops dug into it impervious to shells, mortars, anti-tank fire, flame-throwers, or any other weapon in the Allied armoury. Their ammunition seemed as limitless as their courage. They were apparently undefeatable. This was another bitter moment for the Punjabis; perhaps the worst failure in their whole history. Their dead were littered over the whole hill—one company came back only forty strong—and they hadn't gained a yard of ground nor taken possession of a single bunker.

Failure on the right; failure on the left. Failure by British troops; failure by Indian troops. On the night of the 28th, the battle of Kohima reached another crisis. By all the Intelligence reports, the Japanese were losing men fast; they were sick, demoralized, and half-starved. And yet they still fought like tigers. Still ground every attack on them into the mud. How could 33rd Corps break through? Its battalions were shrunken to the size of companies; its men were weak and exhausted. Hundreds of them should have been evacuated long ago, and how long they could be asked to go on attacking up these steep slopes in the face of merciless machine-gun fire was a question no one could answer.

Also, as Stopford, Grover, Messervy, and indeed everyone who thought about it realized: even when the battle of Kohima had been won the enemy had a series of magnificent defensive positions, running back almost to Imphal. There was Viswema and Kigwema… the great height of Mao Songsang, and the ridge at Maram, almost another Keren in itself. In view of this, how could the advance *ever* reach Imphal? Time was beginning to run out. The men of 4th Corps had been living on short rations for some time now and were weakening too. They had fought long and courageously and were still defying Tanaka's fanatical efforts to break through their defences. But their endurance wasn't limitless. Even if it had been, it would be no good without supplies; and the airlift had run into yet another crisis. By some miracle, Mountbatten had persuaded the Americans to let him keep the seventy-nine transport aircraft till the 15th June—that is, another eighteen days. During that time the reserves would still be dropping; and if 33rd Corps could still not break through, the outlook would be bleaker than it had ever been. In fact, even at this late stage, Mutaguchi's 'private speculations' might not prove so wildly unrealistic after all.

But it so happens time and time again in the history of war that when the crisis is reached, when the result of a battle is poised on a knife-edge, something happens which tips the balance. It may be something spectacular, like Cromwell's charge at Edgehill, or the arrival of Blücher on the field of Waterloo; or it may be something small and unnoticed, something unrecognized till years later. And so it was at Kohima.

The officer taking over the 4th/1st Gurkhas (the battalion that Warren considered unfit for action) was a young twenty-seven-year-old soldier called Derek Horsford. After the failure of the attacks by the Punjabis on Church Knoll on the 25th, Brigadier Loftus Tottenham said that the Gurkhas must have a go. But, as Horsford says: 'I refused, in fear and trepidation, to carry out a third frontal attack and offered an alternative plan—the Gun Spur operation. To my relief Tottenham listened very carefully and agreed the idea, but I remember him saying before I left to plan in detail: "It had bloody well better work".' In the event, it did, and was probably the most brilliantly planned and executed operation in the whole battle.

The sketch map on page 194 shows that to the north and south of Hunter's Hill the ground sloped away in two pointed spurs. The southern of these was known as Gun Spur, and the features on it (starting from the low ground upwards) 'False Crest', 'Nose', and 'Basha'. The slopes of the spur were steep and wooded, and Horsford's plan was to carry out a night infiltration. The tactical position of Gun Spur was important, because it was from here that fire could be brought down on the reverse slopes of Church Knoll and Hunter's Hill. It was no use, however, infiltrating a few men on to the Spur; the force had to be strong enough to resist any counter-attack until the rest of the battalion could join it the following day. And before anything could be done at all, the Gurkhas had to carry out intensive and highly coordinated patrolling so that the entire Jap positions could be plotted, their weak spots pinpointed, and routes through them charted. If surprise wasn't achieved the operation would obviously disintegrate before it started.

The battalion was still situated on Treasury Hill, from which it had a fairly close view of the Jap positions. Briefing the patrols was therefore comparatively easy, but (to quote Major Sir Christopher Nixon, one of the company commanders) 'The execution of the patrols was far more difficult, as once a patrol had left our position it had to descend into a deep jungle-clad valley, cross the intervening nala at the right point, and then in the blackness, scale the precipitous slope that led to Gun Spur.' All patrolling had to be carried out at night, so it was lucky that three nights were available before the operation; it was lucky, too, that the battalion had some excellent N.C.O.s 'who had learned their craft the hard way in the Arakan'. The patrols each consisted of two men, an N.C.O. and a picked rifleman, and their task, in each case, according to Horsford, 'was to report whether Basha, Nose, and an intermediate feature, False Crest, were held by the Japs or not. If they were held, then the patrols were to probe right into their defences and to report the strength of the enemy and the nature of their defences.' The patrols left Treasury just after dark and were ordered to leave the Spur an hour before first light, to avoid any Jap suspicions that the Gurkhas were particularly interested in the position. To quote Horsford again:

> 'The first patrols found False Crest and Nose clear. They then moved along the Jessami track [which rounded the Spur] and found a roadblock and several bunkers 100 yards east of False Crest, and another on the west near Kohima. Basha was found to be strongly defended by a series of bunker positions estimated to be held by thirty Japs. A patrol to Ring [400 yards south of the Spur] reported this also held by thirty Japs, well dug in.'

On the second night the patrols brought back the same information, except that the number of Japs on Basha had increased to forty. During the third night, the patrols brought back the same story, so it now seemed clear that neither False Crest nor Nose was occupied, but that Basha and Ring were. In other words the top and bottom features were occupied, while the two middle features were not.

Having this information, Horsford now worked out his plan, which was that at 1945 hours a company led by Nixon would move along the reconnoitred track to seize and hold False Crest. When this was done he would report by radio: 'In position and consolidating; no Japs around.' Patrols would go on to Nose, to make sure that it was still unoccupied; then on orders a second company would occupy it. Later, when these two forward companies were dug in and firmly established, a third company, with artillery and tank support, would attack Basha soon after first light. The assault companies were to carry extra ammunition, and rations and water, and defence stores were to be carried by men acting as porters. There was also a Gurkha signaller with each company, whose job was to reel out telephone cable as he went along. Horsford says: 'The cable was connected to one terminal of a field telephone which the signaller carried; to the other terminal was connected an earth wire which ran down to the signaller's leg and was connected to a steel spike on to the man's boot, so that when he stuck his spike into the ground the circuit was completed and the company commander could talk to me at any time. This is how I got progress reports.'

By the 29th, when everything was ready for the operation, its importance had grown immensely. The previous day, as it will be remembered, Church Knoll had defied the second series of attacks by the Punjabis; and in three days' time, according to the orders from Stopford, the 7th Division must begin its march south. With the whole 2nd Division temporarily exhausted, and the Queens and the Punjabis still recovering from their heavy mauling, the weight of responsibility on Horsford, his few British officers, and the young Gurkhas under their command, was enormous. But seldom can responsibility have been placed in better hands.

At 1945 hours Nixon fell in his company and they moved down into the valley below Treasury Hill. Here they followed a track in single file, and climbed up to the Jessami road which ran across their front. Here he waited quietly, then began the business of infiltrating on to False Crest quietly and methodically, with each man knowing exactly what was expected of him. First, two Gurkhas crept up on to the objective to make sure that it was still free of Japs. They were followed by a section which went on to occupy a position at the northern extremity of the feature. After them, in quick succession, came the rest of the platoon, then the whole company, which moved up to form a defensive position with all-round defense. To simplify matters, as the operation had to be carried out swiftly in pitch dark, the company commander had worked out a simple clock plan: one platoon occupying from 10 o'clock to 2 o'clock, the second from 2 to 6, and the third from 6 to 10. As soon as the troops were on the ground, Nixon went round with his gunner, adjusted the perimeter where necessary, and arranged a Defensive Fire plan. Wiring was started at once, but not digging because of the noise.

While Nixon's company was so engaged, he sent out a patrol as arranged to Nose, to make sure it was still unoccupied, and this patrol arrived in time to meet the commander of the next company which was concentrated just to the south of False Crest. This company then infiltrated on to Nose and carried out the same drill as Nixon's men had done. Patrols to Basha reported that it was still held, and this information was passed to Captain Carr, who brought his company forward just before dawn, ready to attack it. Everything was ready now; and the

Japs still had no knowledge whatever of the Gurkhas in their midst.

The artillery concentration came down from 25-pounders, mediums, 3.7 howitzers, and tanks. Then, at an agreed time it switched and the company of Gurkhas advanced some fifty yards behind the barrage. The tanks began firing superquick high explosive shells to clear the jungle and, a minute later, changed to armour-piercing shells. As the Gurkhas made their way up the hill the tanks then changed to their Browning machine-guns and fired overhead 'to keep the Japs' heads down'. Once the Gurkhas began nearing the bunkers, the tanks changed back to armour-piercing shells which they fired with great accuracy, only ten yards ahead of the leading files. By a prearranged plan, the men in these were wearing white towels on their backs so that the tank commanders could see them.

Then a snag came. There was a cloud-burst, and Horsford, not being able to see the towels, thought his men were late and ordered the tanks to fire for another five minutes. In fact, the Gurkhas were dead on time and were crouching only a few feet behind the shell-bursts. The result was that a good many of the Japs were still huddled down in the bunkers when the Gurkhas came at them and dozens were bayoneted, grenaded, or dealt with by kukris. Twenty or more rolled out of their bunkers and fled.

After this initial success, the Gurkhas were held up by a string of six inter-supporting bunkers on the crest of Basha, so decided to dig in below them. The action had gone magnificently, not a man being killed, and only twelve slightly wounded. Horsford now came forward with his headquarters and the rest of the battalion, and for the rest of the day the men dug themselves in. It wasn't a pleasant job, as the Japs harassed them with mortars and discharger grenades, and later, after dark, put in a number of counter-attacks. These did not dislodge anyone; and during the 31st the Gurkhas went on 'bunker-busting and raiding'. Here the pole-charges came in useful. Captain Green was shown how to use a Lifebuoy flamethrower entirely by touch in the dark—the battalion had never seen them before—and next morning sallied forth to use it. Unfortunately he couldn't get the flame to ignite and the apparatus merely squirted liquid. Crouched beside him, with bullets singing over their heads, his Gurkha assistant tried putting a match to the jet, but with no success. Green therefore threw the Lifebuoy away and called for another. This one worked, and Green moved forward to deal with a bunker, only to be shot at by another bunker further along, as Woodward of the Worcestershires had been. He received three bullets in the leg and his Gurkha was killed. As he was lying in the open it seemed that nothing could save him, but Subedar Narjang Ghale dashed out into the open, tied up his wounds, and carried him for nearly a hundred yards under heavy fire. For this action Narjang was awarded the Military Cross—but the flamethrowers weren't used again. Fortunately, by other means, not always less spectacular, the Gurkhas were able to reduce sixteen bunkers.

On the 1st June, three Sherman tanks were able to move along the Jessami track, then move up to join Horsford and his men. By then Horsford had been invited to attack Hunter's Hill, but the ground between it and his own position was so bare that it was impossible to poke his head out of the trench without getting shot at. So he asked the tank commander to take him on reconnaissance in order to look at the ground through the periscope. The tank commander agreed, though later regretted it, as the tank received several direct hits from artillery and mortar shells. Luckily they had no effect, but then the tank shot down a steep slope, much to the delight of the Gurkhas who were watching, and it took a long time to get it out. However, having seen something of the ground, Horsford told Loftus Tottenham he wasn't prepared to carry out a direct attack on the feature 'because I knew it would cause too many casualties'. It was therefore agreed that the objective should be pounded by artillery, tanks, and aircraft, until (so it was hoped) the Japs had had enough. Horsford was keen to take the position, however, if he could do so in his own way, and observed it carefully. On the night of the 1st June he kept sending out patrols, and when daylight came on the 2nd it seemed that there were very few Japs left on it. He therefore asked for an artillery concentration, then sent a company up the slope as hard as they could go. In a matter of minutes the objective, which had been disputed so long and had cost so many lives, was in the hands of the Gurkhas. They had completed everything demanded of them exactly to schedule, for the battalion due to relieve them chose this moment to appear.

*

By now the Queens had been on Church Knoll for twenty-four hours. With the rest of the Brigade they had been due for relief on the 1st June, but Loftus Tottenham was anxious to take all his objectives before handing over, and laid on an attack on the morning ofthat day. After an artillery concentration, and with supporting fire from the tanks, a platoon went into action, but were mortared off. However, at 1030 hours heavy rain and mist came down and the Queens went on to the feature again, and this time were able to dig in. The courageous, costly, and decisive role of 33rd Indian Brigade in the battle of Kohima was over.

At about this time also came news that Brigadier Warren's 161st Brigade, which was operating way out on the left flank, had gained three pimples called Lock, Stock and Barrel; and the Royal West Kents had got a platoon up on Firs Hill, where the Lancashire Fusiliers had been roughly handled some weeks earlier. Suddenly the whole picture of the battle had been transformed. As the 33rd Corps Account of Operations puts it: 'The battle... had been one of attrition against the dogged resistance of a determined enemy, capable of taking tremendous punishment. On the 2nd June he was no longer able to prolong the struggle and, somewhat demoralized, the enemy evacuated the Naga Village and withdrew east.'

Yes... Sato was pulling out. But how far back he would take up his next position, and how hard he'd fight to hold it, remained to be seen. But meanwhile the news that there was a chance to break through the ring swept through the tired, depleted battalions and miraculously they found new strength and new determination.

Chapter Twelve

Return to the Chindwin

Sato had decided to withdraw on the 30th, and immediately organized some suicidal rear parties, and put a rearguard of about 750 men under Miyazaki. Several pleas to Mutaguchi for permission to withdraw had brought nothing but abuse and a strongly worded order to stay where he was and keep fighting. During the past weeks, in his great despair, Sato had been signalling Major-General Tazoe, commander of the 5th Air Force Division, begging him for assistance. Finally, about the 27th, with nothing forthcoming, Sato signalled: 'Since leaving the Chindwin we have not received one bullet from you, nor a grain of rice. We are still under attack by the enemy. Please send us food by plane. The enemy are getting regular food supplies and more troops.' Whether Tazoe was under orders not to help, or whether his squadrons were now far too stretched to do anything, it is difficult to say. Nearly half his planes, according to some accounts, were engaged in the attack on the Chindits, and this may well have been one of the determining factors. However, whatever the reason, no supply planes arrived whatsoever, and Sato finally signalled Mutaguchi, advising him that he intended to withdraw. Mutaguchi signalled back: 'Retreat and I will court-martial you.' To this Sato replied: 'Do what you please. I will bring you down with me.' Then on the 31st, having given the order for withdrawal, Sato sent his now famous signal: 'The tactical ability of the 15th Army staff lies below that of cadets.' After this he closed down his radio. Some idea of the stress Sato was undergoing can be gathered from a letter he wrote home to his wife, after watching the tattered remnants of his Division begin straggling away from Kohima. He wrote: 'I cannot see the enemy through my blinding tears.' Ironically, at this precise moment, Mutaguchi was planning yet another attack against Palel, a bastion of the Imphal Perimeter, in which Sato's division was to take a leading part. When he heard what Sato had done, he exclaimed: 'He has lost the battle for me! I will never forgive him.'

Nevertheless, he still went ahead with his operation against Palel, and on the 4th June issued a Special Order of the Day:

> 'After a month's desperate and courageous fighting, we surrounded the strategic position of Kohima. In three months we had the enemy hemmed in round Imphal and the battle situation stabilized. Still all this had not been fully up to the expectations of our nation. This is indeed a most regrettable matter.
>
> Withholding my tears and painful as it is, I shall for the time being withdraw my troops from Kohima. It is my resolve to reassemble the whole army and with one great push capture Imphal.
>
> This forthcoming plan of operations will be the Army's last. You must fully realize that if a decisive victory is not obtained we shall not be able to strike back again.
>
> ON THIS ONE BATTLE RESTS THE FATE OF THE EMPIRE. Officers and men must, however, keep in mind the seriousness of the great task and create a fighting will to win. Everyone must unswervingly serve the THRONE and reach

the ultimate goal so that the Son of Heaven and the Nation may be forever guarded.

MUTAGUCHI Renya.'

While relations between Stopford and Grover had by no means reached breaking point, as those between their Japanese adversaries, they were still deteriorating. When Stopford received Grover's orders for a new operation to try and sort out the Aradura situation, he professed himself unable to understand them, and on the 1st June went forward to suggest a plan of his own. This was to launch 'a wide, sweeping movement to the east' in the belief that any direct assault on the Aradura position was now of secondary importance. Leaving Grover to work out the tactical and administrative problems involved in such an operation, Stopford went on to see Frank Messervy at his headquarters, before going back to his own. Later that night Stopford heard of 33rd Brigade's successes on Church Knoll and Hunter's Hill, and immediately appreciated their tactical significance. The infantry could now be pushed south through the Assam Barracks area, to attack the three features on a ridge about a mile from Kohima, which now constituted the centre of the Jap line. They were called Dyer Hill, Pimple, and Big Tree Hill; and when they had been dealt with the road was open to Pfuchama, a defended village, 4,907 feet high, and Phesema, on the Imphal road, three miles south of the Aradura Spur. Once this hook had been brought off successfully, Stopford and his divisional commanders believed that the Japs would pull out of Aradura.

Once the genera] plan had been agreed with Stopford, Grover gave the job of launching this left hook to Michael West. Though his brigade was weak in numbers, it hadn't received such a bad mauling as the others and was still in good heart. The Dorsets were now back with the Worcestershires and the

Camerons, which gave the brigade an added confidence; the mutual respect and trust between these three battalions was tremendous. The initial orders for the operation were given to West on the 2nd June, but at that time 5th Brigade was still messing around on the Aradura Spur, waiting to exploit any success achieved by 4th or 6th Brigades, and it took a good twenty-four hours to get it concentrated. Meanwhile, patrols were pushed out by 268th and 114th Brigades which, on the morning of the 3rd, reported that Big Tree Hill and Dyer Hill were unoccupied. Grover immediately met Brigadier Dyer, commanding 268th Brigade, who gave him the latest information, including the news that his patrol on Big Tree Hill had run up a telephone line to keep in constant touch. Grover therefore gave orders to Michael West that he should get on to the ridge with all speed, occupying it as far west as Garage Spur, on the Imphal road.

It is worth mentioning here that it was on the 3rd June that the 2nd Division Recce Regiment, under Lieut.-Colonel J. M. K. Bradford, came down off Mount Pulebadze where they had been fighting in an isolated position for nineteen days. The Japs they had encountered, they said, 'were big men, well clothed and equipped, and extremely aggressive, reacting at once to all our own offensive moves'. They were probably men from Captain Watari's battalion of the 138th Regiment, which the Camerons had encountered in their first action on Bunker Hill.

By the afternoon of the 3rd June, the leading unit of 5th Brigade, the Dorsets, was deployed on the lower slopes of Dyer Hill. The Bombay Grenadiers of 268th Brigade had again reported it clear, but Jock McNaught sent out his own patrol under a brilliant young officer with the improbable name of 'Snagger' Highett, who came back exploding: 'Unoccupied! I was bloody well shot up from Dyer Hill, Big Tree Hill, *and* the Pimple!' Whether the Grenadiers' patrols hadn't been where they should have, or whether the Japs were playing their old game of lying doggo, it's impossible to say; but obviously McNaught had to

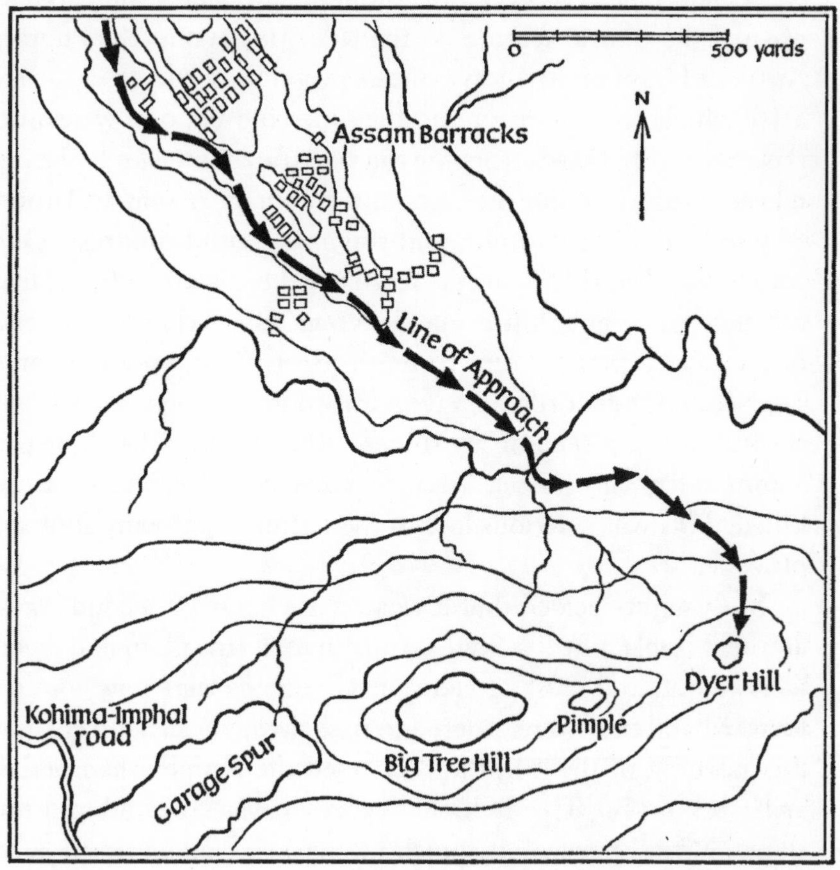

proceed with caution. Just before dark he tried to push forward a company on to Dyer Hill, but it came under fire from the east end of the feature and so McNaught decided to go into a tight perimeter for the night. It poured with rain hour after hour, and the troops had no evening meal, but next morning Clive Chettle (who had distinguished himself in the tennis court battle) took his company and pushed them forward on to the crest. The Japs had evacuated the position in the night, leaving a well-prepared bunker on the reverse slope. McNaught then decided to go for his next objective, Big Tree Hill, which lay half a mile to the west. Before he could get at it, though, it was necessary to dispose of the central feature on the ridge, known as the Pimple. At 0810 hours an artillery concentration was put down on it, after which one company and the Guerrilla platoon went into the attack. Fifty yards from the top the troops came under heavy machine-gun fire, but the company commander sent a platoon to work round to its right, and this made good progress. One section reached the top of the feature, where it killed four Japs, but then the whole hill came alive and the section was forced off, as was a platoon sent to reinforce it. Eventually the company commander ordered a withdrawal and troops came down the hill, being picked off by snipers. Both Davies, the company commander, and Purser, who led the Guerrilla platoon, were killed. This was a serious loss to the battalion, already short of officers.

McNaught decided that it was no use having a second crack at the Pimple until a well co-ordinated fire-plan had been worked out, and West agreed. The Camerons were now coming forward and they were ordered to pass through the Dorsets. On the morning of the 4th, they occupied the Pimple, then put in an attack on Big Tree Hill. The weather was still foul and the slopes were slippery, but somehow the Jocks managed to keep going. The leading company was commanded by Major Angus Douglas, the battalion second-in-command, and directing his troops on the hill, he was shot through the neck and died soon afterwards. He was a small, dapper man, with Highland courtesy, and great wit. He was immensely popular, not only in his own regiment but throughout the whole brigade, and his death brought a tremendous feeling of melancholy. The dying phases of the battle were proving just as bitter as the others.

In the afternoon a fighting patrol was sent out to try and ascertain the strength of the enemy, which was found to be considerable. There was therefore no alternative but to put in a full-dress attack the following morning.

Again a heavy artillery concentration was put down and two companies went into the attack. The going was difficult at first, through thick jungle, and the troops came across a nala which no one had warned them about. By the time they had all succeeded in wading across half an hour had been lost, which meant that the advance took an hour. Apart from seven batteries of 25-pounders, the Camerons were supported by a troop of tanks firing over their heads from the Treasury, the brigade mortars, and two platoons of the Manchesters' machine-guns. They had been issued with smoke grenades in order to indicate their progress, and this device worked admirably. Watching them from his command post, West was able to keep the fire from the Manchesters and the tanks just ahead of the Jocks. One of the Camerons' officers was beside the tank commander with his radio set to report regularly on the progress of the infantry. This arrangement worked excellently too, and the Camerons were full of admiration for the close support they had received. By 1130 hours the whole position was in their hands. The battalion consolidated on the crest and sent out patrols towards Garage Spur which was found to be clear of the enemy.

While the Camerons were engaged in this attack the Dorsets pushed forward a patrol towards Pfuchama. By noon they had reported it clear, and Jock McNaught set off with the rest of the battalion. Like all the hooks that preceded it, this operation involved passing through some formidable country. First the troops had to climb down a thousand feet to the Warno Nala lying in its dark, rocky chasm, then up again along a track which seemed determined to reach the sky. Before the village the track split in two, and when the leading company was misled by its Naga guide, McNaught found himself heading the advance, and had to bring up a second company to put ahead. Towards the summit, the leading troops came under heavy fire, and the situation looked serious as the track was so precipitous that no one could move off it. The whole battalion therefore had to retrace its track down the hill and follow the company which had gone wrong, round the track to the right. Clive Chettle, leading this company, managed to get into the village by late afternoon and reported it now clear. Then it was learned that a platoon of another company had come across some heavily-laden Japs getting out of the village to the north, and killed them. Among their weapons was found a Taisho light machine-gun, presumably the one which had been firing earlier on. The battalion had now been on the move for sixty hours, mostly in the pouring rain, and with no opportunity to brew up char, so was feeling somewhat tired. However, when orders were reached to start patrolling towards Phesema, the village on the Imphal road, where the hook was to be completed, the men somehow found the energy.

The morning of the 6th June dawned bright and clear and even by seven o'clock the day was warming up. It was sticky, too, and the least physical movement brought a rash of sweat. The whole morning the Camerons, 5th Brigade headquarters, and parties from the rear echelons struggled up the steep hill towards Pfuchama. On the narrow track the troops jostled with the mules and several brave characters grabbed hold of their tails to help pull them up. Luckily the mules didn't seem to mind and went plodding on. Towards eleven o'clock the heat and humidity became almost unbearable, and the troops found themselves only able to climb in short bursts. So there was a good deal of crossing and re-crossing and the units became jumbled, though no one worried. All that mattered was to reach the top. Some time before noon the village came in sight and the column wound its way through an ornately carved gateway, ascended a flight of stone steps, and found itself in the village street. Here the tall figure of Michael West was standing, and as the sweating, exhausted troops came by him he shouted: 'Come on, stick it! The Second Front has opened. We've landed in Normandy!'

Feeling this to be such an important moment in history, the staff captain slipped off his pack and, having got his breath, paused for a moment to fix the scene in his memory. That night he wrote:

> 'What a place to be told this news! The sunlight was streaming across the mountains, stretched west and south as far as the eyes could see. Aradura lay opposite, and below Veswema, and far away on the southern horizon the great height of Mao Songsang. Great, green, untamed country, almost as unaware of man's presence on the earth as the day God created it. I gazed for a moment, then thought of Normandy and the men fighting that vital battle there. Their battle seems very far away from our own, but all today I found myself thinking of it... of the Normandy beaches where I have swum so many times, and hoping the troops have got across them. Other people must have felt like this too, as all day the troops have been coming up to our signallers asking "How's it going? How are they doing in France?"'

After tea, Michael West held a conference, producing a message from Grover congratulating 5th Brigade on breaking through the ring of Japanese defences. 'The Jap,' he added, 'is undoubtedly trying to pull out. Our task now is to get hard after them, cut them off if we can and try to let no enemy escape. Flat out everybody.' To achieve this desired end, a company of the Worcestershires were already marching across country towards Phesema. They arrived there in the evening after eleven hours on the move, and occupied the high ground above the village. At 1900 hours the rest of the battalion began advancing to join them. 'It was an extremely hard march,' Major Elliott has written, 'as it was done on a pitch black night, through waterlogged, terraced paddy fields, and the terraces were just too high to step up, which meant climbing up three or four feet every hundred yards or so. However, by dawn we had occupied our objective.'

The road was now cut behind Miyazaki's men on Aradura; and it now remained to be seen if they would pull out, as anticipated.

They did. During the night of the 6th, Patrols from the Lancashire Fusiliers pushing forward on to the lower slopes of the Spur found that the Japs had slipped away, and operations began immediately to clear the road-blocks by Garage Spur so that the armoured column, which had now been organized, could now surge forward. Meanwhile the Royal Scots were on the move early and soon contacted the Worcestershires. By lunch the Royal Norfolk were passing through the Royal Scots; and by evening 4th Brigade headquarters and the Lancashire Fusiliers were established at Kigwema, nearly three miles to the south of Phesema. The whole division was suddenly full of fight and itching to get on again—after Aradura, the men felt things could never be quite so bad again. Brigadier Smith (an Indian Army officer) who came to take over 6th Brigade after Shapland was wounded wrote later: 'I was amazed at the fortitude of these soldiers and their officers, and their amazing powers of recovery. 6th Brigade was really badly mauled on the night before I took over... and yet within a fortnight they set off down the road after the Japs like a real good pack of foxhounds.'

*

In the excitement of getting on the move again, no one noticed that the battle of Kohima had come to an end.... That when the Jap rearguard slipped silently off the rear slopes of Aradura Spur in the darkness soon after midnight, the whole ridge was clear from end to end.

The battle had lasted sixty-four days and seen some of the most stubborn, close, and bloody fighting in the whole of the Second World War. It had been fought across an utterly incredible terrain, in appalling weather. Surely not even the battlefields of Flanders saw such rainfall. The courage and fortitude shown by all ranks and all races, and by both armies had been utterly astonishing. The British, Indian and Gurkha troops had suffered some 4,000 casualties, an abnormally high proportion of them officers. Sato had lost over 3,000 men killed and 4,000 wounded; his division was smashed irretrievably. Yet outgunned, bereft of air cover, and denied supplies of reinforcements, he had fought a great defensive action. Though never succeeding in taking the whole of Kohima, he had given Mutaguchi two months to crack the Imphal box, and even now the road was still cut. No general on earth could have achieved more.

The job of opening the road was to take another fifteen days. Though Miyazaki had only 750 men, the country was in his favour, the road winding up towards Mao Songsang like a snake, and crossing hundreds of culverts and bridges.

Four hundred and fifty of Miyazaki's men were from the 124th Regiment, under Major Ishido, and the remainder from the 58th. Relations between these two regiments had deteriorated even further at Kohima, the 58th maintaining that the 124th had not done its fair share of the fighting, and was unreliable anyway. Only the strong personality of Miyazaki,' one soldier has written, 'held the rearguard together and inspired it to action.'

This action in very favourable country was most effective. Each time the rearguard blew a bridge or culvert and then covered it with fire the whole 2nd Division was brought to a halt.

To reduce delays to a minimum, Grover had thought out the composition of his armoured column very carefully. It consisted of a troop of armoured cars with a sapper officer, a troop of tanks, and then the vanguard commander in a carrier. He was followed by infantry in carriers, then the gunner O.P. officers. After them came more tanks, more infantry, and more sappers. The drill was that when a bridge was found blown, the tanks would engage the enemy with fire, while the sappers got out to do a reconnaissance, and the infantry set off on a flanking movement. Other sappers removed mines and obstacles from the road, often under fire. Once the road was clear and the bridge or culvert mended, the whole column would move on again, but nevertheless the whole job would take at least three hours and often more. Sometimes the infantry had to go up several hundred feet through difficult country to get round behind the Japs.

The difficulties of these outflanking actions were not appreciated by 33rd Corps staff, who kept sending back adverse reports on 2nd Division's progress. 'They're advancing very slowly and being frightened by shadows.... Have advanced only two and a half miles against practically no opposition....' Stopford kept blaming Grover, who in return urged his men forward.

The actions weren't confined to clearing road-blocks. At Viswema Miyazaki prepared a formidable defensive position which was only cleared on the 14th after five days of fighting and patrolling. All this time the rain kept pouring down; and the battalions, through sick, wounded, and killed, kept dwindling and dwindling. When Geoffrey White, who took over the Dorsets from Jock McNaught (who had been promoted to command 4th Brigade) had the battalion paraded, to his horror he found that they could all stand in a single basha.

Stopford's impatience to get on—as at Kohima—is very understandable. The supply position at Imphal was still deteriorating. As early as the 19th May the Chiefs of Staff had been asking Giffard why, with so many divisions employed, 'the fighting is characterized by company and platoon actions'. Giffard replied that the first objective was killing Japs and this had to be done by destroying each Jap in his foxhole. The Chiefs of Staff also criticized the passive role of 4th Corps: Why, they wanted to know, weren't they pushing up the road in force to meet 33rd Corps coming down it? Giffard had to explain that

that wasn't their job. On the 8th June Mountbatten sent a telegram to the Chiefs of Staff in Washington, saying that the air transport at his disposal was insufficient, and that the reserves on the Imphal plain would be down to six days by the end of June. To deal with this situation he planned to step up the airlift, even if necessary diverting planes from the Strategic Air Force; he would also ask 4th Corps to develop their offensive northwards to meet the southward drive of 33rd Corps. Further measures (he added) would be the evacuation of as many sick and non-combatants from Imphal as possible, and the slaughter of local cattle to help with meat supplies. Finally, he intended to investigate the Bishenpur track as a possible supply route.

Slim received a copy of the telegram on his return from the Northern Front on the 12th, and realized immediately how impractical some of the points were. The slaughtering of cattle would have had a disastrous effect on the Manipuris, both from a religious and an economic angle. And the Bishenpur track could not be used until the great suspension bridge at milestone 52 had been repaired. The only way the situation could be saved was by opening the road as soon as possible. In a directive on the 9th June, Mountbatten laid down that it must be open by mid-July, and concerning this Slim has noted: 'I was grateful to him [Mountbatten] for not being stampeded by more nervous people into setting too early a date. I intended that the road should be open well before mid-July, but I was now much more interested in destroying Japanese divisions than in "relieving" Imphal.' If that was Slim's precise aim, it was not shared by other members of the high command. On the 11th June, Stopford received a letter from Giffard announcing that at a meeting at Mountbatten's headquarters it had been proposed that 'we force a large convoy through to Imphal in the same way that convoys were forced through to Malta.' Stopford's remark on reading this suggestion is neither repeatable nor printable. All he could deduce was that, in their frantic hurry to get the road open, some of the S.E.A.C. staff had completely lost touch with reality.

From the 12th to the 15th it poured in torrents; but on the 15th, with Viswema now in their hands, the 2nd Division moved on again. On the 17th, the leading troops passed over the ridge at Mao Songsang, where a major action had been expected, with barely a halt. On the 18th, 5th Brigade rushed forward behind the armoured column a record distance of thirteen miles and halted before a blown bridge, facing the great ridge of Maram. All Intelligence reports now indicated that the Japs were pulling out to the east (where Messervy's column would get them) and indeed some indication of their plight was evident to the British troops as they advanced. More and more corpses were strewn along the road, some of them naked, having been stripped of their clothes by their ragged comrades. Sato was trying to get 1,500 stretcher cases across the mountain tracks to the Chindwin, a task of frightening proportions. The tracks had become quagmires in the valleys and mud-slides on the slopes; and the men carrying the stretchers, like everyone else in the columns, were half-starved and exhausted. The tracks were littered with the arms and ammunition they were throwing away as they staggered and slithered forward. From the 6th June, Sato had lost radio contact with Mutaguchi and had no knowledge as to whether the rearguard had been destroyed, or how close the Allied columns were behind him. When the 15th Army Chief of Staff, Major-General Momoyo Kunomura, came forward to see Sato, he declared himself astonished at the amazing—and in the Japanese Army unprecedented—spectacle of headlong retreat. The object of Kunomura's mission was to deliver Sato an order from Mutaguchi. This told him to stop withdrawing and to send his main body to help the 15th Division, still fighting to the north of Imphal. Sato refused point-blank. He said angrily: 'The 15th Army have failed to send me supplies and ammunition since the operation began. This failure releases me from any obligation to obey the order—and in any case it would be impossible to comply.' When Kunomura reminded him of the possible consequences of refusing to obey an order, Sato retorted: 'It won't worry me at all, if I am put on trial—I will expose the truth. I have got statements here from two generals who agree with me that Kohima was a stupid battle. Somehow I will make Terauchi and G.H.Q. Tokyo realize how foolish Mutaguchi has been.'

This interview (according to Colonel Yamaki who was there) took place in Sato's tent, the staff waiting outside and 'trembling a little when we heard Sato's voice raised in anger'.

The reason why Mutaguchi had sent his Chief of Staff in person was that a few days previously (on the 14th June) he had despatched a signals officer, Lieutenant Nose, who came back somewhat crestfallen with a dusty answer. The actual date of the Sato–Kunomura meeting is in some doubt; the archives in the National Defence College give it as the 22nd June, while other authorities quote the 21st. Colonel Yamaki says that according to his records it happened on the 19th.

The withdrawal continued; and Kunomura returned to 15th Army Headquarters. Later he was censured for having failed to convey Mutaguchi's order as strongly as he should have done; but having seen the plight of the retreating soldiers, he probably realized that the order was quite pointless.

Miyazaki fought on, but with diminishing results. The troops at Maram were given orders to hold it for ten days, but after a brilliant action laid on by Michael West and executed by the Worcestershire Regiment, this formidable position fell in a matter of hours. By the night of the 19th the vanguard had reached milestone 80, and by the next day, milestone 88. Small pockets of resistance were encountered for the next eleven miles but were soon brushed aside. On the morning of the 22nd, men of the Durham Light Infantry moved forward with the tanks of the vanguard, which after two miles came under fire. The enemy troops were small in number, and consisted of walking wounded from a Japanese hospital which had now closed down, pathetic, emaciated creatures, whose orders were to go on fighting till every man was killed. These they faithfully carried out. The vanguard pushed on again, brushed aside another small party, fired at some Japs retreating across the hills to the east, then advanced to milestone 108. Here, according to Sean Kelly of the Durhams, 'the tanks spotted more movement away forward where elephant grass gave way to trees and began to brass it up properly. Soon they stopped. A plaintive message relayed through many sets had reached them: we were brassing up the advance elements of the 5th Indian Division of the beleaguered 4th Corps. Imphal was relieved. We sat alone in the sunshine and smoked and ate. Soon the staff cars came purring both ways. The road was open. It was a lovely day.'

It was a lovely day in many ways. The rain had stopped and the sunlight was again dancing across the mountains. Miraculously, Assam had turned from a soaking, muddy hell into a wild paradise.

That night the trucks rolled into Imphal, and soon afterwards the troops had their first glass of beer for many weeks.

From a tactical viewpoint the opening of the road meant that the 14th Army could now reap the fruits of victory at Kohima, as Imphal was transformed from a beleaguered fortress into a base for offensive operations. The 'twin battles' (to use Slim's phrase) had yielded a double triumph; and the moment had arrived when, as he has said, 'we would pay back all we owed—with interest'.

Four days later, even Mutaguchi had to recognize that the game was up and recommended to Kawabe that his Army should withdraw to a line from the Yu River to Tiddim. Cautiously, however, Kawabe refused to signal his agreement until permission had been obtained from Southern Army Commander, Field-Marshal Count Terauchi, whose headquarters was in

Singapore. He therefore ordered Mutaguchi to fight on, and meanwhile despatched an officer to Singapore. Owing to bad weather, the latter couldn't fly out till the 3rd July, so the hopeless struggle went on. On the 4th, however, Kawabe received the necessary permission to prepare to withdraw, but meanwhile was told to continue his action against Palel. Mutaguchi by now seems to have lost all touch with reality and, with his Army breaking up fast, ordered yet another offensive by the 15th and 31st Divisions. Nothing happened; nothing could happen. And on the 8th July Mutaguchi ordered his battered troops to withdraw east towards the Chindwin. At Kohima and Imphal they had suffered the greatest defeat in the history of the Japanese Army; a Japanese writer, Kase Toshikazu, has even called it: 'the worst of its kind yet chronicled in the annals of war'. The latter is probably an exaggeration; but, surely, not even on Napoleon's retreat from Moscow has a beaten army gone back under such terrible conditions. According to Toshikazu, 'the ranks thinned down daily as thirst and hunger overtook the retreating column... sick and wounded had to be abandoned by the hundreds. In order to avoid capture these men were usually forced to seek death at their own hands.'

Lieutenant Hirobumi Daimats (who has since become famous in Japan as trainer of the Olympic volley-ball team) was a transport officer in 31st Division, and has written of the retreat: 'Most of us were suffering from malaria or malnutrition or both.... If a horse was found wandering it was shot immediately and cooked and eaten, even though we had no salt. Every day we dug up bamboo roots and ate them raw, and they kept us alive for six weeks till we reached the Chindwin.... There were very few of us left then.'

Shizuo Marayama, a war correspondent, has written: 'At Kohima we were starved and then crushed... discipline went, then the troops wavered and we fell into disorder. The regimental officers, N.C.O.s and men trusted each other but they were lied to... then there was that ugly struggle between Sato and Mutaguchi. In the end we had no ammunition, no clothes, no food, no guns... the men were barefoot and ragged, and threw away everything except canes to help them walk. Their eyes blazed in their lean bodies... all they had to keep them going was grass and water. And there were jungles, great mountains, and flooded rivers barring their way.... At Kohima we and the enemy were close together for over fifty days, and could watch each other's movement; but while they got food, we starved.'

Apart from starvation and dysentery, there was the malaria which struck through the ranks. A soldier of the 58th has written: 'The malaria was worse than anyone had expected... it drove some men mad. Usually it was accompanied with diarrhoea, and men would be going forty or fifty times a day, most of them with blood.'

The longer the retreat went on the more the wounded suffered. An N.C.O. has written: 'A soldier who was wounded in the right leg said he could not go on any further, and asked his friends to leave him to die. But they said, "With our wounds and malaria, we'll never reach the Chindwin either," so stayed with him... they thought it better to die with their friend.' Another soldier said after his return to Japan: 'Some badly wounded soldiers put a grenade to their chest and committed suicide.... Sometimes an officer, seeing men suffering, would put them out of their misery with an injection.' This observation comes from a private soldier who survived the retreat: 'The curious thing was that when a man decided to commit suicide he always lay down by the body of another man, or of a group. Men seem to need company, even in death.'

Many of the troops were buoyed up by the hope that once they reached Sittaung they would receive food and proper medical care, but their hopes again were dashed; to quote Marayama again: 'The field hospital on the way to Sittaung was terrible. Patients kept flowing into it before others could be transported to the rear. Only a few men were under cover... most of them were lying outside in the jungle, or slung in hammocks from the trees. All the men had to cover them were overcoats and they would shiver with the cold... many of the men whose arms or legs had been amputated were so far gone that you could not tell whether they were alive or dead.'

Of the 750 men in Miyazaki's rearguard just over 400 survived.

Some years later, a Burmese villager told how he watched group after group of Japanese soldiers as they filtered back through his village. Usually in the evening, having scrounged what food they could for a meal, they would squat in circles and talk. The villager noticed, however, that if a certain word was uttered the soldiers would immediately break off the conversation, and hang their heads in silence. He had no idea what the word meant, and naturally assumed it must be Japanese. Some time later, however, he learned that it wasn't Japanese at all but an Assam place-name. Kohima.

Even as recently as June 1965, when a journalist approached Colonel Kuniji Kato, Sato's Chief Staff Officer, for an account of his experiences, he refused, courteously but firmly: 'Not Kohima...' he said. 'Not that great bitter battle.' Kato had spent most of his time at the main Divisional headquarters, some miles from the action, but even there the bitterness of defeat had so impressed itself upon him that twenty-one years later he still could not bear to talk about it.

General Sato left the 31st Division on the 5th July, having received orders to report to 15th Army Headquarters. In a farewell speech to his staff, he said:

> 'It is clear that this operation was scheduled by the foolish desire of one man: Lieut.-General Mutaguchi, commander of the 15th Army. I do not intend to be censured by anyone. Our 3 1st Division has done its duty. For two months we

have defended our positions against strong enemy forces: and not one of their men during that time passed down the Imphal Road.

Before God, I am not ashamed.

Now I must say good-bye to you. I remember the hard time we had at Kohima and how you helped me do my duty there. I thank you all sincerely.

I ask the forgiveness of those who lie dead at Kohima because of my poor talent. Though my body is parted from them, I shall always remain with them in spirit. Nothing can separate those of us who were tried in the fire at Kohima. Now the moment has come when I cease to be your commander; but I hope we shall meet again at the Yasakuni Shrine. I pray for your health and happiness. Good-bye.'

After making this speech he left immediately for the Chindwin, accompanied solely by his batman. Despite these humiliating circumstances, his feelings were not of self-pity but of rage against Mutaguchi. In his luggage he carried a detailed statement justifying his actions and condemning the inefficiency of the 15th Army. Now he could no longer fight with guns, he intended to start fighting with words. Whether or not one admires Sato as a soldier, it is difficult not to admire him as a man.

Chapter Thirteen

Postscript and Post Mortem

'Only those who have seen the terrific nature of the country under these conditions will be able to appreciate your achievements and especially those of the infantry.'

This sentence is taken from a message written by Mountbatten for issue 'to all ranks on the Manipur Road'. In a few words it sums up a great truth about the battle of Kohima, and explains why the magnitude of the victory bought at such great cost by the 2nd British Division, the 161st Indian Brigade, and the 33rd Indian Brigade, was underrated at the time in Delhi, in London, and in Washington. It does not explain, however, why the role played by Grover's Division should have been so criticized, and even denigrated, both at the time and since. The reasons for this are many and complex; and they are well worth examining.

To begin with, political considerations demanded that the existence of the 2nd Division in the Indian theatre should be publicized as little as possible. (As already mentioned, Congress politicians had been complaining about the expense of maintaining a British formation since 1942.) The result was that British troops reading newspaper accounts of actions they had taken part in were dismayed to find that reference was made solely to 'Indian troops'. The omission was particularly distressing to officers and men in hospital, many of them badly wounded and having suffered great privation during their long journey from the front. Even the victory of the Royal Norfolk on G.P.T. Ridge was allocated to Indian troops in one account. This and other injustices led to a flare-up of all the old jealousies and suspicions between the British and Indian Armies, which had completely died down under fire. In hospitals and convalescent depots, in cafés and clubs and bars, there would be violent arguments and recrimination. Many Indian Army officers—misled by the newspaper accounts and the rumours generated by them—were heard declaring that the British troops of 2nd Division had not captured a single objective; that their abject failure had been covered by the two Indian Army brigades. Arguments concerning the respective merits of various formations have existed since armies began—even Caesar's Tenth Legion excited jealousy as well as admiration—and normally one should not take them so seriously. But in this case one must do so, as ill-informed and biased criticisms of 2nd Division's conduct at Kohima have found their way into books and even the official histories.

Slim called the division 'brave, but inexperienced', adding 'its very dash rendered it liable to heavy casualties'. It has also been called slow, road-bound, and unimaginative; and Colonel Barker has suggested that the root of its troubles 'lay in lack of patrolling experience which was essential to pinpoint Jap bunkers, and also in lack of administrative experience. Nor did they have much experience of working with the Indian Army... whom they looked down on—largely because their experience of Indians was limited to that with Indians in the bazaars.'

These are sweeping criticisms which demand separate consideration.

First, perhaps, one may take the charge that the division was 'road-bound'. At once one must admit that it had a vast number of vehicles— far too many for the line of communications to absorb. As Slim points out: '... its lorries, parked nose to tail, threatened to turn the two-way main road into a one-way track.' But this is not to say that the division stayed tethered to its vehicles, either mentally or physically. Once mule companies and Naga coolies had been allocated, the units moved off the road immediately; the Camerons carried out a flanking march to gain the first objective, Bunker Hill; 5th Brigade were supplied for weeks on end on Merema Ridge and in Naga Village by mule column, Nagas, and air-drops; 4th Brigade were away from the road for weeks during their march round Pulebadze and their subsequent ordeal on G.P.T. Ridge; the Recce Regiment was on Pulebadze for nineteen days; and in the final phase of the battle, 5th Brigade were again away from the road in their hook on Pfuchama and Phesema. Altogether it is true to say that most of the troops, for most of the time, were away from the road and their vehicles; they traversed some of the most difficult country ever traversed in the history of warfare, climbed mountains, scaled cliffs, cut through virgin jungle, and forded rivers. Not until 7th Division were out on their left flank and the advance on Imphal began was the whole division supplied along the road.

The second criticism is that the division was inexperienced. It was certainly inexperienced in the form of warfare that it encountered at Kohima; but one might ask what other troops in the world had experience in such terrain? Brigadier Stevens, the C.C.R.A. to 33rd Corps, wrote after the battle: 'If I was asked what sort of warfare 2 Div have been doing I should quite candidly say that I do not know. It is certainly not jungle warfare as the term implies; it is certainly not mountain warfare, although the hills are very high; it is certainly not ordinary warfare....' It can be argued that the problems faced at Kohima would have come fresh to any formation in any army. It is not true to say either that the division had not been into action; it had fought in Europe in 1940 and been evacuated through Dunkirk, and four battalions had fought in the Arakan in 1943. A large percentage of its officers and men had therefore been in action before. Admittedly the division as a whole had not fought in Burma; but it was highly trained, and its technical services at least had reached a stage of perfection probably unequalled by any formation in the Far Eastern theatre. Even the Indian troops of 33rd Brigade said they had never been so well fed and supplied as when attached to the Division. What is true is that as a Combined Operations Assault Division the formation was wrongly equipped for the battle it was asked to undertake. But that was merely one of the chances of war.

The next criticism is 'lack of patrolling experience'. First it must be pointed out that the division was not seeing jungle for the first time, but had just completed several months' intensive jungle training south of Belgaum. Admittedly there is no substitute for patrolling in contact with the enemy and because of this at least two major mistakes were made. Patrols reported ridges clear, having failed to find the top of them, or being deceived by false crests, and their units later paid the price. But these are merely two examples from thousands of patrols; and there are many examples of brilliant patrolling to counter them. Phillips of the Worcestershires, Cameron and White of the Camerons, Highett of the Dorsets, and many other young officers built up tremendous reputations as patrol leaders. It was brilliant patrolling which led to 5th Brigade's astonishing march on Naga Village, and many other operations. As the casualties among junior officers began to mount, there is no doubt that the standard of patrolling declined somewhat, but, even to the end, there were some outstanding exceptions. The patrols by the Camerons and Worcestershires led to the last and most brilliant victory in the whole campaign, at Maram. On the whole it is difficult to condemn the Division's patrolling.

The charge that the Division's tactics were unimaginative is hard to maintain also. Its moves were often unorthodox; its brigadiers often took great risks. Victor Hawkins twice risked his brigade and twice brought off a brilliant coup. Tanks were used in terrain where no one, not even the tank commanders and the sappers, had believed they could penetrate. Major-General R. P. Pakenham Walsh, in his *History of the Royal Engineers,* pays special tribute to these efforts. And where, it might be asked, in the whole history of warfare has a brigade buried its boots, got into gym shoes, and moved silently by night across the enemy's front? It must be admitted, of course, that many frontal attacks were made, most of them costly; but until one has examined the terrain and explored the alternatives it is useless to condemn the frontal attack *per se.* Sometimes it is unavoidable.

The charge of bad administration is an easy one to make from a distance. Certainly the Division was entirely ignorant of mules as a method of supply; it had never received air-drops; it had never worked with Nagas or coolies. From the start its staff officers had to improvise. But it is difficult to maintain that the tactical course of the battle was affected by any administrative or supply failure, except in one respect: the shortage of 25-pounder ammunition, especially smoke, and the complete failure of 3.7 howitzer ammunition. This matter has been glossed over by professional historians, but as Grover has written: 'This shortage naturally had a definite bearing (and a restrictive effect) on our operations... we were never able to give any operation the full support of the Divisional Artillery, and it was only at the end that we had more than two medium guns. By European ideas, one would hesitate to lay on a set-piece brigade operation with less than the Div. R.A. to support it, some Corps Artillery, and probably an Army Group R.A. (or part of one) thrown in.... The Gunner problem certainly made our task of giving adequate support to the attacking troops, and of neutralizing areas from which they could be enfiladed by hidden Jap M.G.s, more difficult; also that of knocking out bunkers, even when located.' Grover also emphasizes that close air support as laid on in Europe was also impossible because of the time-lag.

The final and probably most serious charge against the 2nd Division is that it was slow. Stopford's staff frequently alleged this, though at least one member changed his ideas once he had walked over the Japanese positions after their capture. Barker suggests the Division was slow due to the fact that mobility was 'more difficult to maintain in the terrain and climate of Manipur than that of an Indian formation'. Most certainly it should be acknowledged that Indian troops are better on mountains than European troops—this was strikingly evident when the Punjabis brought down the 4th Brigade wounded. But it would be difficult to maintain that the Indian formations deployed or went into the attack any faster. This whole charge, in fact, must be related to the country and the enemy. To go back to Mountbatten's letter: 'Only those who have seen the terrific nature of the country... will be able to appreciate your achievements.' Two factors did influence the speed of the Division's build up, but these are never mentioned by its critics. The first is that while it was building forward, it had to keep fighting back to keep the road open to Dimapur; and the second is that its men and equipment arrived from the other side of India, piecemeal, and over a period of some weeks. If the Division could have concentrated before its move to Assam; if Stopford could have relieved it of responsibility for the road, it could have no doubt deployed and moved into action very much faster. But such were the exigencies of war that neither of these things was possible.

Fortunately, some of the more informed critics have been there, and are agreed on one fact; the men of the 2nd Division fought magnificently and with enormous courage. Barker says: 'No division could have fought better, no divisional commander could have proved a better leader.' Slim, who always managed to keep his admiration for British troops under firm control, has said: 'The only trouble with 2 Div. is you were too brave... you were far too brave.' General Miyazaki has said: 'I have a deep respect for the men who fought so determinedly and courageously at Kohima.'

There is no need to defend or reassert the qualities of the other units and formations who fought at Kohima. The Assam Rifles, the Assam Regiment, the regiments of Warren's brigade—the Royal West Kents, the Punjabis and Rajputs, and of Loftus Tottenham's brigade—the Queens, the Punjabis, and the Gurkhas. The scale of their achievements was recognized at once; their share in the victory has never been questioned nor can be. To a man, they were magnificent.

*

For three out of the four generals principally engaged at Kohima it was the last battle. On Tuesday, 4th July, Grover was asked to meet Stopford on the roadside at Maram. Here he was informed that he was to be removed from command of the 2nd Division, and would be found another appointment. Though personal relations between the two commanders remained good, it had been increasingly obvious that Stopford was unhappy about Grover's methods; while Grover did not feel that he had received the co-operation and support from 33rd Corps that he was entitled to expect. At this stage in time it is impossible to probe further into personalities; but it is quite clear that both were highly professional soldiers, and both accepted the immutable law of the British Army: that if two commanders cannot work together, then the junior must go. Grover made no complaint at the time; nor has done since.

But the shock to the 2nd Division was considerable. They had fought to the limit of their courage and endurance, they had won a great victory; they had been showered with congratulations from Mountbatten, from Giffard, from Slim. And now their beloved general was being taken from them. The adjective is not used lightly; for seldom can a general and his division have been so identified with each other. Not only the officers, but the troops, were quite bewildered. When Churchill's representative, Lord Munster, who had come out from England to ascertain what the troops required in the way of comforts, began his meetings the first question the troops asked him was: 'What have you done to our general?' Because of this, or some other reason, Grover received a decoration for his part in the victory. Even today, over twenty years after he left them, the men of the 2nd Division still look on Grover as 'their General'.

General Sato was officially sacked on the 23rd November, 1944, some four and a half months after leaving his Division. On his arrival at Maymyo, he had asked for an interview with Mutaguchi, but was denied this, and preparations for his court-martial were put in hand immediately. These, however, were soon stopped by orders from Tokyo. With the Japanese Army already shaken by its defeat at Kohima and Imphal, it was judged rightly that a public row between the generals would reduce confidence even further, and the General Staff were worried lest the news leaked out to the public. The doctors who examined Sato therefore announced, presumably under orders, that his nervous and mental condition was such that he could not stand trial. He was therefore transferred to the Reserve, and Mutaguchi's threats of vengeance were therefore thwarted. Sato was sent to Java, where he was attached to the headquarters of the 16th Army; his final appointment was with an army District, in Japan. He died of cirrhosis of the liver in 1958.

General Mutaguchi was also sacked, in December 1944, and placed on the Reserve. In January 1945, however, he was recalled and appointed as Director of the Junior Course at the Military Academy. He still lives in Tokyo; still affirms that Sato lost him the battle by disobeying the order to send a regimental group to Imphal. Whether he is right, military historians will no doubt argue in the future. All one can say at this stage is that, like Waterloo, it was 'a damned close-run thing'.

Could Sato have won the battle of Kohima had his anticipation, his grasp, his tactical skill been greater? The answer must be surely, that if he had been allowed to send a regiment to Dimapur, with orders to seize the base and cut the railway, he might well have done. Why did Kawabe order him back? Slim has said that: 'The fundamental fault in their [the Japanese generals'] generalship was a lack of moral, as distinct from physical, courage. They were not prepared to admit that their plans had misfired and needed recasting.' This is undoubtedly true; but at the end of March 1944, Mutaguchi's plans hadn't misfired; they had gone miraculously well, and both he and Sato wanted to exploit their swift success. It was Kawabe whose mental rigidity stopped them; to him, the campaign had to be fought exactly as planned, come failure, or *success*. Such rigidity is surprising in a general as experienced in action as Kawabe and there was obviously a good reason for his decision. Barker has suggested that this was simply his strict interpretation of the Tokyo directive, which was that 'the strategic areas near Imphal and in North-East India' did not include Dimapur. General Matsutani, however, after his researches in the archives of the Imperial Defence College, has pointed out that in all the initial studies for the operation it was anticipated that 31st Division would seize Kohima, then at once despatch a third of its strength, a regimental group, to Imphal. This fact may have unconsciously coloured Kawabe's interpretation of the order; for obviously if a regiment became engaged at Dimapur, forty miles to the north of Kohima, it would be difficult to extract it and despatch it to Imphal as required. In the event, this earlier plan was modified and the whole 31st Division unreservedly committed to Kohima; but it probably remained like a palimpsest on Kawabe's mind.

While dealing with this subject, there is the curious story related by Takahide Hasegawa, according to which Colonel Kato represented his divisional commander at a conference with Kawabe and Mutaguchi, when the precise role of the

31st Division was being thrashed out in December 1943. The dialogue went like this:

MUTAGUCHI: Tell me, Colonel Kato, what is your commander's plan, once he has captured Kohima?

KATO: To hold it with his main body, to stop any movement through to Imphal, then to send a regiment to Dimapur.

MUTAGUCHI: That's foolish! Why should you stay at Kohima? The enemy will be running back to Dimapur. Your job is to get after them.

According to Hasegawa, 'Kawabe remained silent during this conversation, though he did not approve of all Mutaguchi's ideas.' It may well be that Kawabe did not wish to oppose Mutaguchi on this point immediately, but noted his views with the intention of stopping any Dimapur adventure, should it be mooted once the offensive was launched. As already indicated, in Kawabe's rigid conception Imphal remained the main objective, and other objectives had to be judged solely in their relation to it.

*

As far as can be ascertained, the anniversary of Kohima has only been observed formally in one place—Tokyo. On the 26th June, 1965, 700 survivors of the 58th Regiment, members of the Regimental Society, gathered at the Yasukuni Shrine for a memorial service. For this occasion, the officers of the Society had made considerable efforts, though without success, to contact British soldiers who fought in the battle, wishing to send an invitation to them. They still hope that some British soldiers will attend the ceremony on a future occasion. According to one of the leading members of the Society, Captain Susumi Nishide: 'We still have a strong nostalgic feeling for Kohima... something beyond hate and love.' Certainly, so far as these Japanese soldiers are concerned, all bitterness towards the British troops has disappeared. In letters to the author, they have said: Our greatest wish is that our children will never go to war as we did.... Never must the Japanese fight the British again.' This thought will surely find echoes in the breasts of anyone who fought at Kohima, or indeed anywhere in the Burma campaign.

*

'The trees are all young on Garrison Hill, and in Naga Village children are playing. The wet earth and sprouting shrubs have the same spring-fresh smell. And there is no stench. Grass-filled foxholes still mark forgotten fire-lanes and some rusty ration tins and leather scraps have escaped, as too worthless to pick up, a decade of scavengers.... The track which the bulldozers drove up the hillside is now a leafy lane; and houses have hidden the pattern of war till it can be no more traced.'

So wrote an officer returning to the battlefield a few years ago. Since then, the bungalows and houses have spread in disordered confusion along G.P.T. Ridge and up Congress Hill; across Treasury Hill, and down towards the Zubza Valley. They have swept on past the barracks of the Assam Rifles, to lap round the slopes of Big Tree Hill and Dyer Hill. The population of Kohima is so great that in the wettest country in the world there is a water shortage.

The cemetery laid out by the War Graves Commission is sited on Garrison Hill, surmounted by a white cross and surrounded by trees, and the rhododendron bushes which have returned to claim their own territory. In the cemetery there are 1,287 graves, each with a name and rank, and a regiment. There are also private memorial plaques set up by sorrowing relatives, with inscriptions varying from the trite to the powerfully moving.... ' Our only beloved son, who died that freedom might live.' Or simply: 'Good night, daddy.' Many who fell in the hellish jungle-mountains have no known grave, and only an inscribed name bears witness to the fact that they fought in this strange land, so far from home, and finished their earthly journey here.

> 'When you go home
> Tell them of us and say,
> For their tomorrow
> We gave our today.'

This inscription, adapted from the Greek, is carved on the memorial to the 2nd British Division. The stone came from a local quarry and was dragged up the hillside by the Nagas a few months after the battle was over. It is rough in shape and texture, but is very moving; and more important, is right for its setting. The Nagas have cut their own memorial stones from this quarry for centuries. Within the perimeter of the cemetery, or hidden among the hills are the regimental memorials: the Royal Norfolk between G.P.T. Ridge and Aradura Spur, the Royal Welch Fusiliers up on Kuki Piquet, the 4th/15th Punjab on D.I.S., the Durham Light Infantry on Garrison Hill, and the Dorsets near the tennis court. The memorial to the Cameron Highlanders is tucked away in a sprawling houseyard in Naga Village, with the pigs and hens around it. On the stone is inscribed the Cameron lament, 'Lochaber No More'; and, by a happy chance, the sound of the bagpipes still wafts up the hill from the Assam Barracks.

It would be pleasing to say that Kohima is at peace again; but unfortunately, since the British left their Indian Empire, the Nagas have been at war with the Indian Government, struggling for their independence. The rights and the wrongs of their case need not be argued here; but certainly some experienced observers believe that 'the Underground', the Naga guerrilla army, is supported by Pakistan for its own political reasons. If this is so, the prospects of peace in the near future seem very small. But whatever the eventual settlement, one hopes that the Nagas, this strange, courageous race, will be left to enjoy their mountain home, without interference. The Naga Hills have seen enough bloodshed to last for many centuries.

Order of Battle

BRITISH FORMATIONS

THE KOHIMA GARRISON

(On the 3rd April, 1944)

ARTILLERY

One 25-pounder gun with crew from 24 Reinforcement Corps

ENGINEERS

C.R.E. and Staff

G.E. Kohima and Staff

INFANTRY

1st Assam Regiment

One company of the 1st Garrison Battalion Burma Regiment

One company 5th Burma Regiment

Two platoons 5th/27th Mahratta L.I.

One composite company of Gurkhas

Two composite companies of Indian Infantry

3rd Assam Rifles (organized into 7 platoons)

Detachments of 'V' Force

Shere Regiment (Nepalese contingent)

One company of British N.C.O.s and men from the Reinforcement Camp

SIGNALS

221 Line Construction Section
Detachment of the Burma Post and Telegraph Section
Detachment IV Corps Signals Regiment
Detachment from the L. of C. Signal Unit

MEDICAL

80 Light Field Ambulance (from 50 Brigade)
Detachment 53 Indian General Hospital
19 Field Hygiene Section

R.I.A.S.C.

46 G.P.T. Company (less two sections)
36 Cattle Conducting Section
87 Field Bakery Section
623 Indian Supply Section

LABOUR

1432 Company Indian Pioneer Company

MISCELLANEOUS

About 200 British Other Ranks from the reinforcement camp, together with the Administrative Commandant and staff of the unit.
(A total of about 2,500 all told.)

33 CORPS

ARMOUR

149th Regiment, Royal Armoured Corps
150th Regiment, Royal Armoured Corps (detachment only)
11th Cavalry (Armoured Cars)
45th Cavalry (Light Tanks)

ARTILLERY

1st Medium Regiment, Royal Artillery
50th Indian Light Anti-Aircraft/Anti-Tank Regiment
24th Indian Mountain Regiment (from 5th Indian Division)

ENGINEERS

429th Field Company, Indian Engineers
44th Field Park Company, Indian Engineers
10th Battalion, Indian Engineers

INFANTRY

1st Burma Regiment, Burma Army
1st Chaman Regiment
1st Assam Regiment
Shere Regiment (Nepalese)
Mahindra Dal Regiment (Nepalese)

2nd INFANTRY DIVISION

ARTILLERY

10th Assault Field Regiment, Royal Artillery
16th Assault Field Regiment, Royal Artillery
99th Assault Field Regiment, Royal Artillery
100th Light Anti-Aircraft/Anti-Tank Regiment, Royal Artillery

ENGINEERS

5th Field Company, Royal Engineers
208th Field Company, Royal Engineers
506th Field Company, Royal Engineers
21st Field Park Company, Royal Engineers

SIGNALS

2nd Divisional Signals

INFANTRY

2nd Reconnaissance Regiment
2nd Manchester Regiment (Machine-Gun Battalion)
143rd Special Service Company

4th Infantry Brigade:
Brigadier W. H. Goschen until 7th May 1944,
then Brigadier J. A. Theobalds until 4th June 1944,
then Brigadier R. S. McNaught
1st Royal Scots
2nd Royal Norfolk Regiment
1st/8th Lancashire Fusiliers

5th Infantry Brigade:
Brigadier V. F. S. Hawkins until 16th May 1944,
then Brigadier M. M. Alston-Roberts-West
7th Worcestershire Regiment
2nd Dorsetshire Regiment
1st Queen's Own Cameron Highlanders

6th Infantry Brigade:
Brigadier J. D. Shapland until 30th May 1944,
then Brigadier W. G. Smith
1st Royal Welch Fusiliers
1st Royal Berkshire Regiment
2nd Durham Light Infantry

MEDICAL

4th Field Ambulance
5th Field Ambulance
6th Field Ambulance

161st Indian Infantry Brigade

4th Queen's Own Royal West Kent Regiment
1st/1st Punjab Regiment
4th/7th Rajputana Rifles

33rd Indian Infantry Brigade

1st Queen's Royal Regiment (West Surrey)
4th/15th Punjab Regiment
4th/1st Gurkha Rifles

(23rd [Long Range Penetration] Indian Infantry Brigade are not included here as they did not take part in the battle proper. 268th Indian Brigade, which appeared on the final days of the battle, are not included either.)

JAPANESE FORMATIONS

31ST DIVISION

Right (Northerly) Column

One battalion of the 138th Infantry Regiment with one battery of 31st Mountain Artillery Regiment, engineers, signals and medical detachments

Centre Column

Advanced Guard

The 138th Infantry Regiment, less one battalion, and one battalion of the 31st Mountain Artillery Regiment less the troops used in the

Right Column

Main Body

H.Q. 31st Division

124th Infantry Regiment with the H.Q. and one battalion of 31st Mountain Artillery Regiment, together with engineers, signals, a field hospital and a transport unit

Left (Southern) Column

H.Q. 31st Infantry Group with the 58th Infantry Regiment, one battalion of the 31st Mountain Artillery Battalion, engineers, signals and medical detachments

Bibliography

A.J. Barker, *The March on Delhi*. Faber, 1963.

Brigadier F. V. R. Bellers, *History of the 1st King George V's Own Gurkha Rifles,* Vol. 2, 1920–47. Gale & Polden, 1956.

Brigadier Gordon Blight, *The Royal Berkshire Regiment* 1920–47. Staples, 1953.

Ursula Graham Bower, *Naga Path*. John Murray, 1950.

Antony Brett-James, *Ball of Fire*. Gale & Polden, 1951.

Historical Records of the Queen's Own Cameron Highlanders. William Blackwood, 1952.

Major E. B. Stanley Clarke and Major A. T. Tillott, *From Kent to Kohima:* Being the History of the 4th Battalion the Queen's Own West Kent Regiment (T.A.). Gale & Polden, 1951.

John Ehrman, *History of the Second World War: Grand Strategy,* Vol. 5. H.M.S.O., 1956.

Sir Geoffrey Evans and Antony Brett-James, *Imphal*. Macmillan, 1964.

Major R. C. G. Foster, *History of the Queen's Royal Regiment,* Vol. 8, 1924–48. Gale & Polden, 1953.

Saburo Hayashi (with Alan D. Coox), *Koguun: The Japanese Army in the Pacific War*. The Marine Corps Assoc., Quantico, 1959.

J. H. Hutton, *The Angami Nagas*. Macmillan, 1921.

Toshikazu Kase, *The Eclipse of the Rising Sun* (Ed. David Nelson). Cape, 1951.

Lieut-Commander P. K. Kemp, *History of the Royal Norfolk Regiment* 1919–51, Vol. 8. Royal Norfolk Regiment, 1957.

Lieut.-Commander P. K. Kemp and John Graves, *The Red Dragon* (Story of the Royal Welch Fusiliers 1919–45). Gale & Polden, 1960.

R. G. Kent, *United States Army in World War II* (China–Burma–India Theatre). Historical Div. Dept. of the Army, 1955.

Major-General S. Woodburn Kirby, 'History of the Second World War', *The War Against Japan,* Volume III. H.M.S.O., 1961.

Major M. A. Lowry, *An Infantry Company in Arakan and Kohima*. Gale & Polden, 1950.

Henry Maule, *Spearhead Generai.* Odhams Press, 1961.

Vice-Admiral the Earl Mountbatten of Burma, *Report to the Combined Chiefs of Staff—South-East Asia 1943–45.* H.M.S.O., 1951.

Augustus Muir, *The First of Foot* (The History of the Royal Scots). The Royal Scots History Committee, 1961.

Ray Murphy, *The Last Viceroy.* Jarrolds, 1948.

Frank Owen, *The Campaign in Burma.* H.M.S.O., 1946.

Major Mohammed Ibrahim Qureshi, *History of the First Punjab Regiment 1759–1956.* Gale & Polden, 1958.

David Rissick, *The D.L.I, at War.* D.L.I., 1953.

Brigadier M. R. Roberts, D.S.O., *Golden Arrow* (Story of the 7th Indian Division in the Second World War, 1939–45). Gale & Polden, 1952.

Colonel L. W. Shakespear, *History of the Assam Rifles.* Macmillan, 1929.

Field-Marshal the Viscount Slim, *Defeat into Victory.* Cassell, 1956.

Captain Peter Steyn, *The History of the Assam Regiment,* Vol. 1, 1941–1947. Orient Longmans, 1959.

Colonel Masanobu Tsuji (Trans. Margaret E. Lake), *Singapore: The Japanese Version.* Constable, 1962.

Major-General R. P. Pakenham Walsh, *The History of the Royal Engineers*, Vol. 9. Institution of Royal Engineers, 1958.

Lieut.-Colonel O. G. W. White, *Straight on for Tokyo* (The Story of the 2nd Bn. The Dorsetshire Regiment, 1939–47). Gale & Polden, 1948.

TRANSLATIONS FROM:

Toshiro Takagi, *Imphal*. Tokyo, 1949.

Takahide Hasegawa, *Again the Genghis Khan Dream*. Yamicuri Press, 1960.

Takeo Komatsu, *Imphal Tragedy*.

Yukihiko Imai, *To and from Kohima*. Tokyo, 1953.

Colonel Iwaichi Fujiwara, *The Tragic Imphal Operation*.

Toichiro Imanishi, *Burma Front Diary*. Tokyo, 1961.

Officers and Men of the 58th Infantry Regiment, *The Burma Front*. Tokyo, 1964.

Index

Formations: under Brigades, Divisions, etc.
Regiments: British and Indian under their names; Japanese (numbered) under Regiments.
'n' indicates a reference to a footnote.

WATERFORD CITY AND COUNTY
LIBRARIES
WITHDRAWN